PHILIP GREE

AUTHOR OF *LEA*

MINISTERING

ANGLES

How to minister
WHEN 'HOW TO' BOOKS FAIL

FOREWORD BY GREG HASLAM

For list of National Distributors visit CWR's website: www.cwr.org.uk
The author has added his own italics for emphasis in some Bible quotes, and in quoted material from other sources.
Whilst every effort has been made to trace sources quoted, some have not been found, and for this we apologise.

Lyrics on page 221: 'God's Own Fool', Michael Card. Copyright © 1985 Mole Ene Music/Birdwing Music/EMI CMG/Small Stone Media. Administered by Song Solutions Daybreak, 14 Horsted Square, Uckfield TN22 1QG. info@songsolutions.org

Unless otherwise indicated, all Scripture references are from the Holy Bible: New International Version (NIV), copyright © 1973, 1978, 1984 by the International Bible Society.
Other versions used:
ESV: The Holy Bible, English Standard Version, published by HarperCollins Publishers © 2001 by Crossway Bibles, a division of Good News Publishers. Used by permission. All rights reserved.
The Message: The Message. Copyright © 1993, 1994, 1995, 1996, 2000, 2001, 2002. Used by permission of NavPress Publishing Group.

Concept development, editing, design and production by CWR

Printed and bound in Great Britain by 4edge Ltd, Hockley. www.4edge.co.uk

ISBN: 978-1-85345-522-3

When it comes to talking sensibly about the call and task of Christian ministers today, Philip Greenslade's is one of those voices to which I give serious attention. This book represents a wealth of good theology and genuine insight born from experience of ministering in church leadership and out of continuous reflection on this task. It distils living wisdom in a way that makes massive sense to me, theologically and existentially, and will do to many others. I recommend it wholeheartedly to those who are looking for a mature and Christ-centred perspective on Christian ministry.

Dr Nigel G. Wright
Principal, Spurgeon's College, London

How Christian is your ministry? Philip Greenslade brings extensive biblical exposition and wide personal experience to bear as he presents a gentle but insistent call for ministry that is Christ-centred, cross-shaped and culturally critical.

Dr Jeremy Thomson
Director of Higher Education at Oasis College

This is not a 'how to' book. In terms of ministry it is more of a 'why to' and 'what to'. It provides a theological undergirding of the very essence of ministry motivation – servanthood!
This book provides an excellent theological overview of the biblical culture of servanthood. Philip Greenslade writes with a hand in heaven and with both feet on the ground. He provides great study with earthy application. Philip reminds us that in the Person of Christ we see lordship demonstrated through servanthood and we see followership and leadership finding their zenith through this great heart motif achievable only in real relationship with Him.
Finally a book that provides a working theology of ministry that helps redress the balance of assumed positional power. It places the emphasis firmly on those Christlike characteristics of servanthood that are so often overlooked. This is a 'must read' for leaders looking to be effective in all they seek to do in ministry.

Colin D. Buckland
Director of Claybury International

Philip Greenslade writes on church leadership with an authority grounded in his professional practice of ministry, in his experience of training ministers, and in his deep commitment to the God revealed in Scripture.

Revd Canon Professor Leslie J. Francis, Professor of Religions and Education
University of Warwick

In a world of celebrities, statistics and quick-fixes, *Ministering Angles* is an urgent and prophetic call back to the downwardly-mobile path of taking up one's cross and following Jesus into the mess of ministry. By definition, it won't be popular!

Rev Dr Ian Stackhouse
Senior Pastor of Millmead, Guildford Baptist Church

CONTENTS

FOREWORD

In Charles Dickens' classic novel *Great Expectations*, the lovelorn longings and changing fortunes of young working-class hero Pip Pirrin are depicted. Pip is invited by the aged, wealthy and embittered spinster Miss Haversham to visit her secluded mansion and to befriend her beautiful young niece Estella, whom she has coached in the art of vengeance upon all men. Pip is to be her first victim. The long-jilted spinster sits in the sinister, darkened, cobwebbed chaos of her self-imposed prison cell. She morbidly preserves the decayed remains of what was once her wedding banquet, now a heap of dirt. The self-confessed old hag of 'yellow skin and bone', worn down by 'sharper teeth than teeth of mice' gnawing at her, cruelly implements her plan to destroy Pip. Her bitter, vengeful spirit has corrupted even the beautiful Estella, who emulates her aunt's man-hating and loveless attitudes amid the gothic mausoleum of Miss Haversham's shattered dreams.

Years later, his fortunes completely reversed, Pip returns to the dilapidated mansion intent upon rescuing his beloved Estella and snatching her from the accursed and empty house. He enters that same filthy, haunted room where he met the twisted spinster and now occupied by the adult Estella. Outraged, Pip begins to tear down its ragged and dusty drapes to let in the sunlight, sweeping away the rotten remnants of Miss Haversham's grief and faded dreams. He breaks the spell hanging over Estella with passionate revelations of his life-long love for her, and finally draws a line over years of hatred and pain, as the reunited couple leave this 'dead house' and emerge into the radiant light of a glorious new day.

Something very much like this has to happen in the experience of many jaded and faded pastors and churches today, if the people of God are to rediscover Christ's love for His Bride and His passion for lost people everywhere. For this to happen, Christian leaders must display something of Pip's courage, defiance and radical resolve to effect drastic change, renewal and restoration, stopping at nothing less than their Master directs them to do in His desire to awaken His Church from her gloom, to realise her glorious future destiny.

Pastors come in all kinds of shapes and gifting. Some appear to be more exciting than others. Apostles, evangelists and prophets are the most colourful, and usually attract the greatest attention. Some rise to become minor celebrities in the Christian world. But pastors and teacher-theologians are usually ranked somewhat lower. This is a great mistake. Philip Greenslade is one of the finest teacher-theologians I know, and an extraordinarily gifted thinker, speaker and writer. I have known him since I was a young pastor, meeting him at a time of stressful transition whilst trying to lead a very difficult church. I was struggling with the frustration of unfulfilled and desperate longings, alongside the challenge of much needed change, while I was also wrestling theologically with controversial issues related to spiritual renewal and the proper integration of Word and Spirit in the church's life. At that time, Philip was truly a God-send to me, and he still is. He offered me significant help, biblical insight and massive personal encouragement. He literally saved my life spiritually speaking, and helped clarify fresh vision and direction for many years to come, largely due to his own biblical integrity and hunger for spiritual reality – a hunger that still remains. I should add that he is also very prophetic and abounds in rich spiritual insights, in that he has the ability to expound and apply God's unchanging Word to the current situation with an uncanny sensitivity and timeliness. Such prophetic skill is abundantly displayed in its finest form here in Philip's new book, *Ministering Angles*.

Books on leadership have been queuing for our attention for decades now, clamouring for space on our already heavily-laden bookshelves and access to our over-stuffed minds. Most of these books echo the world's entrepreneurial wisdom, and many urge us to advance the success of what we might call 'God's Fortune 500 Mega-church' culture that much of the Church longs to join. And yet, valuable as much of this material undoubtedly is, somewhere along the way anxious, competitive and over-ambitious pastors can mislay their souls in the quest for the Christian equivalent of the mediaeval alchemist's Philosophers' Stone that will turn everything into spiritual gold, thus lining both their pastoral pockets and empty pews with financial prosperity, vast numbers and visible success. Some of this quantitative growth and material prosperity may not be 'success' at all, as Christ Himself defines it to be.

The high incidence of pastoral moral failure, public scandals, and the frequent exposure of money-grabbing evangelists, soberly warns us that all is not well in some places. Add to this the high incidence of spiritual 'burnout' among once fruitful ministries and the wreckage this leaves behind in all-but-destroyed churches, and we have reasons to pause for thought. Often, our driven-ness, man-centred 'vision', relentless abuse of Christ's people, ruthless dealings with perceived rivals and increasing loneliness and isolation, fuelled by our widespread failure to 'produce the goods' even in our own estimation, clearly points to the very real possibility that somewhere along the way many leaders have simply lost their way.

The real tragedy here is that most of these pastors were genuinely called by God to the glorious work of shepherding God's flock. But the world, the flesh and the devil have robbed them of God's presence, His Holy Spirit's aid, and as a result they've mislaid God's agenda. No wonder some leaders finish their race an exhausted shadow of their former selves. Some morph into characters who are just as bitter, disillusioned, twisted, hate-filled, exploitative and unfit for service as Miss Haversham. They may eventually die as faded 'has beens' amid the rotten debris and detritus of a failed ministry, their reputation burnt to ashes by the consuming flames of public exposure, unspeakable shame and inconsolable regrets.

Losing our way is a real possibility for us all. Finding guides who will keep us on track is much harder. But Philip Greenslade may well prove to be something of a 'Pip' to our dusty, cobweb-covered, jaded or disillusioned lives. Philip honestly acknowledges that he is no stranger to failure, pain and disappointment himself, but we can also see that he has been re-visited, re-commissioned and restored by Christ, experiencing the joys of renewed grace and God's high calling upon his life. This has obviously enabled him to 'search out the old paths' and walk an entirely different road than many of his contemporaries who crashed and burned long ago, and whose once successful ministries are now only faded memories. Philip has given years of his life to the extensive study of God's Word and the greatest of the Church's most gifted theologians. He is a man of profound thought, tireless labour and a captivating writing skill – a prophetic teacher par excellence. I have followed his writings and published ministry for many years, and count him among my most inspiring personal mentors. His insights are always fresh, penetrating, prophetic and incandescent with great truths about God, Christ, salvation and the kingdom, along with the central ingredients of effective ministry as Christ and His apostles define it to be.

This present work is no 'run of the mill' collection of predictable platitudes and clichés but, rather, a high vitamin and invigorating tonic for jaded souls and struggling pastors. Philip calls us back to the core realities of our high calling. He rediscovers the old paths that lead us out of the desert wildernesses and into the oases and grand vistas of God's plans for His people. Above all, we are enabled to recover fresh glimpses of Christ Himself, as we hear Christ's voice again gently teaching us, and receive timeless wisdom for the pursuit of a truly Christ-honouring and world-changing ministry. The bedrock realities of Christ's 'upside-down' kingdom are here unfolded in such a way that we may all be turned 'right way up' again.

Another prophet of a former generation, the great American preacher A. W. Tozer, once advised, 'Listen to the person who listens to God'. Philip Greenslade has listened to God, and we can overhear his report of what God told him. No attentive reader can fail to be moved by these studies and then resolve to change in many vital ways. This is one of the very best books on Christian leadership I have read in a long time. It is destined to become a classic. I am so glad that I had the privilege of reading it at a time when I most needed its wisdom, inspiring perspectives and profound help. It has restored my soul, and renewed my conviction that to serve Christ and His people in the ministry of God's Word is the highest calling and privilege any man or woman could possess. This book can help us all to find our true bearings in leadership, whilst warning us against the dangers of hidden rocks and potential shipwreck in ministry. Above all, it offers us the chance to experience the joy of imbibing the very best theology in order to nourish our sometimes starving and depleted souls, souls that need more than spiritual candy floss and high calorie desserts if they are to become fit for the fight that we call Christian leadership today.

Greg Haslam
Minister, Westminster Chapel, London

PREFACE

Pulling into a car space at a roadside diner, I glimpsed through a gap in the trees a patch of green and a man wielding a white stick. A blind man, perhaps, deftly groping his way forward? Or a park-keeper, maybe, spearing up leaves and litter? Moments later from the window-table in the diner I saw a golfer lining up a putt on the ninth tee.
Angle of vision is everything.

This book is written out of a concern that the Church has been looking in the wrong direction for its models of ministry, drawing them, too uncritically, from the worlds of business studies, management theory, therapeutic practice – and, increasingly, entrepreneurship and entertainment. I am convinced that we need to shift our standpoint to one which is more biblical, more prophetic, more apostolic, more gospel-driven[1]; we need to adopt angles of vision which are more Christocentric, cross-shaped, and culturally critical. Of course, these are *my own* chosen angles of vision and are meant to be suggestive rather than exhaustive, a personal point of view on how we do ministry today.
The title of the book is a slight play on the idea of 'ministering angels' (Heb. 1:7,14). This is not another book about celestial beings even though no doubt I have entertained some unawares. Neither we nor our pastoral constituency are angelic but made of the same flesh and blood reality which the Son of God chose to embrace in incarnational identity with us (Heb. 2:14). The title also, quite unwittingly, echoes Eugene Peterson's book *Working the Angles* (Eerdmans, 1987) which no doubt sowed a seed in my mind. No one has reshaped pastoral theology in my generation more than he has, and so I hope he will forgive the unconscious borrowing as a tribute to his significance for my own thinking. In any case, I think I may be reflecting Peterson's sympathies in being drawn to the notion of 'angularity' with its connotations of awkwardness, of being a bit sharp-edged, rough-hewn, *un*smooth – characteristics of a certain 'out-of-sync-ness' or 'against-the-grain-ness'. Given its Spirit-enabled outworking in sacrificial love, tough grace and faithful tenacity, such a stance may well appear otherworldly, even angelic.

Christian ministry is but a focused and intensified expression of the essential paradoxes inherent to Christian existence: honour through humility, power through weakness, life out of death.

As for the subtitle of the book, it sounds a trifle pretentious to me though I adapted it from Donald McCullough's splendid *The Power of Realistic Thinking* (1988). So I have let it stand, if only because it represents the kind of book I would like to have written. Whether this is that book, I leave you to judge. What I am trying to insist on is that the question of Christian ministry is not 'answered' by acquiring new techniques or skills (valuable as these may be) but by raising older questions about 'why?' we do ministry and about the 'who?' of the persons doing it, and 'in what manner?' it is carried out. This book aims to be *that* kind of 'how to' book.

The substance of this book consists of revised and expanded versions of addresses delivered at various conferences, programmes, and graduation events over the past decade. I have tried to eliminate repetition but hope to be forgiven if any remain.

I put on record my indebtedness:

to the late Selwyn Hughes, much-loved founder of CWR, for inviting me to share platforms with him at leadership conferences in Malaysia, India, Sri Lanka, Australia, New Zealand, and at Waverley Abbey House in the UK;

to the Evangelical Alliance and its then UK Director, John Smith, for co-hosting with CWR a series of leaders' events in London;

to Terry Virgo for asking me to address leaders at the New Frontiers International Conference at Brighton over a number of years;

to Professor Leslie Francis (then of the University of Wales, Bangor, now at Warwick University), Dr Paul Rolph, Dr Jeremy Thomson, and Mick Brooks, CEO of CWR, for superintending and supporting my oversight of CWR's first, postgraduate professional development course for clergy, pastors and church leaders, and to those in ministry who came on the course (how good it is to make new friends);

to David Coffey, long-time friend, and erstwhile President of the Baptist World Alliance, who, as Conference President that year, honoured me with an invitation to speak at my alma mater, Spurgeon's College, on the 150th Anniversary of the founding of the college by the famous Victorian preacher, Charles Haddon Spurgeon;

to my friends, especially Trevor Martin, Stuart Reid, Keith Arscott and Ian Stackhouse for keeping me sane by their generous encouragement and good humour; to Greg Haslam for his generous Foreword; to Lynette Brooks and the superb editorial and design team at CWR; to Kathy Overton for administrating my work so efficiently and cheerfully; and, above all, to my wife, Mary, for her perennially positive take on life – where would I be without her?

A friendly critic of my earlier book on leadership, along with generous comments, complained that it lacked jokes. Point taken: though those who know me might find the comment funny. Not least because representing God in any way must in itself be considered one big practical joke, a hearty participation in what the medievals called the long great Easter laugh. Not every one gets the point, though. The esteemed American novelist, Frederick Buechner, who began life by training as a Presbyterian minister, recalls a fashionable dinner party at which a woman leaned towards him down the table and said: 'I hear you are going into the ministry: Was it your own idea or were you poorly advised?'

As for the relationship between this book and my first published attempt to reflect on the topic over twenty-five years ago, I can only hope that a fresh angle of vision may undergird not override what I wrote before. Much water has flowed under the bridge since then, some of it so turbulent as almost to sweep the bridge away with it. But I survive to reflect again on Christian ministry tempered by experience.

My contemporaries and I set out on the road with high hopes and great – perhaps grandiose – visions of the renewal that was coming to Christians, the restoration of the Church, and the revival that was around the corner for the nation. I have seen stunning glimpses of these glorious possibilities and I thank God sincerely for every one of them. I salute the brave pioneers who 'followed the Spirit' in the seventies and eighties and honour those who have lasted the course better than I have.

Realism forces me to say that we have not seen all that we hoped to see. Yet, even conceding this, I am not disillusioned. For one thing, the Light that has dawned on the world can never be eclipsed by anything that is still to happen. 'Blessed are the eyes that see what you see. For I tell you that many prophets and kings wanted to see what you see but did not see it, and to hear what you hear but did not hear it'

(Luke 10:23–24). This was a secret shared between Jesus and His disciples, but true nonetheless. And privately and personally, I am helped by Moses' experience who, when he desired to see the full glory of God's face, was told to enter a cleft in the rock: 'and while my glory passes by I will cover you with my hand until I have passed by. Then I will take away my hand and you shall see my back, but my face shall not be seen' (Exod. 33:22–23, cf. 34:6, ESV).

So by analogy it is with us. We so want to see the full glory of God in our day and at every point along the way but are denied such an experience. Remarkably – as with Moses – what covers our eyes to obscure that glory is not our failures (to be regretted as they are) nor the opaqueness of tragic events (from which God seems absent) but *God's own hand*. Later in retrospect, we see not God's face but *God's back*. And with this angle of vision, seeing God's back, we realise that the glory that has passed us by was gracious and compassionate all the while and that goodness and mercy have surely followed us all the days of our life.

At a recent memorial service, I heard moving tributes paid to an old friend who had been a deacon at the small Baptist church where I arrived as the 'rookie' pastor. It was to him I served my first communion and as I handed him the bread and wine, I noticed his grease-stained hands and blackened fingernails – which were to be expected of a car mechanic. Then I knew, if I had not known it before, that pastoral work had to do with serving working men and women, and with helping them in some small way to become 'saints in ordinary', which Wally was. Nothing has brought me greater joy and satisfaction.

So, to all those I have pastored or ministered to over these past forty years, especially to those I have avoided damaging too much or whose lives I somehow enriched – I dedicate this book to you, in the knowledge that I no doubt received from you more than I ever gave.

Thanks be to God.

Philip Greenslade
CWR, February 2009

SECTION 1

An angle of vision that is ...
... CHARACTERISTICALLY CHRISTLIKE

whoever would be great among you must be your servant ... For even the Son of Man came not to be served but to serve ... (Mark 10:43,45, ESV).

1
SEEING THINGS FROM HIS POINT OF VIEW

We are asking God that you may see things, as it were, from his point of view ... (Colossians 1:9, J.B. Phillips; Mark 10:32–45)

Jesus is God with us; when He acts, God acts God for us; when He speaks, God speaks God to us. As we are drawn to commit ourselves to Him, to follow Him and to listen to Him, we are taught to see things from God's point of view. To find a true angle of vision on ministry we must begin with Jesus Himself. My starting point is a vivid image of Jesus freeze-framed by the evangelists: 'They were on their way up to Jerusalem, *with Jesus leading the way*' – 'and Jesus was *walking ahead of them*' (ESV) – 'And they were amazed, and those who followed were *afraid*' (Mark 10:32, ESV).

'How long have you known Jesus?' I am occasionally asked. Since childhood, I can reply, when my parents introduced me to Him, and when as a curious seven-year-old I opened my heart to him in a small Pentecostal church. The preacher that day was William Booth-Clibborn, a descendant on the American side of the family of General William Booth, who seemed then, in grey, post-war, pre-Billy Graham Britain, an extravagantly flamboyant evangelist in his use of dramatic visual aids to press the case for conversion. In respect to my pietistic heritage which claims a personal relationship with Jesus – much as one has a personal tailor – I would like to say that I have grown to know Him better down the intervening years as I progressed from university student, to Bible seminary (Spurgeon's College), through Baptist pastor and charismatic church staff member, and as I practised my craft as preacher, writer and Bible teacher.

And yet, I have to say, this text resonates with me: because the older I get, the *less I feel I know who Jesus really is*. He seems more scary, much less the cosy figure I trusted as a small boy. The more I get to know Him the more He seems to be striding ahead of me so that I feel, like the disciples, amazed and fearful because He's out there in front with an agenda all His own which I know so little about.

It is some consolation to me that one of my all-time Christian heroes, Oswald Chambers, recognised the same feeling:

> There is an aspect of Jesus that chills the heart of a disciple to the core and makes the whole spiritual life gasp for breath. This strange Being with his face set like a flint and his striding determination strikes terror into me. He is no longer counsellor and comrade. *He is taken up with a point of view I know nothing about*, and I am amazed at him. At first I was confident I understood him, but now I am not so sure. I begin to realise there is a distance between Jesus Christ and me; I can no longer be familiar with him. He is ahead of me and he never turns round; I have no idea where he is going and the goal has become strangely far off.[1]

It is this 'point of view' which we 'know nothing about' that astonishes and frightens the following disciples then as now. The reason why this perspective is unsettling is that Jesus is showing us reality from God's point of view, showing us the way things are in His Father's kingdom. This may not be the way things are now, but this is the way it is in God's kingdom. This is profoundly disconcerting because from our perspective, the Father's is an upside-down kingdom. When the rule and reign of God break into human affairs again in a decisive way, all the social values of society are drastically upturned, all cultural norms reversed; the least shall be greatest, the lost found, the last first, the losers shall be the winners. And so it was with every notion of what a leader looked like and how a leader behaved.

It was His preaching of this upside-down kingdom of His Father that caused Jesus to clash with the established leadership of His day in Israel. His passion predictions single out the current leaders of Israel as chief opponents and persecutors: 'He then began to teach them that the Son of Man must suffer many things and be rejected by the elders, chief priests and teachers of the law ...' (Mark 8:31). It is sobering to recall that it was religious leaders, senior priests, and Bible teachers who led the attack on Jesus. For His part they were the major target of His prophetic rebuke; He denounced those He saw as *mis*leaders, as *mis*rulers of God's people – descendants of the false shepherds Ezekiel had exposed so severely (Ezek. 34). Not surprisingly His fiercest and final warnings were against these 'misleaders' of God's people (Matt. 23:1–11).

Reflecting on Jesus' critique, I see Him warning against:
- *a professionalism* that burdens the people with demands and revels in the social status leadership bestows
- *a paternalism* that plays God and dominates people's lives so that they become dependent on leadership
- *a personality cult* that attracts people to its leadership but distracts them from following Jesus.

Jesus warns against:

(i) *professionalism* – or reliance on an authority that derives only from official status: '... you are not to be called "Rabbi" for you have only one Master [or teacher] and you are all brothers' (23:8). Professionalism is always a danger in Christian ministry, especially if we are paid and set apart for it. To criticise 'professionalism' is not to criticise skill or knowledge, training or efficiency or expertise. What is under scrutiny here, I believe, is an *attitude of heart*, and *a style of living*, which turns ministry into something self-regarding and self-inflating. It is that tendency because you are 'the pastor' or 'the priest' or 'the minister' to stand apart from the people in a vaguely superior way; the result, as in Jesus' day, is that such people urge others to practise what they preach but don't practise it themselves (23:3).

Such leaders tend to be so obsessed with managing an organisation, or so taken up with running a programme, that in order to make it work they heap more and more burdens onto the people (23:4). This can take the form of that straightforward legalism which puts people under the lash of the law or that grinding moralism where we reduce the gospel to exhortations and end up constantly burdening people with another 'ten *demand*ments' of what they must do to be effective Christians. Sometimes it can simply be the pressure we apply to people to do more for the church in a way that eventually wears them down and wears them out. At its worst we can become obsessed with image rather than substance (cf. 23:25), with how things are presented rather than with the quality of the reality behind them; or – even worse – we are taken up with our own status and position in a way that feeds our ego (23:5–7).

The antidote here is to remember that we are 'all brothers' – which democratises everything, relativises hierarchies, and means that leaders are only serving other servants by leading them in the one family of God. From this we might well draw the conclusion – well established elsewhere in the New Testament – that leadership is a 'collective noun' and should always be done in a plural form in a team.

Jesus warns against:
(ii) *paternalism* – or a false way of dominating people: 'And do not call anyone on earth "father", for you have one Father, and he is in heaven' (23:9). In other words, as a leader don't be tempted to 'play God'. It is easy to do this in some settings – especially in the West or if you're under American influence; even to sit behind a desk or behind the closed door of an office can carry its own dangers – subtly, over time, convincing us that we are a somewhat 'godlike' figure to whom people come for the answer to all their problems, and for us to dispense spiritual medicine and 'cure-alls'. Psychologically this is called transference – where people begin to live their lives through us as leaders and end up unhealthily over-dependent on us: and we must *not* let it happen.

Henri Nouwen is worth quoting at length here:

> Real theological thinking, which is thinking with the mind of Christ, is hard to find in the practice of the ministry. Without solid theological reflection, future leaders will be little more than pseudo-psychologists, pseudo-sociologists, pseudo-social workers. They will think of themselves as enablers, facilitators, role models, father and mother figures, big brothers and big sisters, and so on, and thus join the countless men and women who make a living by trying to help their fellow human beings to cope with the stresses and strains of everyday living ... But this has little to do with Christian leadership ... The task of future Christian leaders is not to make a little contribution to the solution of the pains and tribulations of

their time but to identify and announce the ways in which Jesus is leading his people out of slavery, through the desert to a new land of freedom.[2]

Our servant ministry is to accompany people on that journey through what is often a pitiless and barren landscape if only that, like the Baptist, we may prepare them to meet the Lord in it. As Oswald Chambers said: 'The lure the servants of God are made but attracts men to a wilderness where God woos men to himself.'[3] Jesus is striking a very radical and deep note here. What He says should not be minimised as applying only to the holding of clerical titles or status in a superficial sense – in which case those outside the Catholic tradition might feel superior at this point. Nor should these words of Jesus deter us from revering our forefathers in the faith, especially those we call the 'Early Church Fathers'. And it certainly has nothing to do with an arrogant refusal to listen in humility to those older in Christ with much wisdom and experience to offer us.

What we are intended to hear as Jesus' antidote to the failure of leaders in first-century Israel is that we are equal members of the family of God, that He is Father of us all, 'our Father', not just 'my Father'. When John sent his remarkable revelation and prophetic vision as a pastoral letter from Patmos to the seven churches he was overseeing he didn't pull rank but said: 'I, John, your brother and companion in the suffering and kingdom and patient endurance that are ours in Jesus ...' (Rev. 1:9).

Now to the third statement of Jesus; what He is criticising here is
(iii) *personality cults* – where following the leaders becomes more important than following Jesus: 'Nor are you to be called "teacher" [καθηγητησ, leader] for you have one "teacher[/leader]", the Christ' (Matt. 23:10). Leadership can degenerate into a power game. Leaders can make people psychologically dependent on them, by constant promises, or by 'dangling the carrot' about the next revival just around the corner. Subtly and over time we can make people whose primary loyalty is to us.

As has been said, it is a sad thing when men of ideas give way to men of emotional power. Too often contemporary leaders rise to the top of the pile in the Church purely on the strength of their personality. They drive the Church by constant motivation rather than leading by example and truth. They stir with 'hype' rather than steady and consistent hope. They set endless goals and produce new envisioning but usually without any later assessment or evaluation. When exhortation tires, they may even resort to manipulation, a final appeal to 'trust me' or 'feel sorry for me because I'm under attack'.

Anyone acquainted with Pentecostal or charismatic churchmanship will know that in order to stifle disquiet and dissent, however legitimate, the last resort will be: 'Touch not my anointed.'
Gordon Fee comments sagely:

> Surely one of the ironies of my own tradition, the American Assemblies of God … is that every criticism of the ministry in any of its forms, including very bad preaching, was always challenged on the basis of 1 Samuel 24:6. Although Pentecostals might argue that the New Testament analogy of the 'Lord's anointed' is the one who speaks by the Spirit, in fact this becomes a tacit elevation of the 'ordained ministry' to the position of the untouchable king. No wonder the history of such movements, and even more so of independent churches, is fraught with stories of ministerial moral failure. Kings play by a different set of rules and the structures of accountability are seldom in place.[4]

It has been rightly said that none of us is good enough to survive our own unchallenged authority. Believers are sheep, but *His* sheep; *He* is the Chief Shepherd of the flock; we are only under-shepherds. The Church is God's flock, not ours. They are not 'our' converts but 'His'. Spurgeon was once rebuked by a lady who said: 'I know one of your converts, Mr Spurgeon, and he's always drunk and disorderly.' 'Then, Madam, all I can say, is that he must be one of *my* converts because he's obviously not one of the Lord's!'

Oswald Chambers had some perceptive words on this too:

> The servants of God in the Bible never stole hearts to themselves, but handed them over to God … Oh for that man of God who will hand over to God the hearts God has called through him. It is not you who awakened that mighty desire in the heart; it is not *you* who called forth that longing in that spirit; it is God in you. Are you a servant

of God? Then point them to him. Down on your face, down in the dust, oh man of God, if those arms clasp you and that heart rests on you! If that longing, loving heart awakens and finds you instead of God, what a passion of despair will blight you with the curse of solitariness and silence.[5]

'My message and my preaching were not with wise and persuasive words, but with a demonstration of the Spirit's power, *so that your faith might not rest on men's wisdom, but on God's power*' (1 Cor. 2:4–5).

To make an even larger point here, I agree with George Hunsberger that so much of our evangelical understanding of truth and the gospel has been post-Easter and neglectful of the ministry and actual teaching of Jesus. I am reminded of Garrison Keillor's barbed comment: 'Stop being a good Christian and start following Jesus!' Hunsberger says on this larger point: 'Proclaiming a gospel *about* Christ that is not shaped by *the gospel Jesus preached* distorts the gospel by proclaiming only part of its meaning.' This entails the loss of the dimension of the kingdom of God as Jesus declared and embodied it. 'The absence of the gospel Jesus preached', Hunsberger goes on, 'has woefully impoverished the church's sense of missional identity.'[6] Distorted perceptions of how ministry operates are just one symptom of this 'absence'. Only that teaching that leads people to the feet of Jesus is worthy of the kingdom. If the commission is to make disciples, it is not to make them '*our* disciples' but His, and to teach them whatever *He* commands.

There is one teacher of the Church – now known to us as the Holy Spirit Himself: the teachers in the Church are His students.
There is only one Father: leaders in His family are also our brothers and sisters.
There is only one leader, and whatever our gifts, calling, and ministry, we are all following His leadership.
To recognise this is to take to heart the words of St Augustine, the great father of the Western Church, to members of the Church in Alexandria:

When I am frightened by what I am *for* you, then I am consoled by what I am *with* you.
For you I am a bishop; *with* you I am a Christian.

The first is an office; the second a grace;
The first is a danger; the second is safety/salvation.
If I am happier to be redeemed *with* you than to be placed *over* you,
then, I shall, as the Lord commanded, be more fully your servant.

This takes us right to the heart of what Jesus is up to here.
What did Jesus do with leadership?
He prophetically critiqued it in the light of the dawning kingdom of God.
What did Jesus do with leadership?
He drastically redefined it in the light of His Father's upside-down kingdom.

Not that there weren't alternatives: but Jesus refused them and offered to lead God's people in an entirely new direction –

- *not the way of the Pharisees* who promoted holiness by keeping the Law more rigidly and more exclusively: Jesus was a 'boundary breaker' who interpreted the Father's 'be perfect as I am perfect' to mean 'be merciful as your heavenly Father is merciful'.
- *not the way of Sadducees and priests* who made Jerusalem and the Temple ritual the be-all-and-end-all of being God's people: Jesus threatened the dominance of both city and Temple.
- *not the way of the Qumran Covenanters* who withdrew from society to be purer than anyone else: Jesus entered the desert but did not stay there and through His 'table fellowship' gained a dubious reputation as the 'friend of sinners'.
- *not the way of Barabbas – and the later Zealots* who advocated armed and violent revolution: Jesus forbade the sword, preached non-violent resistance and was a peacemaker.

If we ask: 'What did Jesus do with leadership as He found it?', one answer is that He prophetically critiqued it in the light of the dawning kingdom of God and supplanted it with leaders of His own choosing. Then, if we pose the question another way: 'What did Jesus do with the whole idea of leadership?', the answer is that He drastically redefined it in the light of His Father's upside-down kingdom.
And servanthood was His preferred model for leaders (Matt. 23:11–12).
Without downplaying leadership, says Gordon Fee, 'for me the great

problem with a single leadership is its threefold tendency to pride of place, love of authority, and lack of accountability. Whatever else, leadership in the church needs forms that will minimise these tendencies and maximise servanthood.[7] And if we then ask: 'Why "servanthood"?' our texts invite us to draw at least three main conclusions:

1. Leadership takes the form of servanthood because Jesus Himself assumes the role of servant.

'For even the Son of Man did not come to be served, but to serve ...' (Mark 10:45); *'But I am among you as one who serves'* (Luke 22:27).

When Jesus speaks of an alternative kind of leadership He is not suggesting a few new techniques or strategies to be added to the expertise or management skills we already have. He speaks and acts out of His wider mission to restore Israel as the true people of God, to reconstitute Israel by embodying the true servant role Israel was meant to occupy. This was enacted in His baptism when the servant–kingship was bestowed on Him as His vocation: *'You are my Son'* which was the earliest designation of Israel as a people (Exod. 4:22–23). The epithet was later applied to the king who represents both God and people (cf. Psa. 2:7). The statement about sonship is then conflated with the words *'with him I am well pleased'* which are taken from the first 'servant song' (Isa. 42:1). So the word of Jesus 'I am among you as one who serves' is not a scrap of wisdom, a useful tip to go alongside that of other gurus (as if He were a Tom Peters or Steven Covey); not a handy hint offered to us to make our ministry marginally more effective. It is, as John Yoder says, nothing less than 'a capsule statement of Jesus' own key self-definition'.[8]

When Jesus warns the disciples about the way others exercise leadership, distribute patronage or wield power, He is describing temptations He had Himself faced and successfully resisted. 'I am among you as one who serves' describes the *choices He Himself had made* all along the way from His baptism onwards. The choice *not* to win our hearts by turning stones into bread and meeting our every economic need; *not* to make a name and reputation for Himself as a daring man of faith by leaping off the Temple pinnacle presuming on God's Word to save him; *not* to snatch the kingdoms of the world by selling His soul to the devil: this was His personal appropriation of the 'not so among you' principle He urged on His followers. This was His chosen way all through. Whenever another path was offered, He avoided it. After the people saw the feeding of 5,000 'they began to say, "Surely this is the Prophet who is to come into the world." Jesus, knowing that they intended to come and make him king by force, withdrew again to a mountain by himself' (John 6:15).

Matthew was reminded of Isaiah's servant figure when he reflected on how Jesus healed the sick: *'This was to fulfil what was spoken through the prophet Isaiah: "He took up our infirmities and carried our diseases"'* (Matt. 8:17; Isa. 53:4). When Jesus healed people, He warned them not to tell anyone who He was – quite the opposite of what we do with healing testimony – and when Matthew reflected on that he knew he was catching another glimpse of Isaiah's amazing servant: *'This was to fulfil what was spoken by the prophet Isaiah: "Here is my servant, whom I have chosen, the one I love, in whom I delight ... no one will hear his voice in the streets ..."'* Jesus Himself has come to His own conclusion very early on, I suspect.

There is more at stake here than perhaps we first realise. In John Yoder's words, 'What we learn from Jesus is not a suggestion about the strategy or skill in the discharge of those particular leadership responsibilities ordinarily associated with the pastorate ... The difference is not simply between ways to run a battle' – and, we might add, manage a company, organise an event – 'or ways to be socially responsible. It is between *definitions of salvation.'*[9]

Jesus, it seems clear, had seen, in the moving scriptural portrait of the servant of God painted by Isaiah, His own destiny. That strange and compelling biblical image of the servant Israel was meant to be, and was not, the servant that Israel needed to be served by because she was not – it was that image which He deliberately chose as the model for His own life and vocation. Jesus was not, said George Caird, 'the architect of his own destiny, but as a master builder, he followed faithfully the blueprints which he found in the writings of the scriptures'.[10] It is along these lines, I believe, that we can best understand with Matthew what it means 'to *fulfil* what the prophet Isaiah had spoken: it was not the individual but the role which he had in mind, a situation vacant and waiting to be filled by the right candidate.

In Caird's oft-quoted words: 'It was as though the prophet was publishing an advertisement:- "Wanted, Servant of the Lord: all applications welcome", accompanied by a "job description".'[11] We now know there was only one applicant suitable for the job. Christian ideas about ministry are therefore derived not from some idealised ideology but from a biblical and prophetic revelation made concrete in an incarnational model. That lordship is servanthood is not the Gnostic myth of a heavenly redeemer made historical and made human: it is the career of the humble servant of God vindicated and glorified.[12]

Misconceptions[13]

This may be an appropriate point to mention some of the common ways in which the servant concept is misconstrued, and hopefully lay them to rest.

Being a servant of God does not mean being a *dogsbody* – in fact, the servant in the Old Testament world was an honourable figure, often the king's right-hand man. The status of a 'servant' is obviously measured and qualified by whose servant you are. Being a servant of God does not mean being a *doormat*. The servant concept of leadership is no encouragement to lack of self-worth or low self-esteem; it does not denigrate but is intended to dignify our work. Nor is the servant concept of leadership an excuse for abusing people in leadership positions; as, for example, the demeaning treatment of women or patronising attitudes to those in Christian ministry or the idea that the pastor is at the beck and call of the congregation. The minister serves the people but they do not own him or her. God's servant is not there to be trampled on; nor should one allow people to ride roughshod over one. Servanthood is not servility.

It is useful in maintaining the balance of images to retain the hyphen in servant-leader. In this way, we serve precisely by leading. Being a servant does not mean the avoidance of power for fear of abusing it. Certainly, some churches – mostly new or charismatic – are hurt by pastoral domination and abuse of power, victims of 'driven leaders' who impose themselves by force of personality and will, and who are accountable to no one. But – especially in more traditional sections of the Church – churches are more likely to suffer from pastoral timidity. In these cases, whether because the pastor fears his tenure, or his bishop, or is emotionally insecure, the Christian minister becomes a people-pleaser, someone who follows the bleating of the sheep instead of feeding them and leading them. Such pastors mistake servanthood for abdication of their responsibility to fatten the sheep for the sheep's own self-sacrifice.

Servanthood is an attitude of heart and a stance of relationship: it is not meant to be a straitjacket that stifles initiative and creativity among leaders. In this sense, contemporary churches are damaged as much by pastoral default as by pastoral domination. Emotional insecurity can go either way: the way of abdication and weakness and withdrawal, or it can go the other way, manifesting itself in aggressive behaviour, and defensive attitudes which compensate for inner uncertainty.

Hold servant *and* leader together and we may get closer to Jesus, who was able to stoop to wash the disciples' feet without embarrassment or fear of losing face or authority because He knew with certainty where He had come from and where He was going, who He was serving, what the moment was and what was appropriate to that moment. A true servant-leader is able to say 'no', is not afraid to dissent to maintain integrity, who knows when to disagree for truth's sake. Team ministry is a particular test of servanthood. Teamwork demands a humble and sensitive handling of these issues, otherwise servanthood can be the cloak for an unseen control or a wrong kind of peer pressure where leaders so fear to 'rock the boat' that they cross a line where they are no longer true to themselves or to what God has given them to be!
Ron Sider puts it well:

> To be sure, it is possible to confuse biblical servanthood with a groveling self-denial grounded in self-hatred or an inadequate sense of self-worth. Sometimes women, victims of sexual abuse, and oppressed minorities have been so degraded by others that they lack all sense of dignity and worth. Such people think of themselves as *less* than God does. That is not Christian humility and servanthood.

It is self-hatred grounded in sinful abuse. Jesus' kind of servanthood flows from a powerful awareness of our dignity and worth based in the knowledge that the Creator of the universe made us in the divine image, and redeemed us at the cross.[14]

The second conclusion to emerge from the texts:

2. Leadership takes the form of servanthood because it is in the service of the cross.

The key texts make this clear: *'For even the Son of Man did not come to be served, but to serve, and to give his life a ransom for many'* (Mark 10:45).

On this account, our first duty is not to minister but to be *ministered to* by Jesus by being set free through His price-paying atoning death. The cross is the ultimate service He renders to God and to us. The cross is the ultimate outpouring of the servant's life to liberate a world held hostage by sin and oppression.

It is a price, of course, only He could pay.
'But', as John Yoder characteristically says, 'to be a disciple is to share in a quality of life of which the cross is the culmination.'[15] The price is His to pay alone: but the baptism of suffering and cup of cost are to be shared by all in Christian ministry, not only in our willingness to bear the brunt of opposition to the gospel but in our manner and methods of presenting it.

- Evangelists, out of an understandable desire to see people saved, are often tempted to lower the threshold of entry, to soften the cost of discipleship, to offer a padded cross for people to carry, well disguised as something well-fitted, even fashionable.
- Pastoral carers sometimes mistakenly assume that their pastoral task is to make it easier for people to take the costly decisions forced by the gospel so that only minor adjustments are needed to join the Church.

True servants of the cross will avoid these dangers.
Equally, if we are at all tempted to substitute for real repentance a long and heavy list of requirements in order to conform to our way of being a Christian – which don't derive from the gospel but are merely cultural

accretions – then servant-leaders will remember that the cross is pure and total grace whereby He gives Himself unreservedly for sinners.

Our text from Luke 22:20–30 sets this discussion at the Last Supper where John tells us He took towel and basin and stooped to wash the disciples' dusty feet – as an acted parable of what His cross was soon to do! As Jesus reminded them, 'those who exercise authority over them call themselves Benefactors' (Luke 22:25, ευεργεται). 'Benefactors' were a familiar part of the ancient world – dispensing patronage, financing public works, sponsoring events and gifted individuals. And who can deny that 'benefactors' are needed in the Church; without them so much Christian work would atrophy or die. But in that world which Jesus is contrasting with God's kingdom, how cynically do so-called 'benefactors' enslave and oppress, while all the while claiming to be doing good. Wasn't Jesus the Great Benefactor? When Peter summed up the ministry of Jesus – His signs and wonders and acts of compassion – he simply said, 'he went around doing good' (Acts 10:38, ευεργετῶν – the same word as in Luke 22:25).

'Do-gooder' is now a term of abuse. But I am often inclined, when exasperated by high-flown debate about the matter, to protest: 'What's so very wrong with "going around doing some good"?' It is not a bad default position for ministry to take.

If the Son of God loved me and gave Himself for me – how can I not be His willing bond-slave?

I have quoted Oswald Chambers and think of him, brilliant intellectual as he was, artistic and gifted, sowing his life into the arid soil of the Western desert and into the arid lives of the British, Australian and New Zealand troops stationed there in Egypt in 1916, chalking up his unforgettable sermon outlines on an old blackboard in stifling heat in a rough wooden hut, effectively casting his pearls of spiritual wisdom and perception before an audience of rough military men, and finally dying with fatigue as a result. His books still resonate with amazing insights and paradoxical logic and are still in print today, speaking to millions around the world. But he saw none of them and all the books were published posthumously. He knew nothing of the fame or fortune this would have brought him – and I concluded that he must have done it for some other more compelling reason than usually motivates us. What else than that Chambers was passionately in love with Jesus Christ?

Daunting as the lives of such exemplars are, they are the product of the same grace that is at work in our lives. They testify to the unspeakable joy and unmatchable privilege of being Christ's servant and of carrying scars, if scars they can be called, which are only splinters from His cross and of being ablaze with what is – even when at full flame – only a spark from the great burning conflagration of love that consumed Him on Calvary. This cross is the heart of all our ministry. The cross which seems the final constraint of freedom and was used by the empire of the day to oppress and destroy becomes, in His topsy-turvy kingdom, the way to freedom and the path to life.

The third conclusion thus follows inevitably from the texts:

3. Leadership takes the form of servanthood because this is the way things are in God's upside-down kingdom!

As happens too often the disciples fall out among themselves about who's where in the pecking order. This time it results from a request made by James and John to Jesus: 'Let one of us sit at your right hand and the other at your left in your glory' (Mark 10:37).

The brothers assume that Jesus is destined for a kingdom with all its attendant glory and want to make sure of the best seats at the enthronement and top posts in the cabinet thereafter. This does not go down well with the other disciples whose competitive spirit is roused to indignation by the prospect of being upstaged by the sons of Zebedee. The mistake they are all making is to misunderstand the way the kingdom of God works. It doesn't operate along conventional lines – the kind of methodology common to kings and presidents and dictators from time immemorial.

'You know that those who are regarded as rulers of the Gentiles lord it over them, and their high officials exercise authority over them. *Not so among you.* Instead, whoever wants to become great must be your servant, and whoever wants to be first must be slave of all' (10:42–44).

Notice that shattering '*Not so among you*'! No category, whether social, cultural, ecclesiastical, or political will fit His vision of leadership without drastic alteration.

Jesus' '*Not so among you*' thwarts any attempt to institutionalise worldliness in the leadership structures of the Church.

While Jesus is offsetting the way things are in God's kingdom against *Gentile ways of ruling*, His critique is also reminiscent of Old Testament warnings.

I am reminded of Samuel's warning to Israel about the fateful consequence of their choosing a king in order to be 'like all the other nations' (1 Sam. 8).

I am reminded of Rehoboam's tragic refusal to heed the wisdom of the elders he consulted who advised him to respond to the people's plea that he lighten the load his father had imposed on them: 'If today you will be a servant to these people and serve them and give them a favourable answer, they will always be your servant' (1 Kings 12:7).

I am reminded of how the Old Testament historians assess the reigns of the kings of Israel and Judah by giving an almost totally negative verdict: writing off the lengthy reigns of successful and powerful kings in a few dismissive words: 'He did not walk in the ways of the Lord.'

What Jesus makes clear is that the 'alternative to how the kings of the earth rule is not "spirituality" but "servanthood"'.[16] In other words, the alternative to how the world does leadership is not the addition of some 'spiritual' ingredient or devotional dimension but a radical change in the way we conceive of leadership in the first place. It is not so much that we need – as if often said – to 'get Christians out of the church and into the world': they are altogether too much 'in the world' as it is; our task is to get them to act and think like Christians when they are there.

That definite '*Not so among you*' must raise questions, then, about so many of our approaches to leadership and ministry in today's Church.

- the *consumer* appetite, aroused by global capitalism, can so easily distort our concepts of ministry so that even in our evangelistic zeal we become vendors of religious products, albeit dressed up in evangelical and biblical packaging.

- the *therapeutic* culture that seeps out from the West to all parts of the world can be absorbed by the Church so that ministry becomes the offer to meet 'felt needs' rather than an invitation to die to self and rise to new life in Christ, then to learn with others the new skills of how to be human again.
- the *business* mentality can so permeate our minds that we can end up running a religious organisation, taking meetings, setting goals, organising programmes, even employing marketing techniques, rather than caring for and curing souls and creating truly human, new covenant communities.

The Church's primary task – I am more and more convinced – is not evangelism or Church growth or pastoral care and counselling: the Church's primary task is to be an authentic sign, foretaste and agent of the coming kingdom of God – that kingdom previewed and instituted in all its strange and paradoxical glory in the words, and deeds, miracles and mercy, dying and rising of our Lord Jesus Christ! It is a servant-leader who best exhibits this alternative kingdom and its radically different ways of working! *Jesus redefines leadership as servanthood because that is how things are in the upside-down kingdom of God!*

The three points which have emerged from the servant ministry that Jesus modelled and endorsed provide an outline for the three main sections of the book, namely – *Christlike, cruciform* and *culturally-critical.*

Christlike

Under this heading, we explore the shape that Jesus accepted for His own vocation as found in the *'servant songs' of Isaiah* and examine how it can be a valid template for us today. The intention here is to move beyond the idea of slavishly copying Jesus – even if that were possible, given His uniqueness and the 2,000-year gap in cultures between us and Him. What is on the table here is not some sentimental and reductionist transformation of Christology into abstract qualities of inclusivity, unconditional love and general niceness (though heaven knows the Church could do with an outbreak of kindness). While such an approach seems, on the surface, to follow the example of Jesus, it fails, in Andrew Purves' words, in not 'having at its core a vital way in which the church's ministry shares in Christ's continuing personhood and ministry ...'[17]

Rather, what we are seeking to describe involves an imbibing of the Spirit of Christ, an absorbing of His theo-centric mindset, which can occur *only* through *union with Christ*. This is to go beyond *imitation* of Christ to emphasise *participation* in Christ. In the words of Peter Taylor Forsyth,

> When Paul said he had the 'mind of Christ' he did not mean the *temper* of Christ: he meant the *theology* of Christ. And by that he meant not the theology held by the earthly Christ, but that taught him by Christ in heaven. A reference to 1 Corinthians 2:16 will show this at once. 'Who has known (by a gnosis) the mind of Christ that he may *instruct* him? But we have (by faith) the mind of Christ.' That is, of the Lord, the Spirit.[18]

As Forsyth asserted: 'the meaning is that, by the supernatural gift of the Spirit, possessed only in the Church, Paul had knowledge of the intention of Christ, Christ's implicit thought, God's meaning in Christ, the theology of Christ and the cross.'

Cruciform

This section is given over to reflections on Paul's *letters to the Corinthians*. The relevance of the apostle's disputation with the Corinthian 'charismatics' to our understanding of the dynamics of Christian ministry has long been recognised. If Paul is to succeed in defending his ministry (as he aims to do in 2 Corinthians) he must persuade the Corinthians to reconfigure the way in which they interpret the adversities in his life. He must show that his afflictions which seem to disqualify him in the eyes of the Corinthians are God-graced, demonstrations of God's power. 'His reflections on and use of the death and resurrection of Jesus as an interpretive key for his life and experiences as an apostle provide him with the needed criteria to do this.'[19] Only in so far as the method and manner of the messenger are congruous with 'the cruciform nature of the message can the word of the cross occur and so be the power of God' (1 Cor. 1:18).[20]

Recent discussion has framed this theme in terms of *cruciformity*, especially as brought to the fore by Michael Gorman. He defines 'cruciformity' as 'conformity to the crucified Christ' and further explains, convincingly to my mind, that such 'conformity is a dynamic correspondence in daily life to the strange story of Christ crucified as the primary way of experiencing the love and grace of God'.[21] As far as Paul is concerned, Gorman suggests that by 'offering himself as a narrative continuation of the Lord's cross, he invited others to look through him to Christ as the ultimate paradigm of God's love, of cruciform love'.[22] Just as the cross in its evident frailty and folly does not accord with imperial perceptions of reality, so also, Stephen Kraftchick argues, Paul's ministry cannot be fitted into contemporary understandings of power and value. 'Rather the gospel claims that *its reality is the framework for construing the world*.'[23]

The note leads us to a third main point and section in this book:

Culturally-critical

Since the cross was the 'foolishness of God' confounding the 'wisdom of the world', it follows that a ministry generated by the Easter gospel will be humbly and creatively non-conformist. It is important to remember that to be counter-cultural is not to be anti-creational, not Gnostic, in disparaging the goodness of God still gloriously evident in what He has made and continues to sustain. Rather what is being countered is the 'world' in its Johannine sense of human culture and institutions in so far as they are organised against, or without reference to, God – what Walter Wink has aptly termed 'the Domination System'[24]. This was the world that crucified Jesus. With His 'Not so among you' ringing in our ears, we will seek Christological alternatives to the 'world's' attempts to define our ministry for us, however much this raises the stakes. We should expect nothing else. For as Michael Knowles points out in his stimulating study of 2 Corinthians, 'the difficulty and cost of such a ministry match the counter-intuitive, counter-cultural nature of the message and the bitter-sweet, death-and-life challenge that it conveys'.[25]

Such insights are too rich to be fully developed here. But as examples of what it might mean to practise culturally-critical ministry, I offer reflections drawn from the prophet *Jeremiah* on our current obsession with relevance, and from *Paul* on how to translate the '*Not so among you*' into ministry that is *for* its time by being *ahead* of its time. The further implications of all this for pastoral care and for preaching I hope to explore in a forthcoming publication. The three sections of the book show something of the influential links between Isaiah, Jeremiah and Jesus and through Jesus to Paul. The connections made bring the realisation that Christlike servanthood invariably takes a cruciform shape which inevitably will be culturally-critical. Suffice it to say that no one realises more than I do how sharp a challenge this is to our contemporary models of ministry and how sobering a judgment this is on my own life and ministry. I am only amazed how grace manages to achieve its gracious ends *despite* my 'Gentile' ways of doing things. I leave the last word to the late Alan Lewis who advises that

> ... our own 'Gentile' past can scarcely be forgiven unless our churches are willing to allow their ministry and ministers to be transformed by the Spirit into more recognizably Christ-like, that is, cruciform and grave-shaped, patterns.[26]

2
MINISTERING GRACE TO ESTABLISH JUSTICE

(Isaiah 42:1–19 – the first 'servant song')

The word 'service' has undeniably fallen on hard times in the modern Western world. Although the business sector pontificates in its glossy 'mission statements' about 'providing a service', it remains true that real service industries are inclined to offer the most menial jobs at the lowest rates of pay, and tend to be staffed by the poorest people in society, often from immigrant communities. These do the work no one else wants to do but which no one else can do without!

All the more challenging for us, then, that Jesus establishes servanthood as His perennial model of ministry. In doing so, He offsets it against the power structures and institutionalised authorities of His day.

His disciples were not unnaturally impressed by these models of leadership in the world around them. Early on in their relationship with Jesus, the untutored disciples envisage rich pickings in having backed what is so obviously going to be a successful Messianic candidate for office. When their own pride and insecurity break out like a rash, they fall out over who is to be top dog in the new order of things, and Jesus has to intervene to knock a few heads together: You know how secular rulers like to "throw their weight around" … and when people get a little power how quickly it goes to their heads. *It's not going to be that way with you*' (Mark 10:42–3a, *The Message*).

It is still all too easy to get the wires crossed here. I am reminded of a bewhiskered joke I'm fond of told by the late Tommy Cooper. Cooper tells of rummaging in his attic and finding a violin and an old oil painting. He takes them to Sotheby's to be valued by an expert and is told: 'You've got a Rembrandt and a Stradivarius.' That's good, thinks the comedian. 'Unfortunately,' says the valuer, 'Rembrandt couldn't make violins and Stradivarius was a rotten painter!' To spare us any confusion, Jesus ruled out the cloning of secular concepts of ministry for Christian purposes ('It's not going to be that way with you') and, lest we get our wires crossed, explicitly endorsed and exemplified only *one* style of ministry – *servant-ministry*: 'But I am among you as one who serves' (Luke 22:27).

Where did He come by this, and why was it so important to Him? Jesus, it seems clear, had seen, in the moving portrait of the servant of God painted by Isaiah, His own destiny. That strange and compelling biblical image of the servant, which Israel was meant to be and wasn't, merges – like a computer image – into the servant whom Israel needed to be served *by* if ever her vocation was to be redeemed. This was the image which Jesus seems deliberately to have chosen as the mould into which to pour His own life and ministry. And being Jesus' own 'self-definition', equally crucially, *it conforms to the way God chooses to save the world*. In this unique 'fitting of the prophetic bill', this 'fulfilling of Scripture', Jesus stands supreme, but – in another sense – He does not stand alone, but wants His followers to imbibe His spirit and to extend His servant ministry: 'whoever wants to become great among you must be your servant' (Mark 10:43). So, we must draw from the same well of inspiration that resourced Jesus – Isaiah's vivid portrait of God's servant, beginning with the first of the so-called 'servant songs', *Isaiah 42:1–19.*

'*Behold* my servant …' (Isa. 42:1a, ESV). God draws glaring attention to His servant, pushing Him forward, as it were, out of the shadowy background into the public spotlight. This is by way of contrast with Isaiah 41:29 where God calls His people's attention to the insubstantial alternative offered by idols who are false and whose works are 'nothing'. So, rather than hiding His servant away behind the scenes – as servants then and now are wont to be treated – God openly introduces His servant as if in a formal presentation ceremony. Commentators point out that this presentation of God's servant – perhaps before the divine council – is reminiscent of the way kings are presented to their people (cf. 1 Sam. 9:17). In fact, from this point on, the Isaianic servant displays many royal characteristics: not least the task set before kings of establishing justice in the land.

Recalling the context of Isaiah's 'servant' prophecies also helps us to understand the intended impact of Jesus' commitment to this image of ministry. In these oracles, God's Word is addressed to the Babylonian exiles, as much subject to imperial overlordship as was Jesus' first-century audience. It is remarkable then that God puts the emphasis on servanthood as His preferred way of working, addressing an exiled people who in such circumstances might have looked for divine sanction to fight for political power and to use aggression to win them their freedom. Instead, by highlighting His servant in this way, God reminds Israel of her original servant vocation that stretches back to Abraham, to be a blessing to the nations (cf. Isa. 41:18ff.). Now God urges His people not to be afraid (41:10,13–14) and states His intention to renew this servant vocation by focusing it in a mysterious and representative figure. When the real 'servant of God' stepped out of Isaiah's picture, it was to advocate servanthood as the same audacious way of representing the kingdom of God under the constraints of living under Roman Imperial rule. If the focus on servanthood in our postmodern Western world is to succeed in realigning our angle of vision, it will do so not least by diverting our attention from any hankering after the kind of institutionalised power structures that so corrupted the Church of Christendom.

Reflecting further on Isaiah 42, we notice firstly *the servant's distinguishing marks*:

- God *sponsors* the servant's ministry: Here is '*my* servant' (Isa. 42:1). Being a servant in the ancient world was not necessarily to be the miserable slave or dogsbody. To be a servant could put you at the right hand of kings at court. It all depends, of course, on whose servant you are. Who your master is measures who you are; his dignity and stature make yours. So there can be no higher honour than to be '*God's* servant'. Abraham was so called (Gen. 26:24) as were Moses (Exod. 14:31), David (2 Sam. 3:18) and, of course, the prophets (Amos 3:7).

There's a fine hymn of Charles Wesley on the Holy Spirit which has the lines:

Where the indubitable seal
That ascertains the kingdom mine?
The powerful stamp I long to feel,
The signature of love divine.

Charles Wesley, 1707–1778

Just as a great artist signs his painting in the corner with pleasure and pride, so God writes His name on your heart, to own you as His servant. The implication is clear too: God's servant takes orders from God: he is not driven by the world's agenda!

- God *supports* the servant: 'whom I *uphold*' (42:1b). Not surprisingly, God promises to back His servant with His full resources. The servant will not operate in His own strength but is a standing sign in the world of one who has no visible means of support except God alone. If God fails, so does the servant; if God lets the servant down, the servant falls. 'If anyone serves, he [or she] should do it with the strength God provides' (1 Pet. 4:11).

- God *selects* the servant: 'my *chosen one*' (42:1c). The true servant of God is never self-appointed but comes by royal divine appointment. This is the basis for the servant's sense of security.
  To be chosen is to be cherished and deemed precious.
  To be chosen is to be loved.
  Being chosen does not exclude others, but immediately includes others in the compassionate scope of ministry.
  Says Henri Nouwen, 'When love chooses, it chooses with perfect sensitivity for the unique beauty of the chosen one, and it chooses without making anyone else feel excluded.' Nouwen goes on, 'I beg you, do not surrender the word "chosen" to the world. Dare to claim it as your own even when it is misunderstood. You must hold on to the truth that you are a chosen one. That truth is the bedrock on which you can build a life as the Beloved.'[1] To be chosen is to be a sign of God's choice in the world – and, we might add, a sign, surely, that God's choices, not ours, are the best guarantee of our human freedom.

- God is *satisfied* with the servant, the one 'in whom *my soul delights*' (42:1d, ESV). This is the secret of energy and peace: to serve out of

39

a heart flooded with the love of God. Knowing the Lord's approval fortifies the servant against human disapproval and denigration and against the vanity that seeks self-satisfaction as its only goal. Nourished by God's endorsement, the servant can withstand criticism and rejection. Of Jesus, Samuel Chadwick once said:

> Everybody else disapproved. At one stage or other of his work, everybody lost faith in him … [But] however terrible his lot, however hard his task, however disappointing his toil, however deep his humiliation, however faithless his friends or bitter his enemies, he never doubted God loved him.[2]

And this assurance of God's delight surely lifts servanthood too out of mere function and duty and into the realm of relationship. It is no coincidence – as Isaiah reminds us – that Abraham, God's servant, was also called God's *friend* (Isa. 41:8). No wonder Jesus was able to supervise the graduation of His disciples from 'servants' to 'friends' (John 15:14–15).

- God puts His *Spirit* on the servant: '*I will put my Spirit on him*' (42:1e). Since the Spirit of God in the Old Testament is a virtual synonym for the power of God, it is all the more striking to see *how* that power operates as unfolded in what follows. Sufficient weight is seldom given to the fact that everything Jesus said and did He carried out by the empowerment of the Holy Spirit bestowed on Him without measure. Equally, sufficient weight is only rarely placed on the fact that the same Spirit is as available to us (in our limited measure) as it was to Him.

It is this empowerment of the Holy Spirit which explains the description that follows of the paradoxical *way* in which God's servant conducts ministry.

Secondly, then, notice *the servant's manner and method of operation.*

- *self-restraint* (42:2): '*He will not shout or cry out, or raise his voice in the streets.*' Here is early biblical evidence that the Holy Spirit produces the fruit of 'self-control'. It is not as though the servant exercises no public ministry of speaking or preaching or even protest – if so, Jesus would not have qualified to fit this picture.

But the servant is not a hectoring demagogue. True servant ministry does not engage in self-promotion; does not draw needless attention to itself; does not believe its own publicity; does not see God's service as an ego trip; does not – as Oswald Chambers said – go into the showbusiness. In short, servant-ministry seeks the Master's glory, not its own. And this public restraint is simply the sign of a true and deep *reticence*. Such reticence is the wisdom which knows when not to overstep the mark, which knows where the boundaries are and where to draw the line. Eugene Peterson observes of reticence:

> An enthusiasm for God's unlimited grace requires as its corollary a developed sensitivity to human limits. We have to know when and where to stop. In a work in which God is intensely active, we have to be cautious, reticent lest we interfere in what we do not understand.[3]

Peterson goes on to quote Wendell Berry who says he knew a barber once who refused to give a discount to a bald-headed man, explaining that his artistry consisted not in cutting hair off but in knowing when to stop! More importantly, we need to make space for the Spirit. 'The words of Jesus: "It is for your good that I leave" should' – says Henri Nouwen – 'be part of every pastoral call we make. We have to learn to leave so that the Holy Spirit can come.'[4] And with self-restraint and reticence goes …

- *sensitivity (42:3): 'A bruised reed he will not break, and a smouldering wick he will not snuff out.'*

Whether from Jewish Holy War, Christian Crusade or Muslim 'Jihad', power has a tragic history, even in religious hands, of furthering the cause of conquest rather than compassion. From power-mad kings to military dictatorships to religiously inflamed suicide bombers, power is crudely misused to trample on people, to abuse them, to oppress them, to obliterate them. So often does this happen in our power-hungry world that it is hard to envisage power harnessed to any other purpose. 'The style of the Servant', says Old Testament scholar Paul Hanson, 'stands so starkly in contrast to the ways of the nations that it must be regarded either as foolishness or as an intriguing alternative to a failed strategy.'[5]

Servant-ministry is God's alternative strategy: it handles people like valuable china. It seeks not to break lives but to make lives. And it is not deterred by the fragility and faltering faith of those it ministers to. Here is power under the leash: power brokered by sheer goodness, power that is not harsh or clumsy, authority that is not brash or boastful.

The servant moves in the Spirit with tact and tenderness. Is there some vestige of human dignity under that abused and broken personality? Is there a flicker of hope or expectation that God can act, dimly perceptible in the darkness that engulfs a life? Don't despise it: start there. Don't rush in with idle words or promises where angels have the good sense not to tread! Cup the hands of ministry around that needy person as you would around a candle in the wind. Tread softly lest you tread on someone's discarded dream. In Daniel Berrigan's words, 'be a gentle footfall on the earth'.

- *strength of purpose* (42:3b–4): 'he will not falter or be discouraged'. In other words, never mistake the servant's meekness for weakness.

There is a well-known play on words in the Hebrew here. The true servant will minister to crushed reeds and flickering flames but will not in the process be 'broken' or 'burn dimly'! In modern jargon the pressures of ministry are often classified as 'having a breakdown' or 'burning out'. But true servant ministry need not 'break down' or 'suffer burnout'. Practise vulnerability with the vulnerable as we must, but it is possible not to be utterly crushed or discouraged in the process. Needy people can wear you out. Marriage counsellors often tell how wary they have to be that they do not – by transference – take the marriage problems they are dealing with back into their own relationships. But for true servant ministry it need not be so. Here is the mysterious power to absorb pain without being destroyed by it. In John Oswalt's words,

> God's answer to the oppressors of the world is not more oppression, nor is his answer to arrogance more arrogance; rather, in quietness, humility, and simplicity, he will take the evil of the world into himself and return only grace: that is power.[6]

Here is a heart replenished 'at the secret source of every precious thing'. No one has said it better than John Bunyan in *The Pilgrim's Progress*:

> Then I saw in my dream that the Interpreter took Christian by the hand and led him into a place where there was a fire burning against a wall, and one standing by it, always casting much water upon it to quench it; yet did the fire burn higher and hotter. Then said Christian 'What means this?' The Interpreter answered: 'This fire is the work of grace that is wrought in the heart; he that casts water upon it to extinguish it and put it out, is the devil; but in that thou seest the fire notwithstanding burn higher and hotter, thou shalt also see the reason of it.' So he had him about to the back side of the wall, where saw a man with a vessel of oil in his hand, of the which he did also continually cast (but secretly) into the fire.

Bunyan identifies this man as Christ who maintains the work begun in the heart. It was precisely this extraordinary combination of toughness and tenderness that Matthew saw exemplified in Jesus – especially in the way Jesus handled the poor and needy, and healed the sick.

Thirdly, notice that *the servant's mission and objective is ...*

- '*[to] bring forth justice ...*' (42:1,3–4) – this is the one priority! Here is a truly prophetic conjoining of piety and politics. 'Justice' (*mishpat*) is the covenant love of God in its social dimension. Walter Brueggemann states it well when he says that justice is the 're-ordering of social life and social power so that the weak (widows and orphans) may live a life of dignity, security and well-being'.[7] God's servant ministry contributes to the building of God-filled communities of truth, righteousness and faithfulness – where widows and orphans, aliens and strangers, women and children, the poor and oppressed, are particularly welcomed – where spiritual and social 'exiles' can find a home, and where everyone's gift and potential is set to be developed and grown. To show, to bring, and to establish justice – this is the ultimate reason for the servant's ministry.[8]

The big question raised by the prophetic oracle is whether there is anyone that fits the servant's 'job description'. In Isaiah's day it was evidently not Israel! Israel is unqualified to bring the light of saving justice to the nations: 'Who is blind but my servant, and deaf like the messenger I send?' (Isa. 42:19) – as blind and deaf as those she was meant to bring light and revelation to. This is tough talk, but it has to be to break through the apathy and self-absorption that holds God's people captive and makes them strangers to their own history and destiny. Only tough talk can puncture the complacency with which God's people refuse to face the fact that it is their own sin that has brought them into Exile, and that they need the revival that only true repentance will launch. So where is a fitting candidate for such a servanthood as so brilliantly described here by Isaiah? The evangelist Matthew felt sure he had found the answer (see Matt. 3:16–17; 12:15–21). Here was a 'job vacancy' waiting to be filled until the Man from Nazareth stepped into and out of the Jordan River. There, Jesus was anointed as Servant-King – King with the royal covenant commitment to David echoed in the words of Psalm 2 ('You are my Son'), and Servant to carry the nation's destiny and vocation as the one with whom God 'delights' (Isa. 42:1).

Jesus is the servant God has always been waiting for. Jesus is the embodiment of Israel, gathering into Himself all that Israel was meant to be. He embodies the covenant (Isa. 42:6b). In Him the covenant faithfulness of God and the faithful response of a covenant partner are joined. Now, at last, the light of God's revelation and grace may shine forth from Israel to the nations of the world.

Can the Church, now licking its wounds in post-Christendom trauma, rise to the prophetic challenge of Jesus to be this servant ministry? The question posed by the Early Church Fathers – what has Athens to do with Jerusalem? – finds its corresponding question today: what has pastoral care to do with politics? The answer, surprisingly, is – 'everything'. The world longs and waits for God's justice: for 'the order of compassionate justice that God has created and on which the wholeness of the universe depends'.[9] In its broadest sense it is synonymous with salvation. In every respect, as Yoder observes, it is a 'justice of grace'.[10]

Christian ministry – whether in leadership, preaching, pastoral care or counselling – is not ultimately, or even primarily, about therapy. It is not in the business of making people feel better about themselves. It is not in the business of soothing the 'angst' of middle-class believers and returning them a little more comfortably adjusted to the hedonistic, consumerist lifestyles that caused their stress first time round. Servant ministry – yours and mine – is in the service of a God who is about opening blind eyes and freeing prisoners and restoring His people to covenant health and community, and all to His glory (cf. Isa. 42:7–8). To that end, servant ministry is funded by the gospel. I repeat what is for me almost a mantra: If it doesn't take the cross and resurrection of Jesus to effect the transformation we seek in providing care or giving counsel, then it isn't Christian caring or counselling we are offering but some form of self-help. Every servant ministry – even on the intimate, micro-scale of counselling and pastoral care – is carried out under the aegis of our Lord and Saviour Jesus Christ, who by the Spirit seeks to make disciples who will make a difference, communities of servants, with tough minds and tender hearts, who will in small but significant ways be a sign and foretaste and agent of the coming kingdom of our just and righteous Lord. However small-scale our ministry seems, we dare not settle for being part of anything less.

I leave you with my motto, which has sustained me in many failures and occasional successes of Christian ministry over thirty-five years:

> I sink under what has to be done for the world until I realise it is all less than what has been done and put into the charge of our faith and word.
>
> P.T. Forsyth

3

MAKING A SECRET LIFE COUNT FOR PUBLIC MINISTRY

(Isaiah 49:1–13 – the second 'servant song')

Faced with the challenge of choosing a way of saving the world, you would be hard pressed to come up with a scheme as incongruous as servanthood. And without being melodramatic, it is the world's destiny that is at stake. It was for this large reason that Jesus opted for servanthood in preference to 'Gentile' ways of ruling and running the world. The contrast He draws between worldly ways to rule the world and His own is not a mere clash of styles. The difference is between 'definitions of salvation'. The contrast is between domination and the meekness and patience of service; between the lust to control and the desire to set free; between the instinct to coerce and the disposition to persuade. In the 'Gentile' system, 'every concession is a defeat';[1] in the kingdom of God forbearance is a tactical retreat in the strategy of love. The self-serving propaganda and spin that would ensnare and deceive, is supplanted in the kingdom of God by costly truth-telling that sets us free. In contrast to the closed system where politics is the 'art of the possible', the Spirit of God opens up new possibilities from old impossibilities.

It is in this 'altogether different' order of things that servanthood operates. In this order, we proclaim the new world, we do not produce it; we are witnesses, not engineers. And this is precisely where the burdens of servanthood are felt most keenly – in the contradictions between the large scale of the task and the seeming fragility of the agents, between the universal and the particular, the public role and the private persona. Even God's unique Servant was not immune from this: 'Now is my soul troubled. And what shall I say? "Father, save me from this hour?" But for this purpose I have come to this hour. Father, glorify your name' (John 12:27–28, ESV).

The disparity between 'Gentile' ways and God's way is registered as painful perplexity in the servant's heart. The tension requires to be resolved by the fresh confession of faith, by the honest admission of weakness, and by the recommission and reassurance of God. Which is what we find here in the second 'servant song'.

The 'song' opens with the servant's own testimony (Isa. 49:1–4).

First we hear the servant *calling on the world* (Isa. 49:1), claiming the attention of distant nations. The servant plays his part on the world stage because it is the world's story that is in process of being rewritten. The story is that of the world's one Creator-God and the salvation of the world. Nothing less than this is at stake.

The servant begins to tell his own story and, in doing so, he can only start before his birth when, he says, 'The LORD *called me from the womb*' (49:1, ESV).

This is the language of a prophetic calling – as Jeremiah felt it (Jer. 1:4–5) and as Paul himself later acknowledged (Gal. 1:15). Not surprisingly, then, when the servant reviews his own life and ministry (49:2–3) he sees himself above all as

- the *mouthpiece of God's word: 'He made my mouth like a sharpened sword'* (49:2).

Unlike Cyrus, the other agent of God's plans at this time, unlike any other military conqueror for that matter, the sword is not a literal sword, a weapon of war in his hand, but the sword of truth in his mouth; the sword of God's powerful prophetic word. Again, it is clear how the servant as portrayed by Isaiah represents what Israel was meant to be – the nation that lived by the Word of God alone, whose exclusive privilege shared by no other nation was to have heard God speak (Deut. 4:12,15, 33). The seclusion of the wilderness had been intended to teach Israel to live not by bread alone but by every word that proceeds from God's mouth (Deut. 8:3).

- The servant is the *handiwork of God's secret dealings: 'in the shadow of his hand he hid me'* (49:2).

This suggests the preparation of a life hidden away from open view, a season of special training, but in secret away from people's gaze. These are the servant's private dealings with God that count for so much in his public ministry. One thinks of Moses prepared for forty years with the flock, or of David's years of fugitive existence before becoming king, and then, by extension, of the thirty years spent growing up in Nazareth for the ultimate Servant of God, and of Paul in his desert seclusion. It is in the shadows where God shapes our lives that our public service is formed. Christians in earlier generations referred to this as 'having a history with God'. In that intimate interaction between the servant and God is where the sword in the scabbard, the arrow in the quiver is kept rust-free, and sharp. And all this is so that the servant can be on the cutting edge of God's plans with the only weapon given to the servants of God – the sword of God's Word of truth.

- Everything in these secret dealings and shaping of the servant's hidden life by God is with one end in view – to make the servant what God's people as a whole are intended to be, the *showcase of God's glory* (49:3b).

It is beginning to look as if this servant – as portrayed by Isaiah – is called to represent and embody all that Israel was intended to be. Now Isaiah makes this explicit. 'He said to me: "You are my servant, Israel, in whom I will display my splendour."'

At this point disagreement has often broken out among scholars between those who say the servant is a *corporate image*, a picture of Israel, or ideal Israel, and those who say the songs of the servant progressively reveal an *individual* servant. Yes: the servant is Israel (41:8ff.) but has a ministry to Israel (as here) and cannot even be identified with the faithful remnant *in* Israel because he ministers to them as well (49:6b 'those … I have kept'). Failing to resolve this, many scholars give up and suggest it is a vague image capable of many interpretations. But as we have already begun to see, both are in a sense true. In other words, the servant represents God but also stands in for God's servant people. Furthermore, 'Israel' was a name first given to an individual, the father of the nation, Jacob (Gen. 32:28; 35:9ff.). In Isaiah 49:3 then, the sense is that the servant is being *designated* 'Israel' once again. 'From now on I call you "Israel"'. In John Oswalt's words: 'The Servant is going to function as Israel ... and will be *for* Israel and the world what Israel could not be.'[2]

The 'song' now outlines at least four obstacles the servant has to overcome:
• *futility* – 'I've wasted my time' (49:4)

The servant experiences the intense discouragement that inflicts all of us involved in ministry: '*I have laboured to no purpose ... in vain and for nothing.*' And '*yet*' – an even stronger article of contrast intrudes, overcoming the 'but' at the start of the verse; the 'yet surely' breaking into the servant's own thought processes. The servant appears to be wrestling with a personal sense of pointlessness, searching deep within himself for a meaning to what he's doing. By an effort of will, he reconnects with God's perspective on things, refocuses on the rewards God hands out, and is enabled to reaffirm his commitment to leave the success of his ministry in God's hands.

• *weariness* – 'I'm utterly worn out' (49:4): '*I have spent my strength*'

God's servants do get tired serving God, and it is no sin to admit it. Some brands of so-called 'faith-teaching' tell you that if you were really spiritual, you would never feel tiredness or futility; and in any case, if you did, it would be lack of faith to confess it. What nonsense! Trust in God is trust in the final outcome, not the immediate result (49:4b).

• *small-mindedness* – 'I want to stay in my comfort zones' (49:6)

Putting it that way may seem hard on the servant as the text presents him, but we can all identify with this. In fact, verse 6 reveals an amazing turn of events: 'It is too small a thing for you to be my servant to restore the tribes of Jacob and bring back those of Israel I have kept. I will also make you a light for the Gentiles, that you may bring my salvation to the ends of the earth.'

Imagine you work for a large company, representing their business interests – in, say, the UK or Malaysia – and you're not doing too well.

Things aren't going very successfully, your sales figures for the last few years have been on the slide. Finally, you are called into the chief executive's office, and you enter, half expecting a strong pep talk about 'the need to improve your performance', perhaps fearing a demotion or, with luck, a sideways shift to a less demanding job, or – there lurks at the back of your mind the worst-case scenario – 'We are downsizing', or, with mock regret, 'We will have to let you go' (or whatever other office-speak is now current for 'You're fired!'). Instead, an extraordinary thing happens: the managing director announces that he considers your current local job too small for you, and so has decided to enlarge your area of responsibility to include the world by making you the firm's *international representative*. Something similar is happening here with the servant. Do we need any more convincing that God's kingdom is an upside-down kingdom, which stands the world on its head? Jesus scandalised the religious 'trade unions' of His day when He told the story of an employer who paid the workers hired at the eleventh hour the same wages as those who had toiled all day. But that's just the way it is in God's economy of grace.

It is significant to notice that the first goal of ministry here is to 'bring ... [God's people] back to him' (49:5b). In my view, it remains the primary work of servant ministry always and in every way to deepen the relationship between God's people and God Himself. It is striking to consider Paul's prayers for the churches to which he is writing and to realise that he prays basically for one thing and one thing only: he prays not so much for Church growth or for new miracles, but that his readers may know God better. We may at any one time consider ourselves to be successful or unsuccessful. But if Isaiah 49:6 is any guide to the footsteps we follow in, then we can with boldness lose our small-mindedness and embrace God's world vision and mission.

- *self-denigration* – 'I get no recognition' (49:4). Such is the lot of God's servant – to go unregarded and unrecognised.

But if God's servant wonders where to find vindication, honour and strength if not from the Lord, his Master, the answer is at hand: 'Yet what is due to me is in the LORD's hand ... for I am honoured in the eyes of the LORD ...' (49:4b,5b). Servants trust to a superior valuation; they play to an audience of one. So the humble will be exalted in God's way and in God's time (cf. 1 Pet. 5:6). So the servant's mission is enlarged. The servant is to be a *light* to the nations and a living embodiment of the *covenant* to the people (Isa. 49:6,8). Once again, we see how the servant himself *is* the covenant – so that only in him can the covenant relationship and blessings be enjoyed. In his own person, the servant is an answer to prayer (49:8b) and the trigger for God's grace to explode into action. The servant's ministry and message to the exiles is now poetically celebrated (49:8–9). This is couched in the language of the Jubilee Year (Lev. 25) and its down-to-earth practicalities ought not to be spiritualised away.

The servant brings:
- *security for the unsettled* – by seeking to 'restore the land' (49:8c) and so to give dislocated people a place to be and grow once again;
- *hope for the dispossessed* – by reassigning 'desolate inheritances' (49:8d) and as a matter of justice, redressing wrongs, and making reparation where possible;
- *freedom for the imprisoned* – by calling on the enslaved to 'Come out' (49:9a) – inviting exiles to leave their 'Babylonian captivity' (however we may currently construe it) as once Israel left Egypt (cf. 48:20) and to enter into a newfound, God-given freedom;
- *reality for the darkened* – by urging those hiding in darkness to 'appear' (49:9b, ESV), to stir those 'keeping a low profile' to show their faces – which probably means: 'Exiles, don't let yourselves be totally assimilated to the Babylonian way of living: reassert your true identity, dare to be different as God's people, step out into the light of God's new day of grace and favour.'

The servant now becomes a shepherd, *an agent of Yahweh's pastoral care* in making *provision for the needy*, offering *protection for the vulnerable*, and showing *pity for the wanderers* (49:9b–10c). The influx of those returning to God's people is from all points of the compass so that the homecoming of God's people from Exile is only a token of a larger homecoming of all nations to the One Lord (cf. Matt. 8:10–12).

There is a pattern in the first two 'servant songs', in which the description of the servant's calling and role is followed by a *reassurance* from the

Lord given as here in a direct prophetic oracle (cf. Isa. 42:5–9). So here, the servant's ministry is guaranteed by the LORD, the Redeemer of Israel, the Holy One (49:7), a God of comfort and compassion (49:13). God's compassion for His people once again causes cosmic praise to break out. The whole natural world is caught up in the redemption that is coming to Israel again. Is this exaggerated, poetic language? Perhaps, but there is almost certainly something more going on. Scripture always makes a close connection between the fall of God's human creatures and the blight that has fallen across God's good creation whose ground is cursed. Similarly, there is a mysterious but wonderful link between our redemption and the restoration of God's whole creation. In the Exilic prophets – Isaiah, Jeremiah and Ezekiel – salvation is pictured as 'new creation', but a new creation which means not only 'new people' but 'new heavens and new earth' on which the best New Testament commentary is surely Romans 8:19–21.

If this is not reassurance enough, the servant ministry is bolstered further by the Lord's recommitments to its cause.

Servant-ministry is reassured …
… that the Lord *is faithful* (49:7) – what would all our good resolutions amount to if they were not backed by the unchanging faithfulness of God?
… that the Lord *shows His favour* (49:8) – now is the Jubilee Year to end all Jubilees, the time of God's salvation, the dawning of the great and long-awaited day of grace.
… that the Lord *will not forget* (49:14–15) for 'at the heart of the work of the servant is eternal love which lives to forgive, redeem and restore'.[3] 'I have engraved you on the palms of my hands' (v.16) – in contrast to what might be expected where a master's name is stamped on the servant, here the servant's name is indelibly engraved on the master!

The servant is further assured …
… that the Lord *enlarges His family* (49:19–21). God's people will be surprised by joy, and will ask: 'Where did these children come from?' But then isn't that precisely where the faith story started, with Sarah and Abraham, a childless couple past the age of childbearing, in whom God works wonders? Isaac was a miracle baby: Israel was born a child

of impossibility. 'Look to the rock from which you were cut and the quarry from which you were hewn; look to Abraham, your father, and to Sarah, who gave you birth. When I called him he was but one, and I blessed him and made him many' (Isa. 51:1–2). So the enlarged family created by grace will rally to the flag God sets up (49:22) and God's most implacable foes will become the unwilling midwives to the countless new births God wills (49:23). However much the Church plans evangelism and growth, it is good to be reminded that God gives the increase and gives it often beyond our planning and prayers and imagination.

Which is also a reminder that a true prophet is not one who infallibly predicts the course of events. Nor is this the picture of a God whose will runs on mechanistic lines: that is fatalism. Prophecy is definitely not 'history told in advance'. That makes God a control freak. What Isaiah shows us is a God of real and intense feelings, involved in real and intense debate with His rebellious people. He pleads and warns, provokes their slumbering imagination and prods their apathetic faith. When they pray, He can be entreated. He loves them less than He loves His own name and righteousness, but in the end remains faithful to His unchanging purpose to have that worldwide covenant family He has always set His heart on. That, of course, is why, by a miracle of life out of death, we are here at all. This is the God we serve.

> The God encountered here is one passionately opposed to injustice, deeply committed to righting wrongs, captured by love for his creation, and drawn into the agony of involvement. The God encountered here is one we can picture in the streets of our crime-infested cities, in nations exploited for the resources they can supply to affluent societies, in wards consigned to persons lost in delusion.[4]

Finally, the servant is reassured that *this* God *will fight for His people* – '*I will contend with those who contend with you* …' (49:25). God will fight to right the world's wrongs and to bring about the peaceable kingdom. How that battle will be strangely fought and paradoxically won is already being adumbrated in this 'servant song' and will be made more explicit in the final two 'songs'. Meanwhile, three reflections come to mind:

Firstly, Isaiah's vision of God's servant was a 'job description' for a post which surely remained unfilled until the ministry of one who can amplify the echo of Isaiah's voice and say, 'I have brought you glory on earth by completing the work you gave me to do' (John 17:4). In the strength of His undoubted and unambiguous 'mission accomplished', we are asked to go and do likewise in our measure and in all the ambiguities of the unfinished task ahead of us.

In proclaiming this servant as Lord, Paul was fulfilling his commission to bring light to the Gentiles by declaring that the great day of salvation had dawned and that 'now' was the time of God's favour (2 Cor. 4:4–6; 6:2; cf. Acts 13:46–48; 26:15–18). As we wrestle with doubts and misgivings, not least about ourselves, we who are the servants of the Servant can joyously toss our caution to the winds and proclaim and practise the day of grace that is here.

Finally, even as we share in this level of the servant's ministry, we do well to remember that public effectiveness depends on a secret life with God. The counsel of the saintly Robert Murray M'Cheyne, who should know, is worth considering:

> Do not forget the culture of the inner man. How diligently the cavalry officer keeps his sabre clean and sharp; every stain he rubs off with the greatest care. Remember you are God's sword – it is not great talents God blesses so much as great likeness to Jesus. A holy minister is an awful weapon in the hands of God.[5]

4
BEING TOUGH-MINDED AND TENDER-HEARTED

(Isaiah 50:4–11 – the third 'servant song')

Words seem frail weapons of our warfare, fragile bearers of the weight of truth, insubstantial enactments of reality. But words are really all we have.

'... *to know the word that sustains the weary*' (50:4).
This statement seems to me to encapsulate the aims of servant ministry, be it preaching, pastoral care, or counselling. Each of its three terms is shorthand for whole tracts of truth and practice.

1. By '*word*' is not meant the verbal equivalent of Elastoplast – which, by the hasty application of glib clichés, attempts to heal the wound of people lightly. By '*word*' we mean the whole process and content of engaging others with wisdom and patient skill by which we reconnect them to their defining story.

2. By '*weary*' we do not mean only those who are mentally or physically exhausted – though they, too, deserve our compassion and help. Isaiah was addressing the people of God exiled to the strange land in Babylonia. Exiles are always in danger – both individually and as a community – of losing any sense that they are in any way a special people. They can easily grow tired of trying to be distinctive and to retain their unique identity and values. This was the Jewish exiles' danger, then: they were under pressure to succumb to the propaganda and lies and advertising

of the empire that was now dominating them; they were threatened with being defined by the pagan culture all around them.

David Kettle notes a recent advert, in America, in which a smiling three-year-old girl addresses the readers: 'What's a customer?' she asks. 'I don't know, but he sounds really important. My dad says the people at his office work all day just to make the customer happy. And he told me that when customers need something, everyone in the office tries to get it for them. That sounds great. When I grow up I want to be a customer. Then I will be really important.' What is funny coming from a three-year-old is weary cynicism in a thirty-three-year-old burnt-out company executive already growing tired of our culture's devaluation of what human beings are made of, and made for.

3. In this light, what does it mean 'to sustain'? Walter Brueggemann rightly points out, in commenting on our text, that the 'sustaining word to the weary is not just any pastoral word: it is a word energising the exiles to their own distinctive identity in a context where the identity is at risk'.[1] This surely gets to the heart of a 'sustaining ministry'. Isn't the aim of Christian counselling, pastoral care, or preaching to enable those being cared for to realise with *renewed minds* who they truly are, and to rise to their full potential? Isn't it our intention to sustain another *heart* so that it is strong enough to bear the truth it needs to face? Doesn't a servant ministry seek to encourage and support and so to strengthen another's *will* that it can bear the weight of the tough but healing decisions that have to be taken on the road to recovery? In doing so, isn't it our hope as Christian counsellors, pastors or teachers to speak a word which will rekindle jaded *imaginations* so that the weary can envisage an alternative scenario to whatever has closed them in and lowered the ceiling of their dreams? Our purpose in all this is surely to reignite in resigned hearts a fresh spark of hope that change is after all still possible, starting with them and starting now!

And what of those we minister to whose judgment is clouded, who are utterly bedevilled by self-deception and who are not even sure of themselves any more, or what is true or false? Then we may aim – in Randall Nichols' lovely phrase – to 'loan them a sense of reality'[2] so that this borrowed sense of what is real may for a crucial while be a reliable bridge across what had seemed an uncrossable chasm shrouded in impenetrable darkness. Thus, for the emotionally weary, numbed and flattened by painful experience, we have a sustaining and life-giving word of good news:

> Down in the human heart, crushed by the tempter,
> Feelings lie buried that grace can restore
> Touched by a loving hand, wakened by kindness,
> Chords that were broken will vibrate once more.

Fanny Crosby, 1820–1915

Christian pastoral care or counselling – indeed, pastoral preaching – shares this goal of the servant ministry: to seek to restore another's crushed sense of self-identity so that they venture out once more on the path of becoming the person they really are – a member of the people of God, a human being made in God's image for God's glorious best.

What qualities are needed for a servant ministry of 'sustaining the weary with a word'?

Three words spring to mind from the text before us. The first is *vigilance*: 'He … wakens my ear to listen …' (50:4).

In a painful reflection on what led up to Exile, the prophet recalls that when God came and called, *there was no one to answer*! (50:2). Does this mean that God has lost His power (50:2b)? No, of course not, but God is looking for those who will pay attention to Him. As William Willimon puts it, 'we are the only listeners God's got'.

And amidst a people whose complacency has made them hard of hearing (cf. Isa. 42:18–19), maybe there is someone who is *listening*, who is *ready to answer when* God calls and *is available* for God's service? This is usually the priority in personal ministry: not to speak but to listen – to listen, of course, to the people you care for but first and foremost to listen to God. Speech patterns tell us a lot about what drives or governs a person, and so it is with the servant of the Lord. Isaiah notes this characteristic in all the songs: noting the servant's *'gentle speech'* (42:2) with no barbed or wounding words. At the same time, it is '*incisive speech*' (49:2) – not blunted by compromise or fudging and not in the least insipid; rather it is 'pure speech' (53:7,9) – pure, in not being tainted by self-interest, or hedged about by self-defensive qualifications. It is truthful and faithful speech.

So here the Lord gives 'an instructed tongue' – '*the tongue of disciples*' (NASB); 'the tongue of those who are taught' (ESV). Vigilance is a mark of discipleship. This is where we learn 'how to sustain the weary with a word …' God gives to His disciple-servant a word to sustain those who are being worn out by the demands of the domination system. What we offer in pastoral care, in counselling, in preaching, is not mere therapy – still less stroking. Because we are disciples, the word we offer the weary is not any word, no idle word, no glib counsel but the word of an instructed tongue; we offer the wise and careful and timely words of someone who has been trained and taught and instructed in the truth of the Lord that alone can truly set people free.

To be a wise and faithful counsellor then is to be a faithful listener to God. God gives an open ear – '*He wakens me morning by morning, wakens my ear to listen like one being taught*' (50:4b). God seeks to develop in His disciple and servant-counsellor a well-trained ear which listens 'morning by morning'. This phrase occurs in the prophets as a metaphor for a prophetic appointment. Jeremiah uses this 'morning by morning' phrase of the prophets who keep the channels open on a daily basis to hear all that God has to say to them and to speak through them (eg Jer. 7:25). In which case, only a warm bed or inattention stands between me and being a prophetic counsellor or prophetic pastor. Young Samuel, you recall, began his training to be a prophet by being discipled to remain vigilant whenever God spoke: 'Speak, LORD, for your servant is listening' (1 Sam. 3:9–10). As A.W. Tozer often urged: 'Listen to the person who listens to God.' But how do we find the space and time for this in-depth listening? I suggest that perhaps this is really a matter of *an attitude of the heart.*

As the lover says of her eagerness to hear the footsteps of her beloved outside the door: 'I slept but my heart was awake' (Songs 5:2). So it is a sign of love, where lovers can't stop thinking about the loved one, where mothers seem to have a mysterious radar that alerts them to every stir or murmur of the sleeping baby, and where servants of the Lord are discipled to the alertness of how to 'pray without ceasing'. Be vigilant, then, and listen continuously to God – this is the first requisite of a servant of God.

The second characteristic of the servant of the word evident here is *vulnerability* (50:6–7). The need to be vigilant is matched by the need to be vulnerable. If the servant's speech patterns show his vigilance, his body language – if we may put it like that – shows how vulnerable God's servant has to be. Love makes God's servants open to hurt. The greater the sensitivity to God, or to other people, the greater the capacity for suffering. The lower your ideals, the fewer your disappointments. Here in this violent cameo – the brutal beating, the contemptuous spitting in the face and the tearing of hair from the beard – are miserable humiliations which call to mind the persecution of the Jews in Nazi Germany. No one suggests that physical brutality or suffering awaits us in Christian ministry; and yet, who knows what lies ahead? Certainly for Christians in many parts of our intolerant world, the description is no metaphor. But, in some strange way – if on an infinitely lesser scale – all true servants of God must enter into the fellowship of His sufferings and feel the pain of His wounded world. This is unavoidable in the kind of work we are called to.

There is an old piece of rabbinic dialogue:

'I love you, Rabbi ...'

'Do you know what hurts me, my son?'

'I don't understand ... I only try to tell you what you mean to me and you ask me confusing questions ...'

'But, my son, this is no confusing question ... for *if you do not know what hurts me, how can you truly love me ...?*'

Even more so, surely, since we are followers of God's suffering servant, Christian ministers can surely never remain entirely detached or removed from the pain they seek to resolve. We often enter deeply into people's traumas. Effectively to sustain the weary we must be willing to be vulnerable ourselves and come close to the fire!

In doing so, we run the risk of being overwhelmed as we come face to face with shame and humiliation, and stand alongside victims of abuse and violence.

But the servant's courage is remarkable and may inspire us to believe that we may sustain the weary without being worn out ourselves.

The servant is empowered to withstand the evil that threatens to engulf him and is nerved to stay courageously determined to do God's will. So he stands his ground without fleeing: he is bruised without flinching; he sets his face like a flint. And so he is able to help and save.

> It is one of the mysteries of life that those with the greatest ability to encourage the distraught are often people who, far from being exempt from suffering, discover special gifts of empathy and empowerment precisely in their own valleys of personal suffering.[3]

The final note that springs from the page is *vindication*: 'He who vindicates me is near' (50:8).

This is the kind of ancient law court scene much favoured by the prophets, in which God as judge adjudicates between His people and their oppressors. When He declares in favour of those who believe in Him and trust Him as their covenant partner, then, in this sense, He justifies them by faith.

The servant is confident he will not be disgraced or put to shame or let down but that the Lord of the covenant will vindicate him in the end. His accusers, he believes, will not last the pace but will 'wear out like a garment' (50:9). His advocate will never leave his side and is always 'near' (50:8). In other words, the servant is ready to leave the outcome of his ministry entirely in God's hands. This surely is our consolation still. The servant work we are engaged in, and for which we have been trained, is not ours at all: it is the Lord's work.

It is noteworthy how often the prophet draws attention to this by his use of the very specific title 'the *Sovereign* LORD' as if to emphasise who is really in charge here. The 'Sovereign LORD has given me an instructed tongue', 'the Sovereign LORD has opened my ears', and twice – 'the Sovereign LORD helps me', 'It is the Sovereign LORD who helps me' (50:4–5,7,9).

Whatever form our ministry takes, we take comfort from remembering that it is the Lord's work that we do and always remains so. He can be relied upon to help us and sustain us in doing it. When in long and protracted and difficult counselling, for example, we may dare to believe and go on believing that God is at work in the persons we are seeking to sustain. We may probe like spiritual detectives alert to detect signs of God's working and, when we discern them, have the humble wisdom to ride with them and cooperate with Him where He is working.

Our faith will be tested here: but *there really is no alternative*. The clarity of the servant's discipleship and patient determination in itself forces a decision on the world. The servant's testimony sets out a clear choice either to walk by faith in the dark, obedient to the light of God's word, or to walk by the light of one's own self-kindled fire, trusting in one's own ideas – which is the road to ruin (50:10–11).

Admittedly, life without God's light is capable of being clearly and comfortably mapped out, with family, career and retirement planned, and with a standard of living guaranteed by technology and the availability of consumer goods. Much of this is the outcome of the so-called 'Enlightenment', and who is not grateful for the blessings of modern science? But, left to itself, such a life ends in moral ruin and spiritual bankruptcy. The self-determined life is the self-destructive life. Admittedly, too, even serving is not all plain and simple, not always reducible to clear steps or graspable principles. Life even for God's servants – perhaps especially for God's servants – can be baffling. But when the natural light fails, then we need the light of God's revelation as never before. Then we learn as never before what has always been true – that we walk by faith not sight in what Henry Vaughan deemed the 'dazzling darkness' of the Easter event.

No Christian, of course, can read Isaiah's moving words without thinking of the One who so perfectly exemplified them – our Lord Jesus Christ, the final and complete servant of God. He lived the continuously vigilant life, only speaking what He had heard His Father say. He was willing to bare His back to the scourgers who lacerated Him and humiliated Him as enraged soldiers are wont to do to helpless prisoners in their charge. But He set His face like a flint to go to Jerusalem to penetrate to the very bottom of our brokenness and rebellion and pain in order to bring us healing and salvation. His Easter victory was a stunning vindication of God's cause and with it, a vindication of His own servant ministry and, in turn, a vindication of the work of all those who in whatever way faithfully follow Him. Go and be His disciple, then. Be vigilant, keep listening for the wisdom that He gives. Risk being vulnerable. You will be vindicated and so you may find rest for your own souls and hear and speak the word that sustains the weary in our world.

5

BEARING WOUNDS THAT BRING WHOLENESS

(Isaiah 52:13–53:12 – the fourth 'servant song')

The burning question for faith in every generation is: how will the kingdom of God come?

Isaiah has already raised hopes in his generation for its coming (52:7). And, for his contemporaries, another question jostled for an answer: how will the sins of God's people, which have brought them to Exile, be dealt with? The prophet answers both questions in this highly paradoxical picture: *through the suffering of the servant of the Lord*. Salvation lies in 'the power of the powerless servant, the wounded healer who brings wholeness'.[1]

Isaiah 52–53 is, for Christians, almost holy ground, uniquely trodden by the ultimate servant of the Lord, our Servant-King. But remarkably, Jesus Himself – Mark 10:45 – puts it firmly within the orbit of our discipleship and within reach of the outworking of our ministry and leadership. The path that He trod is unique to Him and 'yet', says William Lane, 'his submission to the servant's mission is here proposed as an example to the Twelve, who are summoned to pattern their lives on the humility of the Son of Man'.[2]

Isaiah tells a moving and incredible story of the career of God's servant from lowest humiliation to highest exaltation. In it, we face the price that has to be paid to establish servanthood as the paradoxical principle of leadership in the kingdom of salvation. The 'arm of the LORD' is the same servant-figure we have met before; what we see here of the worldwide consequences of His work after apparent failure, the human one exalted to the highest place, the courage and faithful obedience that enters into suffering for the sake of others – it's all been there in embryonic form before. Now, Isaiah gathers all the threads into one concentrated and stunning vision. The poem begins – and ends – on the note of exaltation.

Exaltation: 52:13–15

God resolves to exalt the servant beyond humiliation in an astonishing reversal of his career. The phrase *'raised and lifted up'* is language used only three other times in the Old Testament – all in Isaiah (6:1; 33:10; 57:15) and only of God.

In line with the programme established earlier with the prophet, God proposes to humble the exalted and exalt the humble (2:10–12,17–18). This reversal of fortunes which marks the replacement of the kingdoms of this world with the kingdom of God is focused in the career of the servant of God. God's strategic plans hinge on his humble servanthood and obedience unto death. He will stoop to conquer, and descend into greatness. It is likely that the so-called 'hymn' of Philippians 2:5–11 is shaped by this fourth 'servant song'.[3]

But at first nations will react to his shameful appearance with revulsion. They will be shocked by the servant's disfigured face of suffering. The servant seems unrecognisable as an individual; indeed he doesn't look like a human being at all (52:14). But if this is shocking, the sceptical world will be even more shocked by his elevation. How can someone who has seemed so much the loser be declared the winner? This is surely an unprecedented thing – unheard of before (52:15c)!

In the first *story section* (53:1–3), the prophet shows us the servant dumbfounding the disbelieving who are slow to catch on. Disbelief is not surprising since to understand this enigmatic figure and the crucial role he is playing in God's saving plans requires divine revelation. Initially no one believes this strange story. A believing community who understands the servant and sings his song is brought into being by divine revelation so that they see this mysterious suffering as the demonstration of the 'arm of the LORD' previously promised and prayed for (51:9). The servant in his helplessness and weakness is shown to be the Lord Himself in His strength.

If we are ever tempted to water down the gospel to make it easier to accept, it is vital to face the fact that – granted all necessary communication skills – if our message is not inherently unbelievable, it is not true and not worth believing. God's mighty arm then moves to save (52:10) but when it does, it takes this strangely paradoxical form of suffering servanthood. So from the outset the message of the servant is a test for faith:

His origins are inauspicious, emerging as 'a root out of dry ground' (53:2). His beginnings are unremarkable, arising amidst barrenness, growing out of overwhelming ordinariness.

And in his appearance he is not especially attractive with 'no beauty or majesty to attract us to him' (53:2b). Usually deliverers are dominating personalities, commanding figures, with personal magnetism, the handsomer the better so as to look good on TV. But this one has no external glory, no regal paraphernalia, nor can the compelling hold he has over his followers ever be explained psychologically. And if he turns heads, it is away from him.

But worse than mere indifference, the *reception* he receives is openly hostile and he is 'despised and rejected ...' (53:3). Rejection can start small: being looked down on, the patronising glance, innuendo about your parentage or sneers about your racial origins, misunderstanding by family, ostracism from those who know you best and finally, perhaps, from husband, wife, lover or close friend, a kiss of betrayal – surely the unkindest cut of all.

The servant is considered *worthless* – 'and we esteemed him not' (53:3d). Perhaps as a child you were continually put down by dominating parents and your self-esteem was never healthily nurtured by their proper esteem for you. Perhaps you minister to those on whom society sets no value, or perhaps you feel your ministry goes largely unnoticed and unappreciated. So many lives become ciphers, mere cases and dry statistics. The road from here is downhill all the way to hell on earth. Leo Alexander, the psychiatrist who represented the US medical profession at the Nuremberg trials of the Nazi leaders as war criminals when seeking to explain the psychology behind the Holocaust of the gas ovens said: '... it all began when it was believed that there was such a thing as a life not worthy to be lived'.[4]

The servant in Isaiah's graphic image is being educated in sympathy by the curriculum of suffering. He is becoming acquainted with grief. I doubt whether anyone carries real spiritual authority who has never suffered. But the servant of God is gaining inside information, firsthand experience of the full range of the human condition. A century ago, J.H. Jowett observed: 'Every addition to spiritual insight widens the exposure of the soul and sharpens its perception of the world's infirmity and the sense of its own restraints ...' The emotionally deaf, of course, hear no discords; the emotionally blind see no ugliness; only the connoisseur of fine feelings, like an expert in fine wine, tastes the vinegar when he sips the cup of life. Sometimes even we instinctively steer clear of severe sufferers – perhaps because we don't know what to do or say. So the suffering servant of the Lord enters the depths.

Suddenly the note changes as we reach a turning point in the poem. Here is *the logical heart of the song* (53:4–6) and with that one word, '*Surely*', theology is set to music. As has been said, when life is a picnic we play at religion; when life is a battlefield we grope for a theology. Here is that theology. God gives an explanation for the servant's sufferings: 'his wounds heal your wounds'. These are the *only* sufferings for which we are ever given an explanation and so we had better pay attention to their rationale if we are in any way to link our sufferings to them.
'Surely' expresses that burst of satisfaction when someone gets the joke or gets the point. It captures that 'Oh! I see ...' moment. It is a further shock but this time a glad surprise to discover that contrary to all previous opinion and rumour the perplexing pain endured by the servant is mysteriously the path of salvation. Suddenly we are made to see the connection between '*him*' and '*us*' that alone makes any sense of what the servant is going through. If sickness is what afflicts him, it is *our* sickness we see in *him*.

If sin is what he is being punished for, it is *our* sins we see *him* carrying. Hearing this it begins to dawn on us, as never before, that we need a saviour and might just have found one. The realisation dawns that only wounds heal wounds. As the horticulturalist grafts one plant onto another by cutting both and binding the wounds together, so the Lord binds our shame and guilt and pain onto the stock of the servant's life at the point where the servant is hurt and wounded. The servant suffers because 'we all, like sheep, have gone astray', blind to the consequences of our own choices. But the shepherd picks his prize lamb for the sake of the rogue sheep in the flock. And all of this is in the line of service for the servant as the will of the Lord is made effective through him.

The second *story section* (53:7–9) heightens the drama.

Every servant-leader knows the times when speeches and sermons are inappropriate, and when 'actions speak louder than words'. The sequence in this stanza of the poem describes the servant's trial (53:7), death (53:8) and burial (53:9).

His trial, in which he is 'oppressed and afflicted' echoes Israel's experience under the harsh conditions in Egypt. To such oppression the servant submits willingly. He is not at the mercy of fate or inexorable evil forces. He goes knowingly, and willingly but wordlessly. He is not a victim caught on the wheel of destiny but amazingly remains 'a person of worth and dignity in the most degrading of circumstances'.[5]

It is *willing* obedience that gives lasting saving power to self-sacrifice.

Of all the prophets, it was Isaiah of Jerusalem who knew the efficacy of the animal offerings slain on the sacrificial altar (cf. Isa. 6:1ff.). Now, nearly fifty chapters later, Isaiah receives the increasingly emphatic revelation that the deepest problem of human sin cannot be finally eradicated by the blood of bulls and goats. This is as far as Old Testament vision goes in peering into the sun for an atoning answer to the problem posed by deep-seated sinfulness.

Sin as failure is one thing: 'I was out of order' we admit, as if we were mere machines which for a moment fail to function properly.

Sin as iniquity is something else again as there is in us a deep inner perversion and twist, a cross-wire that perverts our best intentions. Even then, perhaps drugs or psychotherapy can partially enable us to cope.

But sin as moral wilfulness, rebellion and high-handed transgression

(53:8c) can only be compensated and atoned for by a consenting, holy, obedient, free will (cf. Heb. 10:1–10).

'By oppression and judgment he was taken away' (53:8a). For Israel this was no injustice since she was suffering for her sins: for the servant it was unjust since he was innocently suffering on behalf of others. And as for his contemporaries, his generation, they neither understood what was going on nor imagined he had any future. And so the servant dies: 'cut off from the land of the living' (53:8b) – 'cut off' by a violent death and, perhaps also, short of that, 'cut off' socially and emotionally from the world where real people know what life is really about. Perhaps the servant enters into the realm of the emotionally dead, inhabited by those who have lost touch with reality, the misfits who no longer feel part of normal society, the outcasts pushed to the extreme margins of acceptability. Maybe the servant crosses over into that twilight zone of the acute schizoid condition of those who feel nothing except peculiarly 'split off' from the sights and sounds and colour of a life they only observe from outside. But the servant's discipled tongue (cf. 50:4ff.) does not let him down: 'like a lamb to the slaughter, and as a sheep before her shearers is silent, *so he did not open his mouth. … nor was any deceit in his mouth*' (53:7,9). Though he had done no violence he was buried with the rich – and the wicked rich at that.

Exaltation 53:10–12

In a resounding paradoxical resolution, God gives the humiliated servant a place above the strong and mighty not least because of the amazing results which flow from his self-giving.

The heavily theological language used here – of guilt offering and substitution, of sin-bearing sacrifice, of being identified with sinners and of intercession – is plainly the priestly terminology of Leviticus 16, the Day of Atonement. But there is nothing formal or symbolic about the servant's self-giving for 'he poured out his life unto death' (53:12b). 'What a phrase', commented P.T. Forsyth, 'as if the limpid waters which transfigure every pebble ran off and left but the muddy bed and debris of death.'[6] Forsyth goes on to emphasise that the servant pours his whole life-energy into this project: 'What he did drew upon the very citadel of his personality and involved his total self. The foundations of his great deep were broken up; his whole personality was put into his work.' The outcome is salvation (53:10). Just as the Lord's desire was satisfied in Cyrus returning the people to the land (44:28), so the Lord is delighted in the servant bearing the sins of the people which brings them home to the Lord.

Compensation is surely required for this extraordinary ministry. And when it occurs, it will be on a scale commensurate with the servant's sufferings. The suffering servant's lack of descendants due to his premature death (53:8) will be made good in an amazing fruitfulness (53:10) so that 'he will see his offspring' of many children. The servant will enjoy life out of death or beyond death – 'he will … prolong his days' (53:10). His seeming failure will in fact be seen to have been instrumental in accomplishing the great redemptive purposes of God. His hard, unsatisfactory labour in dark places will give way to 'light' and he will be satisfied by the outcome – this knowledge will give him great satisfaction. As the 'righteous servant' he will restore many to covenant status and integrity. 'Therefore' he will descend into greatness, a conquering servant with the spoils of his holy war, the servant king of kings. And all because he interceded for others!

The servant who leads this new Exodus out of Exile back to God is, in one sense, a new Moses. In Isaiah 42 the servant is a *royal* figure, in chapters 49 and 50 a *prophetic* figure, and in chapter 53 a *priestly* figure. In fact only the king can incorporate his people's vocation and destiny the way the servant does.

How is Isaiah 53 *in any way a pattern for our ministry today*? Surely it is unique to the servant of Isaiah's vision and, with biblical hindsight, applicable to the Lord Jesus Christ? Yes, if by that we mean a servant whose life and death has world-atoning significance. In this, He treads the winepress alone. But, as we have seen, Jesus Himself puts Isaiah 53 at the heart of His instruction on leadership (Mark 10:35–45) and so encourages us to make some connection between His servanthood and ours.

What might these tentative connections be?

1. Our ministry is necessarily incarnational. Who we are and what we are counts. We model to our measure the character and feelings of God in our humanness. We embody the covenantal relationship.

2. Our ministry must identify with the people. We are neither their Saviour nor Lord but to our measure we take their cause upon ourselves as their representatives.

3. Our ministry is called to follow in His footsteps, even if this involves suffering (cf. 1 Pet. 2:21–25).

4. Our ministry is necessarily shaped by the cross. We minister into and out of the cross so that dying to give life is the operating principle of our ministry to others (2 Cor. 4:10–12). The cross is a whirlpool of redemptive self-giving that sucks us into its own dynamics. The cross sets up a magnetic field which draws us into the fellowship of His sufferings. This may not be martyrdom or persecution or even outright hostility. We may be only singed by the raging inferno of divine love that burns at Calvary; our vexations may be mere splinters from the wood of His cross, mere irritations, when it comes to it. But the cross is the beating heart of servant ministry. This does mean, at the very least, that our ministry taxes our deepest resources, draws on our vital energies, expends the central reserves of our personality. Ministry is not a function or even only a gift; it is a vocation, a vocation that exhibits character as much as charisma. Theologically, this makes sense since – contrary to much popular triumphalist thinking – the cross does not cancel out the resurrection; the resurrection endorses the cross as the truly human way to live.

5. Our ministry will inevitably encounter pain and suffering – in many cases what looks like innocent suffering. Our wisest contemporary pastoral theologian, Eugene Peterson, advises that our pastoral task is not to explain suffering away or minimise it. Nor, what is worse, he insists, to attempt programmes of 'grief management' which he labels 'offensive'. We have no business, he insists, interfering with another's suffering or manipulating it, or by treating it as a 'problem', denying others the chance to find grace in it. Rather, our role, like the suffering servant, is to enter into it, to taste the absurdity of it, and to share it in

the spirit of the One who 'has borne our griefs and carried our sorrows'.[7] There may be no explanation for our own sufferings, but in so far as we are given an explanation for *His*, we may find meaning for our own, and – better still, more often than not – find God mysteriously present in the midst of our pain.

6. Our ministry, if modelled on this pattern, peaks in prayer and intercession (Isa. 53:12). As such, our servant ministry is part of the wider movement of the Church and creation. The new Exodus imagery of Isaiah 40–55 lies behind the New Testament vision of salvation. Romans 8 shows us that the guidance we receive is not so much individual but that the Spirit – like the fire and cloud for Israel – is leading the sons of God (the Church) through the wilderness of the present age to the new world to come. Our contribution to this process on the way – in mysterious interaction with a groaning creation – is through suffering, groaning, intercession and hope. We need to keep before our eyes Eliot's image of the 'wounded surgeon' whose 'bleeding hands' express 'sharp compassion of the healer's art' ('East Coker').

Into this fourth 'servant song' we venture only tentatively. But what was uniquely true of Him is true, derivatively, for us: actions do speak louder than words. Redemptively, Christ's mission is accomplished. But this is, perhaps, our part in what Paul called making up the 'shortfall' in the Messianic suffering of Christ (Col. 1:24).

Final reflection on the 'servant songs'

We have suggested that a study of Isaiah's four so-called 'servant songs' brings us closer to the 'mind of Christ'. Reflecting on them reinforces the disparity Jesus set up between the way the Gentiles make rulership work for them, and the way His Father makes servanthood His way of restoring the world to His benign rule. Maintaining this disparity is the necessity laid on us as servants of Christ. Before you step from the platform onto an arriving Tube train on London's Underground rail system, an amplified voice routinely warns you to 'mind the gap'. Echoing Isaiah, Jesus would warn us to 'mind the gap' that exists between these two contrasting ways of doing things.

If his ways are not our ways, and his thoughts not our thoughts then we must reach across the gap, and speak across the gap, but we must resist the temptation to close the gap. If we are to stay faithful to the model of the suffering servant and indeed to share in his exaltation, we need faithfully to maintain what John Yoder calls 'the congruence between our path and the triumph of Christ'. To quote Yoder in full:

> The standard by which we measure our obedience is therefore Jesus Christ himself; from him we learn that brokenness, not success, is the normal path of faithfulness to the servanthood of God. This is not to glorify failure or some sort of heroic uselessness, but to claim, as confession that can only be made in faith, that true 'success' in Christian obedience is not to be measured by changing the world in a given direction within a given length of time, but by the congruence between our path and the triumph of Christ.[8]

SECTION 2

An angle of vision that is ...
... PARADOXICALLY CRUCIFORM

The cup that I drink you will drink, and with the baptism with which I am baptised, you will be baptised, but to sit at my right hand or at my left is not mine to grant, but it is for those for whom it has been prepared ... whoever would be first among you must be slave of all. For even the Son of Man came not to be served but to serve, and to give his life as a ransom for many (Mark 10:39–40, 44–45, ESV).

6
CROSS-EYED VISIONARIES

(1 Corinthians 2:1–5)

I look back on my seminary education with warm nostalgia. But others have a different take on their history. Woody Allen blamed his problems on his early education when he went – he said – to a school for mentally disturbed teachers. He tried to catch up later by taking a speed-reading course: 'I read *War and Peace* in twenty minutes. It was about Russia.' He tried short cuts: 'I cheated in the finals of my metaphysics exam: I looked into the soul of the boy sitting next to me!' Lenny Bruce said: 'I wouldn't want you to think that ours was a tough school, but we had our own coroner. We used to write essays like "What I'm going to be if I grow up"!' The very English humorist, J.B. Morton, wrote to *The Times* to object to the attack being made on the fagging system in English public schools: 'In all my four years [at public school]', he wrote, 'I can only recall eleven deaths from fagging!'

Initiation rites, too, are a strange business. In order to join one cult in the ancient world, you stepped down into a pit dug in the ground which was covered with a grid and a bull was slaughtered over you so that you were drenched in its blood and thus initiated into the group. When I arrived at Spurgeon's College in the 1960s things had thankfully moved on a bit! Newcomers like myself were simply dunked fully clothed in a bath of cold water – which I figured later was appropriate enough for a Baptist college. William Willimon points out the oddness of what we Christians do by commenting that when you join the Rotary Club they give you a handshake and pin a badge on you. When you join the Church they take all your clothes away, throw you in the water and half drown you! The womb is the tomb – as he puts it.[1]

Reunions are equally odd in their own way. They are strangely ritualistic affairs. There's a dinner; dance, perhaps; much joshing and time at the bar; faded snapshots are given a fresh airing – 'Remember him?' we say to each other, 'I wonder what happened to him?' Our Christian reunions are odder still for being held not annually, but in most cases weekly! We eat and drink, of course. We remember Him and wonder what became of Him. Yet for us, the remembrance is so sharp, so sweet that it's almost as if His living presence is all around us – and that presence itself is so compelling that we half expect Him to walk back in again … all very mysterious, especially as we claim to be eating His flesh and drinking His blood – which is odd, to say the least!

But it is right for us to emphasise the strangeness and oddness of what we are about. Because at the heart of our initiation and our reunions is a death. And odder still, it's not just any death, but a particular kind of death, a terrible, agonising and disreputable kind of death – death by crucifixion.

Martin Hengel's research[2] has shown that, in the first century, death by crucifixion was a means of execution reserved for hardened criminals, for runaway slaves and political revolutionaries! At the start of our story, the cross was a total scandal, a PR disaster on a grand scale; not the cosily familiar image and talisman of salvation it has since become. 'Seeing Salvation' was the magnificent Millennium exhibition at The National Gallery in London, celebrating 1,000 years of Christian Art. Undoubtedly one of its highlights was Salvador Dali's surrealist masterpiece 'Christ of St John of the Cross'. The painting is a stunning visual tour de force. Dali shows the cross suspended over the earth – in fact, over Port Lligat in eastern Spain where the painter lived. He achieves dramatic effect by having us look down on the cross as it hovers above the ground and onto the top of Christ's head and forearms portrayed as those of an Adonis figure like the stuntman who modelled for it. Beautiful as it is, it is unfortunately not a Christian painting at all. Dali, who may have been into esoteric mysticism at the time, has missed the whole point. His cross is hygienically detached from human sorrows, floating free of reality, unearthed, unconnected with the sin and evil which Christ so radically engaged. *It is a pretty picture, but not a true one.* It symbolises for me that romantic view of the cross as a nice talisman, a lucky charm but one which comes with no offence and carries no satanic government health warning.

Given the real scandal of the cross, it is remarkable, then, that the cross is so central to our very existence as Christians – a magnet for sinners, and even confused artists, ever since. But *'Christian faith stands and falls with the knowledge of the crucified Christ.'*[3]

Hence Paul's single determination: *'I resolved to know nothing while I was with you except Jesus Christ and him crucified'* (1 Cor. 2:2). This does not mean, of course, that he had changed his message from what he had been preaching earlier – for example, at Athens; still less does it mean that he had only one topic for his sermons – the crucifixion; or one theme to his theology – the atonement. What he means is that he has no other way of 'knowing' anything except through the lens of the cross.
Paul is *cross-eyed*, not because he had a squint – though some people think he did – but because he sees everything in the light of the cross, and in that light everything is drastically re-evaluated.

In Richard Hays' words, 'Paul has taken the central event of the Christian story – the death of Jesus – and used it as the lens through which all human experience must be projected and thereby seen afresh. The cross becomes the starting point of an epistemological revolution' – that is, a revolution in the way we know reality. He adds: 'For everyone who grasps the paradoxical logic of this text, the world can never look the same again.'[4]

In order to see how this affects Christian ministry, we have to appreciate something of the broader scope of Paul's argument.

The cross reconfigures the entire cultural landscape. It does so, Paul believes, because *God has always intended to subvert the 'wisdom of the world'*. God had previously made His intentions clear through the prophets: *'For it is written: "I will destroy the wisdom of the wise; the intelligence of the intelligent I will frustrate*' ' (1 Cor. 1:19; citing Isa. 29:14). God has now done what He said He would do, supremely in the cross of Christ. In the cross, God has undermined the wisdom of the world. By the cross, God trounces the wisdom experts of the day (1:20). Whether Greek or Jewish 'sage', whether Toranic scribe or contentious Corinthian debater, God has made them all look utterly foolish by His action in the cross. 'The wisdom of the world' represents the prevailing ideologies of a society organised in opposition to God. This approximates the same sense in which the apostle John uses the term 'world' (*kosmos*) not to refer to the theatre of God's creation where God's glory shines but to organised human society where it is ignored or denied. That Paul suggests Jewish scribes might be placed in this company is provocative and, if true, tragic.

The 'wisdom of the world', like conventional or proverbial wisdom, is based rigidly on general revelation, of observation of the way things are. Precisely that which the Corinthians tended to exalt and overvalue, God has always intended to debase and undermine. In the cross, God has thoroughly repudiated it.

This subversion of the world's wisdom in the cross has sustained knock-on effects:

- In the case of the world's salvation, God's action in the cross demolishes the world's ideas of how it might save itself through its own wisdom and power (1:21–25).
- In the case of the Christian community, God cancels all worldly valuations of people (1:26–31).
- In the case of Paul's ministry, God bypasses all worldly methods of communicating a message (2:1–5).

In turn, each of these 'knock-on' effects has a divinely intended outcome:

- God determines in the cross to 'destroy the wisdom of the wise ...' so that the world is shut in to believing the 'foolishness of what is preached' if it is to be saved (1:21).
- God radically reverses social values in choosing 'nothing people' to populate His Church 'so that no one may boast before him' (1:29).

- God rejects all humanly devised ways of pressing home His case to the human heart precisely 'so that your faith might not rest on human wisdom but on the power of God' (2:5, TNIV).

In each case, the intended outcome brings glory to God. The cross is a great 'no' before it is a great 'yes'. What are the implications of this for Christian ministry? In 2:1–5 Paul has four distinct 'nots' – by which he makes *four disclaimers about Christian ministry, its message and its methods.*

Firstly, he comes …

- *not* with '*eloquence or superior wisdom*' – not presenting merely human ideas or regurgitated second-hand sagacity – *but the firsthand 'testimony of God'* (2:1, ESV).

Whether we translate 'testimony *about* God' (NIV) or, more likely, 'testimony *of* God' (ESV), Paul is a mouthpiece for revelation received from God. Paul regards Jesus Christ and Him crucified as the centrepiece of God's own witness to Himself. The cross reveals the decisive action which God has taken against all sinful human pretensions. God, through the cross of His Son, has testified to the fulfilment of His long-held intention to undermine all worldly wisdom and pretensions. The cross is the testimony to God's drastic revision of the way we humans configure the world in our cleverness and sophistication. Now let's not misunderstand Paul's point here: he is not placing a premium on ignorance nor is he belittling genuine intellectual understanding or disciplined thinking – no one does this better than Paul himself – far less is he endorsing the 'heart not the head' mantra fashionable in some Christian circles.

What he is saying is that the cross demolishes all godless ways of thinking about the world. Where is the consultant, where is the spin doctor, where is the TV pundit, tabloid editor; where is the sophisticated, *Guardian*-reading, opinion-former? They are made to look utterly foolish by God's way of saving the world through the cross of a broken Messiah.

God's way of doing things, demonstrated in the cross, is very definitely *not* the way the world does things. Hidden though the wisdom appears, obscured by the ugly suffering, here in the cross is the firsthand revelation of who God is and how God saves.

Secondly:
- In his ministry, and especially in his preaching, Paul is *not projecting the power of his own personality but the compelling personality of 'Jesus Christ and him crucified'* (2:2).

All the things the Corinthians were so taken up with are radically reassessed in the light of the cross. Among their chief obsessions were the powerful personalities who regularly visited Corinth and were now dominating the Church, Christian superstars – as they thought – who performed impressively, offered slickly packaged messages, promised big things for the Church, and guaranteed dazzling and sensational experiences of the Spirit, compared to which Paul's gospel seemed small beer indeed. Sadly, such attitudes seem to have rubbed off from the culture climate. Eloquence and rhetoric being popular pastimes in Greco-Roman society, rhetoricians were the superstars of the day. These itinerant celebrity orators staging public-speaking contests, placed more emphasis on style than substance. They were judged by their performance. The more flamboyant, the wittier, the flashier they were, the more the public loved them. Hype not hope was the staple diet on which the rhetoric fans fed. Again, regrettably, the Corinthian Christians appear to have been assessing their Christian leaders and preachers by the same criteria. They were over impressed with the charismatic preachers who had recently impacted the Church claiming to lead the Corinthians into higher realms of spiritual knowledge and wisdom to which they had the exclusive rights, so weaning them off the rather plain gospel that Paul had preached to them. Paul pales beside these glowing personalities (2 Cor. 10:10).

All Paul admits to is the weakness and *'fear and ... trembling'* with which he had first come to Corinth. Perhaps Paul had felt the natural anxiety of facing a big task. But not so much, I suspect, as the result of a nervous disposition as out of a deep sense of awe and astonishment at being the agent of the divine disclosure of salvation (cf. Phil. 2:12). With this commission, Paul was no match for his super-spiritual, self-confident rivals. But to play the personality game would, for Paul, have betrayed the gospel.

And the third 'not':
- *not 'with wise and persuasive words'* – not showing off his rhetorical skills – *but relying on the 'demonstration of the Spirit's power'* (2:4).

Paul surely did not intend to discourage thinking, or studying, or preparing with all the creativity and flair we can muster in order to communicate the gospel as effectively as possible.

But he is surely urging strongly that this should be done as servants of the Holy Spirit awaiting His move, and attendant on His choices. Ironically, it is those churches which most profess the Holy Spirit which seem to have the least trust in His operations. The cross is still a scandal, still shocks us, because if we make the gospel too user-friendly we have lost the plot. The cross is the answer to my personal need for forgiveness of sins – thank God for that – but it is much more than that: it constitutes a God-made revolution in the way we are intended to look at everything. After the cross nothing is ever meant to look the same again. Christ crucified launched a cultural revolution that changes the way Christians live in and look at the world.

In the light of the cross, think how *evangelism* might look! When we make a fresh resolution to know nothing except Jesus Christ and Him crucified, it begins to seem faintly ridiculous to spend the amount of time and energy we do trying make this message palatable, wearing our brains out trying to simplify it and make it easily digestible. As if unbelievers were in any position to pass judgment on this. I thought the whole assumption was that none of us can do this but we must repent and die as quickly as possible in order to see it. It is difficult to sustain the idea that you can easily assimilate this gospel of a crucified Christ to the way people are and fit it into their predetermined lifestyle. This gospel centred on the cross does not come naturally to us, we have to die and be raised to embrace it. The gospel cannot be located on existing maps of reality, nor can it be fitted into existing consumerist agendas, nor can it be translated into the language people are already using to define their lives. And, according to Paul, when people seek miraculous signs of divine power and others seek rational plausibility, the gospel of the cross refuses to accommodate itself to their demands.

What might so-called *'seeker-sensitive' services* look like through the lens of the cross? What kind of 'seeker services' might be appropriate to a gospel of the cross which deliberately disappoints those who seek sensations of spiritual power to give their jaded middle-class lives an adrenalin rush that might justify them believing in this God – or those who seek rational proof of God's existence and a plausible response to the questions they demand God answer on how to make their self-centred lives work a bit more efficiently?

And what of our own habits and practices? *The Corinthians were charismatic Christians who had lost touch with the cross.* The issue is not whether or not a song that features the cross is occasionally sung (normally of the 'he died for me' type); the graver issue is whether the determination has taken hold to 'know nothing except' through the lens of the cross. The Corinthians were too assimilated to their own culture. They had carried over from their pre-conversion days the fascination with wisdom and rhetoric and public displays of rhetorical skill.

Finally, the fourth important disclaimer:
• *not so that people come in the end to put their faith in the human agent, but that their faith and confidence may 'rest on … God's power' alone* (2:5).

To be resolved to know nothing except Jesus Christ and Him crucified is to *know God in a completely new way*! In strongly endorsing Martin Luther's distinction between a 'theology of glory' and a 'theology of the cross', Alistair McGrath states that *'The cross marks the end of a particular way of thinking about God.'*[5] In Christ's crucifixion, God not only effected salvation but revealed His essential character: 'The Cross is thus definitive for a proper Christian understanding of God.'[6] What kind of God is this who saves the world by the weakness and folly of a crucified carpenter from Nazareth? Left to our own devices, we would never have come up with such an idea. Even more to the point, to believe this message is to throw ourselves into the

hands of a God whose power is defined by the cross:
'*... that your faith might ... rest ... in the power of God*' (2:5, ESV).

This power is the power Paul has already defined as the weakness of the cross. Faith is faith in a God construed as foolishly weak, as a powerless God by worldly standards. But only this God is adequate for the tragedy of our world. After the most pain-wracked century in history we can better appreciate Bonhoeffer's view from his Nazi prison that 'God allows himself to be edged out of the world and on to the cross', and that 'only a suffering God can help'.[7] To resolve to know nothing except Christ and Him crucified alters the way we think and talk about God Himself. God suffers our history with us, He has chosen to work out His salvation from inside our skins, in our flesh and blood reality. The cross must at least mean this. God's tears flow with ours. His wisdom entered our world to face the anguished irrationality of unjust suffering and the ultimate absurdity of death itself. But instead of offering us an explanation, He insisted on sharing it all with us. God's strength is made perfect in our own human weakness and death because it was first perfected in that of His Son. Now with hope and faith we reach out for a nail-scarred hand that has endured the worst that evil can do. Who would you rather trust – the theoretical God who, in His inability to change, is unable to feel and so keeps His divine distance from it all, and so hugs His omnipotence and triumphalism to Himself having never got His hands dirty; or, the real God whose Son's scars are the tokens of a suffering and victorious God?

And the demonstrations of the Spirit we receive from His hands are all the more holy and precious for having cost so much.
As we resolve to know nothing except Jesus Christ and Him crucified, the power is released to change us and make us new.
Occasionally, He lends us wings to fly. If He thinks we are humble enough to be trusted with them, He gives us foretastes of the age to come – samples of His many tongues, whispers of His voice in prophecy and hints of the greater healing yet to come: and all to surprise us with joy, giving us unexpected courage to embrace the cross and so be broken bread and poured-out wine for others. But finally – always and for ever it will be 'Jesus Christ, risen and reigning, and him for ever in the virtue of the crucified'.

The cross, then, its fact and message, radically subverts ...

- conventional ways of 'knowing' (1:18)
- traditional methods and expectations of 'saving' (1:22ff.)
- rational ways of defining 'Godness' (1:24)
- established structures and orders of society along the lines of power, nobility, prestige and cleverness (1:26ff.)
- classic methods of 'communicating' and 'persuading' (2:1–5)

If the message of the cross implies all this, then Christian ministry can hardly fail to be *culturally-critical*. More of this later, but for now, it serves to highlight one further unavoidable implication for Christian ministry: *its total reliance on the Holy Spirit*. This has already been mentioned in the disclaimers considered above. But Paul's reference there to the 'demonstration of the Spirit' (2:4) must be singled out for special attention. Everything hangs on this. Christian ministry is a ministry of the new covenant and only the Holy Spirit makes us competent in advocating and nurturing it in the Church.

My ministry as a young Baptist pastor was completely transformed when I was 'baptised in the Holy Spirit'. Should anyone want to take issue with my semantics, I would urge you not to let terminological fussiness rob you of this surging reality. The Holy Spirit really is the indispensable requirement of ministry.

How is Christian ministry, then, made effective with a demonstration of the Holy Spirit? This may refer to the fact that the apostolic proclamation of the gospel is often attended, now as then, by evident signs and wonders, healings and miracles (cf., eg 2 Cor. 12:12; Rom. 15:19; Heb. 2:4). But it surely alludes, primarily, to the compelling way in which the gospel comes to people, born of deep conviction in the speakers, carrying deep conviction in the speaking and creating deep conviction in the hearers (cf. 1 Thess. 1:5). As John Taylor remarked in his classic book on the Holy Spirit, 'our need is not more wonders but more wonder' – and I would add that more wonder might well evoke more wonders![8] It is significant that Paul develops his discussion of the demonstration of the Spirit not by examining external evidence of the Spirit's activity but by exploring what seems almost like a 'psychology of conversion' (1 Cor. 2:6–16). Rather than talking about healings and exorcisms and the like, Paul probes the miracle which occurs in the human heart to convince it of the truth of God.

In celebrating this, we should first note several definite refutations that serve to show the distinctiveness of the message of the cross and 'cross-eyed ministry'.

Paul makes four firm rebuttals:
If Christian ministry speaks wisdom among the mature in Christ, it is
(i) *'not the wisdom of this age' – which is coming to nothing* (2:6).

There is a 'true wisdom' available for the mature, which is the wisdom of the cross. This was not of human devising but is God's 'secret' wisdom (2:7) which is *'hidden'* – inaccessible to human reason unless and until God reveals it. Crucially, it was *'decreed before the ages'* (2:7, ESV) and is therefore not the product of any age. Because it is not tied to any cultural fashion, it cannot be made obsolete by any cultural progress or advanced scientific progress. All the more reason not to risk cultural widowhood! Stoicism, Epicureanism, Marxism – all the seeming immoveable ideologies then and now have passed or are passing away, giving place in every age and culture to a divine strategy and gospel that is enduring (cf. Eph. 1:10). The God we serve has no need of option B; His is always plan A!

The wisdom Christian ministry deals in, secondly, is
(ii) *not the wisdom of 'the rulers of this age' – who are also 'doomed to pass away'* (2:6, ESV).

The 'wisdom of the world' would normally be the preserve of the 'rulers of this age' (2:6). Scholars have suggested that the book of Proverbs was sponsored by Solomon, and was compiled by the king's men in grey suits who formed his civil service retinue. It guarded bureaucratic order and was regarded as the unchallengeable way things are. The Wisdom literature is usually seen as reflecting an 'upper-class ethos'.[9]

Be that as it may, it would be in line with the fact that ancient conventional wisdom inevitably came within the purview of the powerful and influential and tended to be accumulated and catalogued by court officials, state advisors, and government think tanks (cf. Matt. 2:2) –

utilising the international trade in wisdom ideas. Rulers rarely recognise counter-order wisdom, especially when it comes from 'below', from the poor and oppressed. They are predisposed not to notice the power of the powerless. As for the victory of the victim, who can blame them for not 'getting it'?

Nevertheless, since God's wisdom is unequivocally *centred on the cross*, it utterly confounds the powers (2:8). Had they 'understood' this, the rulers of this age would not have killed Jesus, but – as it is – with all the resources of this world's wisdom at their disposal they did not understand. Herod and Pilate unwittingly brought about their own downfall (cf. Acts 2:23ff.). In Ben Witherington's judgment, 'Christ was crucified in part because the rulers of this world relied on their traditional and conventional forms of wisdom, not on the revelatory message about the wisdom of God, and so crucified Christ in ignorance'.[10] This makes the fact that God's secret wisdom was '*for our glory*' all the more ironic and all the more to be relished (2:7b). The glamorous rulers of this age are 'coming to nothing' (*katargeo*), but believers in Christ, however socially marginalised, are destined for glory (cf. Eph. 2:6ff.).

An eschatological sea change has taken place with the Easter event. '*This* age' and the 'rulers of *this* age' are 'coming to nothing', 'doomed to pass away' (ESV) because the age to come has already broken decisively into the historical process, relativising all the old ways of knowing and ordering the world (cf. 7:31; 10:11). Just as the *old ways* of perceiving reality as wisdom or folly must be discarded, so the *old order of things* with its institutions, power structures, including politics and government, and the inherited forms of family life are radically called into question. At the very least they have a case to answer at the bar of God's revealed wisdom. The revelation of God's wisdom in the cross *relativises* all purely human values.[11]

The third rebuttal derived from the revelation of God's wisdom and power in the cross is

(iii) *that 'No eye has seen, no ear has heard, no mind has conceived what God has prepared for those who love him'* (2:9).

Beyond where empiricism and rationality can take us, beyond all human comprehension and expectation, there lies what can be known only by the perception of love. Paul's statement echoes Isaiah 64:4 and is usually cited exclusively at funerals to refer to the promised glory of our future existence. But this usage is only subsidiary to its primary application to the here-and-now experience of the Holy Spirit whereby what has been prepared in the hidden past has now been made known to the lovers of God. This can only mean the revelation of God's saving love in the atoning cross of His Son. All that gloriously awaits God's people in God's future will, for ever, be a fruit of this cross.

A mature *'HolySpirit*uality' relishes the awesome privilege of being party to the secret of God's wisdom in the cross and to being reconciled to God by the crucified Christ.

Paul's fourth rebuttal builds on the others by concluding that the secret wisdom of God centred on the cross is inevitably understood …
(iv) *not by 'the natural person' but by 'the spiritual person'* (2:14–15).

Paul's distinction is often wrongly used to suggest that Paul is teaching that there are two kinds of Christians – carnal or spiritual – those with, and those without, the Spirit. This cannot be right; it contradicts everything Paul says elsewhere and would fail to serve his purpose here.

Paul does accept that there are different levels of Christian maturity but never suggests – either here or elsewhere – that some Christians are 'spiritual' or 'have the Spirit' while others do not. It is precisely because he acknowledges that the Corinthians do indeed have the Spirit that he urges them not to live or behave or react or relate as if they did not. Rather the sharp antithesis of the natural (*psychikoi*) as over against the spiritual person (*pneumatikoi*) is not then a differentiation between two classes of Christian but a clarification of the distinction between those *without* and those *with* the Holy Spirit. *The natural person* is a human being with normal human faculties and physical life but without the Holy Spirit. *Unaided by the Spirit,* such a person, however morally good, however brilliant and well educated, does not accept the things that come from God and sees no reason to do so. The natural person is liable to regard such things as foolishness (2:14) and cannot understand, since like is known by like (2:11).

To remember this in Christian ministry is not to put a premium on ignorance. It is to recall what Michael Polanyi has taught us by his insistence that knowledge is gained of an object only when we adopt a humble stance appropriate to that object. All the more so should this be true since God is not an object within His creation, susceptible to empirical test or rational proof. When we approach God, what is evoked is a willingness to wait on divine revelation, to rely on the Spirit's illumination of heart, and then to reach out to Him in receptive faith.

The person who does this is acted on by the Holy Spirit to become a 'spiritual person' with the developing capacity to examine and judge all things. Such a person can discern God's ways and actions and appreciates His gifts. The range and scope of what the average Christian considers and values, talks about and relishes, is astonishing and makes so much of the vaunted wisdom of the world shallow and narrow. In this positive sense, the Spirit makes Christians an enigma to the world (John 3:8).

Christian ministry then can be effective only in so far as it remains culturally-critical, with a healthy discernment for the wisdom of the world and of the natural man, and only in so far as it recognises its absolute dependence on the prior and enabling ministry of the Holy Spirit.

From Paul's rich exposition, four aspects of the Spirit's role stand out:

Firstly, Christian ministry works because the Holy Spirit acts as the *revealer* (2:10). The Holy Spirit reveals what God has already accomplished in Christ through His death on the cross. The Corinthians who have the Spirit should have seen this clearly but their lens has been blurred by cultural mist. Preoccupied with the Spirit as a source of *power*, we may undervalue His primary role as an agent of *perception*. The Holy Spirit 'enables us not by making us supernaturally strong but by opening our eyes'.[12]

Secondly, if we inquire further as to how this wisdom can be communicated to us by the Spirit, Paul answers to the effect that the

Spirit is the *researcher* (2:10). The Spirit 'searches all things, even the deep things of God'. The Spirit shows us that there is nothing deeper in God's fathomless wisdom than the cross. The Spirit is the revealer because He is the *researcher* who plumbs the depths of God's unfathomable wisdom, and brings to the surface the deepest wisdom, namely the secret strategy of the cross. The emphasis on the depths of God's wisdom echoes earlier biblical witnesses (eg Job 28; Dan. 2:22–23, cf. Rom. 11:33). The mystery of the cross is the deepest layer of wisdom in God and can be plumbed only by the Spirit of God.

Evangelical and Pentecostal history is awash with 'Higher Life' or 'Deeper Life' movements or programmes of advanced 'revelation-knowledge' that only their advocates have the patent for. No doubt, these are often well-intentioned efforts to rouse lethargic Christians. But they verge on Gnosticism in suggesting access to an elite brand of knowledge on their terms which is off limits to the ordinary Christian.
Paul is surely arguing that, to the contrary, there are no deeper truths accessible only to an elite but that God's profoundest wisdom is made known in the cross. This cross-founded wisdom is not merely 'milk' that Christians can move on from, but constitutes both the initial 'milk' and the further 'solid food' necessary to Christian maturity. The teaching of the cross and its implications for discipleship can never be outgrown (1 Cor. 3:2).

We can be sure of our ground here because *only the Spirit of God knows God at this depth* (2:11). Paul risks an analogy. He is not offering an elaborate ontology or psychology. The comparison he draws is predicated on the simple idea that 'like understands like'. Paul holds this to be true for the mystery of personality. Just as by our human spirits we are self-aware, so, by the Spirit of God, God knows Himself. The Holy Spirit is essentially the 'interior expression' of God's own being.[13] The Holy Spirit is, as it were, the *self-consciousness of God*.

And this is just the Spirit we have *received* – the Spirit who is the *revaluer* (2:12). This third point in the argument is an added reassurance to Christians everywhere, not least the Corinthians. We have not received the 'spirit of the world' but 'the Spirit who is from God'. By this extraordinary grace, we can share in God's own self-knowledge, and participate by faith in a measure of God's own self-certainty. If the gift of God's Son is an unspeakable gift, the gift of God's Spirit is scarcely less so (cf. 2 Cor. 9:15). Again, Paul would emphasise, the chief value of the gift of the Spirit is in enabling us to *understand* the things of God – in particular, the secret of the cross as manifesting God's saving power and wisdom.

The Holy Spirit *revalues* for us what we have disdained or underestimated. Nothing is more shameful or dishonourable than death by crucifixion. But the Holy Spirit empowers the message of Christ's cross to us to such effect that what was once so reviled is revalued as infinitely precious. So it was for Paul, who now glories in what he once despised. And if the greater includes the lesser, then praise is due to the Holy Spirit who renews our appreciation for *all the good things* that God has freely given to us, whether in nature or grace, and thus inspires us in thanks and praise (2:12; cf. Rom. 8:32).

As a final reassurance to Christians in ministry – especially to those involved in training others – Paul insists that such a ministry works with words and works through teaching. The Holy Spirit is the *re-educator* (2:13). God's once hidden, now revealed, wisdom – encapsulated in the message of the cross – is imparted to us not in words of human wisdom but 'in words … taught by the Spirit, interpreting spiritual truths to those who are spiritual' (2:13, ESV). The Spirit renews our minds, reprogramming us with truth into a cruciform mindset that is not conformed to the world (cf. Rom. 12:1–3). *The Holy Spirit is the true teacher of the Church behind all the trainers, teachers and preachers in every generation in the Church.*

Here, then, is a 'cross-eyed' angle of vision on Christian ministry.

So the wisdom of God, the word of the cross, and the ministry of the Spirit are all conjoined. Each facet casts light on the other. God's wisdom is foolish until revelation and divine illumination show us otherwise; the cross is God's hidden glory until the Spirit-anointed message shows us that the seeming weakness of God is His power, and the foolishness of God is His wisdom. So the spiritual person remains open but focused;

on the one hand, open to all the truth the Spirit leads us into by which He glorifies Christ; on the other, focused, as if 'cross-eyed', on Jesus Christ, and Him crucified.

To risk mixing metaphors, every believer in Christ is bifocal: with a wide-angle lens and telephoto lens. Openness in the Spirit does not presume to match wits with God (1 Cor. 2:16; cf. Isa. 40:13). It stays humble-minded, God-aware, intellectually modest, respectful of God's mystery, conscious of the limits of its own knowledge, and intensely curious about the world. Focusing, at the same time, on Jesus Christ and Him crucified, the 'spiritual person' has a cast of mind which is the very 'mind of Christ'. The mind of the Christian is being renewed by the Word and the Spirit so that it makes its own the very thoughts and outlook, indeed theology, of Jesus Christ (cf. Phil. 2:1–5ff., which shows what it ought to mean to think this way, cf. 1 Cor 1:10).

Specifically, to have 'the mind of Christ' is to have a *cruciform mindset*. To have this mind is to repudiate the wisdom of a world that exalts style over substance, gloss over reality; that honours power, cleverness, strength of will, attainments and success and measures relationships by such criteria. 'One who receives this mind perceives anew who God is, that is the self-giving God of the cross, and is thus re-orientated toward reconciling service to God and the world.'[14]

Douglas Webster speaks truth when he says,

> The resurrection does not cancel out the meaning of the cross. It confirms the real scandal of Jesus' death. Shallow Christians who use the victory of the empty tomb to justify a life of worldly happiness and success have failed to grasp the meaning of the cross. It confirms the real scandal of Jesus' death. Shallow Christians who use the victory of the empty tomb to justify a life of worldly happiness and success have failed to grasp the meaning of the Resurrection. They want the glory of the resurrection without the fellowship of Christ's sufferings.'[15] (cf. Phil. 3:10)

We live this life of faith with all its delicate balances and creative tensions. The key to true spirituality, to summarise Paul's stance, is maintaining the critical balance of the experienced 'now' and the still-to-be experienced 'not yet'. This 'now' but 'not yet' tension is in essence the dynamic dialectic of the cross and the resurrection. Which is why, significantly, Paul brackets his discussion of the issues with major teaching on the cross (1 Cor. 1:17ff.) and resurrection (1 Cor. 15). Dissolving this tension has at least two consequences; either Christians slide back into a defeatist, powerless, uncharismatic, joyless, imitation-of-Christ kind of spirituality which claims too little and undervalues the present availability of the 'powers of the age to come'; or – moving in the opposite direction – Christians go off the radar screen of sanity into a triumphalistic fantasy world of charismatic arrogance which claims too much for the now and fails to live in hopeful but humble recognition of what is yet to come.

Maintaining the 'now – not yet' tension which reflects that between cross and resurrection is vital to balanced Christian living and to sane and effective Christian ministry. Maintaining that tension faithfully reflects the tension between Good Friday and Easter Sunday. In one real and vibrant sense, faith lives 'on the yonder side of convention', in the glow of new creation. Christians inhabit the Easter side of things where they can enjoy the risenness of Jesus pulsating through them. But, in another sense, equally real, we still inhabit a Good Friday world – a world of unfulfilled dreams and broken promises, of innocent suffering and politically and religiously motivated violence. In that sense, we exist poised between Good Friday and Easter Day. *We are 'Easter Saturday' people.* We endure the world's 'longest day' suspended between the deep darkness where our divine assailant defeated our 'Jacobness', and the full midday light of the new day towards which we limp even as princes with God with the rising sun behind us.

In this liminal state, we enact faith by carrying our cross with Easter hope and cheerfulness; we enact in mortal bodies His rising and dying in sure and certain hope of the resurrection from the dead. This tension must never be dissolved if we are to live a truly Christian existence or exercise a truly Christlike ministry. As Alistair McGrath says,

> 'knowing that the one who was crucified was raised by God allows us to see the present world in a different light and gives us certain

crucial insights into the nature of weakness, suffering, persecution, and death – but it does not allow us to pass from the present into the heavenly world. We remain where we are – but are allowed to see things in the light of the cross and resurrection.'[16]

It is with this angle of vision that cruciform, culturally critical ministry is carried out. What enables any of us, in any way, to carry this out is the superior wisdom and surpassing power of God brought home to us by the Holy Spirit Himself. Alan Lewis rightly asks, 'How can we live such a story, which promises new personal identity, without the rejuvenated prayer of invocation for the Spirit, who creates new life and gives one energy, incentive, and maturity?'[17]

Whether for initiations or reunions or for the faith-walk in between, we pray '*Veni Sancte Spiritus*'. The Holy Spirit makes all the difference.

7

SERVANT-LEADERS

For we do not preach ourselves, but Jesus Christ as Lord, and
ourselves as your servants for Jesus' sake.
(2 Corinthians 4:5)

'Paul modeled himself on the ultimate servant leader, Christ.' That is one scholar's judgment and there is much to commend it.[1] Paul's own servant ministry in following that of his Servant-Lord, Jesus, was a deliberate and risky 'stepping down' in a society which was very much concerned for the 'up and up'. Becoming a servant was not top of the ancient world's list of chosen careers.

That Paul's leadership took the form of servanthood was a daring thing to do in the context of 'an ongoing cultural struggle for status, power and control in a world in which power was clutched in the hands of a few'.[2] As is evident from the Corinthian correspondence and from elsewhere in his letters, Philippians 2:5–11 in particular, Paul believed Isaiah's vision of the humbled servant of God, exalted to the highest place as Lord, to have been fulfilled in Jesus Christ. And it was this Jesus, humbled, crucified, buried but raised and exalted on high as Lord who served as the model for Paul's ministry. It is likely, then, that in deriving his concept of ministry from Jesus, Paul is drawing, as Jesus was, on the Isaianic portrait of the servant of God.

In line with this, it is fascinating to note that there are several direct verbal echoes of Isaiah – especially of Isaiah's 'servant songs' – in this section of 2 Corinthians.

- Just as the servant refused to be discouraged despite the pressures upon him (Isa. 49:4), *so Paul is emboldened by the new covenant ministry given to him not to 'lose heart'* (4:1).
- Just as the servant was commissioned to bring 'light to the Gentiles' (Isa. 42:6; 49:6), *so Paul saw his ministry as bringing the light of the knowledge of the glory of God in the gospel and face of Jesus Christ* (4:4–6).
- Just as the servant was encouraged by the promise of hearing the year of the Lord's favour announced (Isa. 49:8), *so Paul in the dawning of that great day is able to urge the Corinthians to embrace God's present grace because 'now is the time of God's favour, now is the day of salvation'* (6:2).
- Just as the servant was 'made a covenant' to the people (Isa. 42:6; 49:8), *so Paul is a 'minister of the new covenant' and can even claim that through Christ's death for our sins, he and all believers have been made an embodiment of the covenant righteousness and faithfulness of God* (3:3; 5:21).
- Just as the servant's mission and suffering was part of the prophet's promise of God 'doing a new thing' (Isa. 43:19) and bringing a new creation – 'new heavens and a new earth' (Isa. 65:17) – *so Paul sees himself as an ambassador of that 'new creation' which has already begun to happen* (5:17).
- Just as the prospect of the servant backed up the prophet's call to the exiles to 'Come out' of Babylon, separate themselves from ungodly cultural values, and return to the Lord (Isa. 49:9; 52:11, adding daughters to the Davidic covenant promise from Isa. 49:22), *so Paul is ministering through preaching and prophetic pastoring to keep the Church from assimilating to its own 'Babylonian' cultural captivity and to make it distinctively different as the holy people of God* (6:17–18).

Finally,
- Just as the servant's mission was given eternal value by suffering (Isa. 53), *so perhaps Paul's 'hardship catalogues', his lists of what he has endured for the sake of the gospel, are his way of identifying with his Servant-Lord, and taking up his quota of what is available in the sufferings of the Messiah* (2 Cor. 4:7ff.; 6:3ff.; Col. 1:24).

William Webb summarises his extensive research of this point by saying: 'The collective image found in 4:1–6 of Paul as (suffering) "servant" who brings light-into-darkness, and glory-light proclamation to those who are blind, *can hardly be mistaken as other than one which mimics the Isaianic servant.*[3]

Second Corinthians 4:4–6 is a key starting point for exploring what it means to be a *servant-leader*.

(i) To ask the question: why are servant-leaders needed? is to ask a question about the servant's *mission*.

In brief, the servant in the cause of Christ is commissioned to show the world who God really is: to bring 'the light of the knowledge of the glory of God in the face of Christ' (4:6). This is in line with the role given to the servant of God in Isaiah 'to be a light for the Gentiles' (Isa. 42:6; 49:6) and accords with Paul's own call. Luke evidently construes Paul's Damascus Road encounter as more a commission than a conversion. '"Who are you, Lord?" "I am Jesus, whom you are persecuting … Now get up and stand on your feet. I have appeared to you to appoint you *as a servant* and as a witness of what you have seen of me and what I will show you. I will rescue you from your own people and from the Gentiles. I am sending you to them to *open their eyes* and turn them *from darkness to light*, and from the power of Satan to God, so that they may receive forgiveness of sins and a place among those who are sanctified by faith in me'" (Acts 26:15–18). Subsequently, when Paul and Barnabas have to justify reaching out to Gentiles they do so by assuming the role of the servant of Isaiah: 'I have made you a light for the Gentiles, that you may bring salvation to the ends of the earth' (Acts 13:47).

The gospel shows us who God really is, which is why it is the focus of such bitter spiritual warfare. God is redefined as the God who is only truly known in Jesus Christ. The war Paul fought was a *theological battle*. Paul fought fiercely against every false view of God, and sought to bring every thought captive to the God known in Jesus (2 Cor. 10:4–5). The weapons employed in this fight are not the 'carnal' weapons of coercion or conquest but the 'spiritual' weapons of preaching and persuasion which rely for their effectiveness on divine revelation. 'The god of this age has blinded the minds of unbelievers, so that they cannot see the light of the gospel of the glory of Christ, who is the image of God … For God, who said, "Let light shine out of darkness," made his light shine in our hearts to give us the light of the knowledge of the glory of God in the face of Christ' (4:4–6).

'Light' and 'glory' are evidently key words here. The phrase, 'God, who said, "Let light shine out of darkness"' is taken by many commentators as a clear reference to Genesis 1:3: 'And God said, "Let there be light," and there was light.' More recent study, however, has convincingly argued that while this may be in the background, the immediate reference is likely to be to the prophet Isaiah's use of light and darkness imagery to speak of the coming day of redemption. 'This would suggest,' says Tim Savage, 'that Paul understands his glory as the fulfilment of prophecy and thus as eschatological light.'[4]

In other words, the light referred to here is the light not of the old creation but of the new creation, the light of the coming day of Messianic salvation. When this day dawns, 'The people walking in darkness [will] have seen a great light' (Isa. 9:2). Just as the new covenant supersedes the old, however glorious, this new creation light will eclipse the light of the old creation: 'The moon will shine like the sun, and the sunlight will be seven times brighter, like the light of seven full days, when the LORD binds up the bruises of his people and heals the wounds he inflicted' (Isa. 30:26).

'Arise, shine, for your light has come, and the glory of the LORD rises upon you … The sun will no more be your light by day, nor will the brightness of the moon shine on you, for the LORD will be your everlasting light, and your God will be your glory' (Isa. 60:1,19–20).

Where the false god of this age cloaks the world in darkness (2 Cor. 4:3), the God not only of creation, of the 'age that is' but the God of 'the age to come' floods the world with light.

Now follows a tight sequence of thought. The light God gives is the revelation of who He really is; the light is the knowledge of His glory. How does this light enlighten us?

The means by which this light of revelation illuminates our darkened hearts and blinded minds is the preaching of the gospel. *This gospel is the gospel that proclaims that Jesus is Lord, and that in His glorified face the very glory of God shines forth.*

This face of glory is now the illumination of Paul's heart. Everything Paul does, says and thinks, he does 'before that face'. When he looks at the Church, he does not see merely a collection of difficult Corinthians but the very Body of Christ for whom Christ died, and for whom Paul gives thanks. When he worships, he acts not only on feelings but stands transfixed before that glorious face and, in doing so, is transformed from one degree of glory to another. So when he preaches, he does not preach himself as if looking in a mirror posturing for a better self-image, he is proclaiming Jesus as Lord, who is the image of God. When he undergoes hardship, he rejoices because it's the light that matters – and the light exists as treasure in Paul like a lamp set in its modest clay container, the container being a humble servant not drawing attention to itself but holding forth the treasured light.

(ii) To ask the question: to what do servant-leaders bear witness? is to ask a question about the servant's *message*.

Paul's answer is to point to the 'gospel', at the heart of which is the proclamation of who Jesus really is: 'Jesus is Lord'. The concept of 'gospel' has two chief sources.

Firstly, 'gospel' is a term drawn from *Isaiah's prophecies* where it encapsulates the comforting message to Israel that God is returning as King (Isa. 40:9). 'Gospel' (*basar*) here finds its key meaning as describing the good news of the dawning of the kingdom, the gracious day of salvation when God would come to re-establish His peaceful and life-changing rule (Isa. 52:7ff.; cf. Isa. 61:1ff.). Paradoxically, the restoration of God's saving rule will come about through the agency of the humiliated, dying, and subsequently exalted suffering servant of God (Isa. 52:13–53:12).

Secondly, the term 'gospel' is lent impact by its currency in *Imperial policy*. At the time Paul wrote to the Corinthians, the Roman emperor would customarily make public announcements to the effect that 'Caesar is Lord' (κυριοσ) of which the whole Greco-Roman world should take notice. The *Pax Romana* was the peace that Rome offered in return for total submission to its military and economic power, and crucifixion was the ultimate sanction used to establish and enforce that 'peace'. The paradox at the heart of the gospel – Lordship through servanthood

– which is political but not ideological, ought always to shape the way in which witness is born to the message.

Ron Sider tells of an experience he had in Malaysia (quite by accident, I read his account a week before going there). He recounts tragic examples of perverted evangelistic work – in particular that of the Spanish Inquisition when missionaries to South America massacred anyone who refused to be baptised into the Church, and forced conversions to Christianity at the point of a sword. Sider adds a personal testimony.

> The difference between that kind of evangelism and servant evangelism as patterned after Jesus struck me recently while I was in Malaysia. One Sunday morning I was swept up in praise to the Risen Lord as I stood and sang passionately in a charismatic Chinese worship service. I do not remember the song. But suddenly it hit me that I stood in the middle of the largely non-Christian continent of Asia in the predominantly Muslim country of Malaysia, singing that Jesus is Lord of all the earth, the only way to salvation. The audacity of the claim overwhelmed me. Slowly I began to reflect on *evangelism as servanthood*. The evangelism of marauding medieval crusaders or conquering colonial armies has no integrity. But servant evangelists who humbly, sacrificially minister to all the needs of people of other faiths do have integrity when they invite them to accept the only Saviour of the world.[5]

This seems to me a word of wisdom that enables us to 'indwell' this text. How can we preach the unique Lordship of Jesus in a multi-faith society or where another religion is dominant? Only as we faithfully proclaim the message of His unique Lordship *'with ourselves as your servants for Jesus' sake'*, that is, backing up our witness by acting as servants to those we seek to submit to His Lordship.

We serve with love and mercy and good deeds and acts of compassion even while we remain uncompromising about the unique Lordship of Jesus, and salvation as exclusively through Him alone.

As servant ministry bears witness to the gospel of the Lordship of Jesus, it makes *two complementary appeals*:
- Come home to grace (6:1-2)
- Come out of 'Babylon' (6:17, cf. 6:14–7:1).

The first appeal is to *come home to grace* (6:1–2). Paul serves as an agent of the new covenant (3:6), a minister of reconciliation, and an ambassador of the new creation (5:17–21). So Paul urges the Corinthians not to miss out on the grace of God, or waste the joys and opportunities that come with God's day of favour and salvation. He makes his appeal by citing the second 'servant song': 'In the time of my favour I heard you, and in the day of salvation I helped you' (6:2, citing Isa. 49:8). God's day of favour and hour of salvation is not just a past tense event but a present reality – a 'now is' that we must continually appropriate. Isaiah 49:8, it may be recalled, is Yahweh's answer to the servant's lament over his apparent ineffectiveness (49:4). So Paul – pressured by tough circumstances and the problems in the Church at Corinth and so tempted to 'lose heart', and writing to Corinthians who are tempted to squander the good which the day has brought them – urges them to draw on the same resource of grace that replenishes him.

Paul is supremely confident in the new covenant, the new era of salvation, the new exodus to a new creation that has been inaugurated in the death and resurrection of the Lord Jesus Christ. He is desperately keen for his fellow members in Corinth not to neglect all this. Ever since Paul, it has been a constant battle to keep the Church enjoying the grace of God. Where is the old legalistic heaviness we knew and loved? Where are the cramping rules and regulations? This freedom in Christ is scary. If this is freedom, it feels like a wild and scary place and, as with the Israelites, the urge is strong to return to Egyptian slavery and to being under law. Life was miserable then but at least there was a regular routine and somebody else told us what to do. What is a charismatic church if not one where grace (*charis*) and forgiveness, acceptance and truth-speaking in love prevails?

'All the believers were one in heart and mind. No-one claimed that any of his possessions was his own, but they shared everything they had. With great power the apostles continued to testify to the resurrection of the Lord Jesus, and *much grace was upon them all*' (Acts 4:32–33).

If the first appeal is 'Come home to grace', the second is: 'Come out of "Babylon"' (6:14–7:1). Once more, Paul mirrors the Isaianic servant in appealing to the Corinthians in this way. This second appeal complements the first. His urgent 'Come out' (citing Isaiah 52:11) is an exhortation to the 'exiled' Corinthians to 'separate' themselves from the uncleanness of 'Babylonian' (Corinthian) cultural assimilation.

If the Corinthians have the courage to cut loose from their inbred attachment to the social conventions and mores of their Greco-Roman culture, they will come home to the true reality of the kingdom of God. There they will find the warm welcome of grace sufficient to sustain them as 'exiles' in their cultural distinctiveness. There the Father of grace and glory 'will receive' them afresh and bind them together into His royal family according to the terms of the fulfilled and now inclusive Davidic covenant (6:18, cf. 2 Sam. 7:14).

Find God's grace every day and you find the courage to break with the standards and expectations of the society around you without joining a monastic sect. To live under God's favour is to retain your God-given flavour ('salt') which is the wisdom to live differently as God's holy people without condemning others.

How culturally distinctive, then, are our ministry styles, our leadership aims, and our understanding of what the Church is meant to be? Paul's servanthood was a risky venture in the context of what was – to cite Witherington's words – 'an ongoing cultural struggle for status, power and control in a world in which power was clutched in the hands of a few'. But it is just this non-conformist, servant lifestyle that Paul commends as true in his own experience (6:3–10). It is life lived for Christ 'against the grain' of popular culture. Servant ministry commends itself by its unusually irrepressible response to hardship, by its unlikely tenacity in accepting privations, and by its unfashionable commitment to the godly virtues of sincere love, patient endurance and courageous truth-speaking. In our measure, and whatever form our Christian ministry takes, we are, like Paul, servants of an upside-down kingdom, of a cross which turns accepted notions of power and wisdom on their heads, of grace that will never add up on the cash tills of legalism; we are servants of a Servant-King. If there is glory in this – which there is, the glorious light which attaches to the new covenant – 'it is a paradoxical glory, visible only to those whose pride has been shattered through judgment, a judgment precipitated by the re-creating energy of this very light'.[6] It's hardly surprising that we live paradoxical lives as we seek to prove ourselves:

genuine servants of God whatever we have to go through: true to our word, though distrusted; ignored by the world, but recognised by God; terrifically alive, though rumoured to be dead; beaten within an inch of our lives, but refusing to die; immersed in tears, yet always filled with a deep joy; living on handouts, yet enriching many; penniless yet in reality having everything worth having.[7]

(iii) Taking these reflections further is to ask the question: How do servant-leaders minister? – that is, to inquire about the *manner* in which such a ministry conducts itself. In particular, this raises the delicate issue which surrounds the whole notion of servanthood; namely, the balance between, on the one hand, a necessary self-assertion in ministry that overcomes passivity and indifference, takes initiatives and acts creatively – and, on the other hand, a called-for self-denial that avoids ungodly self-denigration or self-hatred but gives itself for others in non-self-serving ways.

Firstly, it is clear that servant-leaders are *not to be self-promoting*: '... we do not preach ourselves' but 'ourselves as your servants for Jesus' sake' as 'servants of God we commend ourselves in every way' (4:5; 6:4).

It is possible without straining one's interpretive ears to hear an echo in this decisive 'not ourselves' of that definite 'not so among you' with which Jesus ruled out worldly ways of leading in His Church. Paul is perhaps echoing these words of Jesus also in the first Corinthian letter when he says that in the service of the gospel he is willing to adapt to whatever audience he has to work with: 'Though I am free and belong to no man, I make myself a *slave to everyone*, to win as *many* as possible' (1 Cor. 9:19). David Wenham is one scholar who thinks it plausible that the phrases '*slave to everyone*' and 'as *many* as possible' directly echo the language of Mark 10:44,45.[8]

Of course, Paul's conviction that ministry is not a means to self-projection is not intended to stop the sharing of personal testimony or the use of one's own experiences to illustrate the embodied truth of what is being proclaimed. Far from it. In fact, Paul gives more spiritual autobiography in this second letter to the Corinthians than almost anywhere else. What does this tell us, say, about how and why we witness?

We should not testify to our experiences but we should testify *out of our own experiences of what we bear witness to.* That surely is the implication of what Paul says when he describes the light of God shining in the heart to give the knowledge of the glory of God in the face of Jesus Christ (4:6)? Whether or not Paul is referring exclusively to his Damascus Road encounter, he is clearly talking about what he and the Corinthians have experienced – and are still experiencing – '*in our hearts*'. This language of experimental faith, which the Wesleys were to term 'felt religion' and which is, Paul testifies, '*in our hearts*', undoubtedly connects back to the glory of the new covenant reality of which Paul is a minister and which was new precisely because it was the covenant written 'on tablets of human hearts' (3:3).

If Second Corinthians is anything to go by we can suggest *two qualifiers* about sharing your personal experiences in ministry:

Avoid boasting about your exalted spiritual experiences especially as a way of sounding more spiritually impressive or in order to bolster your authority. To brag of receiving five angel visits – and all before breakfast – is scarcely credible and in my experience is intended only to intimidate people into thinking the boaster is an exceptionally spiritual person and must therefore be unquestioningly obeyed. It was against just such manipulative practices in Corinth that Paul was fighting. In fact, when it comes to his own spiritual experiences, Paul is remarkably reticent – only going so far as reaching the 'third heaven' before shutting up shop and refusing to say any more about what he regards as 'inexpressible things … that man is not permitted to tell' (2 Cor. 12:3–4).

If public relations is unavoidable then emulate Paul and advertise your weaknesses. This is Paul's preferred method of giving his testimony as in the account of his trials (4:7ff.; 6:3ff.).

'If I must boast,' he says, 'I will boast of the things that show my weakness' (11:30); 'I will not boast about myself, except about my weaknesses' (12:5). And the reason for this is 'because God's power is made perfect in my weakness' and the more Paul talks this way rather than promoting himself, the more the God of sufficient grace gets the credit.

To say this is not to advocate a hard-hearted, tight-lipped attitude to ministry. Quite the reverse. Paul's testimony encourages us to be *frank and open in speech and expressing feelings.* 'We have spoken freely to you ... and opened wide our hearts to you. We are not withholding our affection from you' (6:11–12). In imitating Paul at this point, servant-leaders will want to avoid spurious displays of emotion. Some pre-modern preachers, like their modern TV evangelist counterparts, could actually turn on the tears and make themselves weep at the right places to order.

Despite the dangers, Paul would encourage us as servant-leaders to humble ourselves and show our feelings for Jesus, our passion for the gospel and our compassion for the people. If we are not excited by the truth, no one else will be. One nineteenth-century preacher wrote of 'the romance of preaching'. Nowadays, it's more likely to be a manual on techniques of communication skills you'll be handed. There is a romance to this because we are telling a sensational and moving love story, not reading from a telephone directory or car repair manual. So if you are speaking – then wing it and sing it and relish it as you tell it truly. If you are caring by its light then woo people and win their hearts to love God as God did through the prophet Hosea; plead and persuade as Paul did the Corinthians (5:11,20).

Servant-leaders' style – their manner as well as their message – reveals whether they are exalting the crucified Lord or conforming to the false gods of cultural appropriateness.

(iv) Which leads us to the question: what compels servant-leaders to minister as they do? – the question of *motivation.*

In answer to this question, Paul mentions two factors which energise his ministry: *the fear of the Lord and the love of Christ* (2 Cor. 5:11–15).

Knowing what it is to *fear the Lord*, with an expectation of having to appear before the judgment seat of God, generates in Paul a healthy desire to please the Lord at all times and gives a life-or-death edge to the witness he bears to the gospel. Nothing could be more currently unfashionable in our flip and ironic age than to talk of the fear of God. Nor should we allow the concept to be hijacked by the apocalyptic doom-mongers of the fundamentalist and science fiction prophecy movements. History helps here. A few years ago I attended a cathedral commemoration of the 1662 Prayer Book and was struck by its deep sense of sinfulness and awareness of judgment and the world to come. It would be self-defeating, as well as unbiblical, for modern evangelicalism to strike this note entirely from its ethos and vocabulary. As James Denney once commented: 'We need something to suppress self-seeking, to keep conscience vigorous, to preserve the message of reconciliation itself from degenerating into good-natured indifference, to prohibit immoral compromises and superficial healing of the soul's hurts.'[9] Humble fear of the Lord stirs Paul to persuade his hearers and not simply to offer the gospel to them with a cool 'take it or leave it' casualness. Fearing the Lord adds 'spiritual adrenalin' to our witness, and brings an urgency and an imploring appeal to our ministry.

The second motivating factor which Paul mentions is *the love of Christ*. 'Love', here, despite its possible ambiguity elsewhere, is clearly Christ's love to us. As 'fear' frees us, so 'love' binds us – fear of God frees us from the fear of man. Fear frees us because what we are responding to – what we are accountable to – is love. For the 'love of Christ compels' (συνεχει) – controls, constrains, hems us in, as an inner compulsion that energises servant ministry. Christ's love as a suffering servant in the cross induces in Paul a kind of 'holy madness'. Relishing such love sometimes makes him appear 'out of [his] mind' (εξεστημεν – lit. 'standing outside of' himself; 'ecstatic', 5:13). But even when, as usually, he appears quite in control of himself, he is, he says, governed by this overmastering love. Such compelling love gives colour to servanthood, delivers it from being a tepid, timid, non-activist stance in the world. Contrary to current thinking, a God-fearing motivation is at one with a love-driven ministry. As Paul can say, 'Christ's love has moved me to extremes' (*The Message*).

Nor can such passion be diluted and reduced as it often is in our modern therapeutic context into a generalised and undifferentiated 'unconditional love'. The constraint of Christ's love in the cross hems us in to a doctrine of atonement. Christ's love in the cross does not generate merely some sentimental admiration but fuels Paul with a burning conviction, an impassioned logic *'because we are convinced that one died for all, and therefore all died'* (5:14).

The best and last thing to be said about servant-leaders is that they are in the grip of such love. None of us, said James Denney, should be strangers to 'that omnipotent constraint which enchained and swayed the strong, proud spirit of Paul'. There is 'not a soul in the world' which 'ought not to be pouring out its life for Him who died in its place, and rose to receive its service'.[10]

8
COMPETENT INADEQUATES

... who is equal to such a task? ... Not that we are competent in ourselves ... but our competence comes from God. He has made us competent as ministers of a new covenant. (2 Corinthians 2:16; 3:5–6)

Is there anyone involved in Christian ministry who has not at some point wondered whether they are equal to the task? Is there anyone who has not felt the challenge to be beyond their resources and skills? Is there anyone who has not asked with Paul: 'Who is sufficient for these things?' (ESV).

In a wise and deeply honest book, the much-respected Christian psychologist, Larry Crabb, admits his confrontation with the question. 'For years,' he writes,

> I hid the *inadequacy* I felt as a counsellor behind a professional demeanour, technical jargon, and sound psychological methods of treatment. Recently I have made a truly liberating discovery. I *am inadequate.* My sense of inadequacy is not the effect of deficient intellect or poor training, nor is it a symptom of emotional disorder. It is a painful admission of what is true. On my own, I can make nothing of importance happen. I can help no one.[1]

My interest in this chapter is to explore the possibility that such an admission can be the turning point in realising that being inadequate does not stop us being competent.

In his letters, not least in Second Corinthians, Paul is never averse to telling his *own personal story*. But he invariably does this with the shape and intention of the *bigger story* in mind – the 'macro' story of God's history with Israel. This aspect of what has been called *'Paul's narrative thought-world'* is evident here. In exploring our particular line of interest, it is useful to start by noting the connection between Paul and the prophet, Jeremiah.

Elsewhere in his letters, Paul describes his vocation in terms strongly reminiscent of Jeremiah's as a pre-birth call of God which recognises God's claim at the deepest, subconscious level of one's personal history (Gal. 1:15; cf. Jer. 1:5). More pertinent to our particular concern, Jeremiah's mission is mirrored in Paul's, although with significant omissions. Jeremiah testifies to being appointed 'to uproot and tear down, to destroy and overthrow, to build and to plant' (Jer. 1:10).

This commission is weighted towards its *destructive* aspects – four negative verbs as against two positive ones. Crucially, for our purpose, the two *constructive* tasks – 'build and to plant' – are later said to be reserved for a *future era of restoration* (Jer. 24:6) *characterised by the establishment of a new covenant* (Jer. 31:28, cf. v.31ff.).

After the 'Exile' has taken place, with its final uprooting and ultimate demolition of judgment now passed, the constructive tasks of ministry associated with the era of the new covenant can take place. Believing this era to have been inaugurated by Easter and Pentecost, the apostles are summoned to the constructive aspects of the task (as promised to Jeremiah) in their new covenant ministry. In his clash with the Corinthians, Paul goes out of his way, albeit with a measure of irony, to forswear the negative aspects of ministry in favour of the positive ones: 'For even if I boast somewhat freely about the authority the Lord gave us for *building you up rather than pulling you down*, I will not be ashamed of it' (2 Cor. 10:8). The emphasis in his ministry is clear: '... the authority the Lord gave me for *building you up, not for tearing you down*' (13:10).

I pause here to note that it is always easy to 'knock' the Church. It is not difficult to tear down its traditions, expose its deficiencies, dismantle its institutions; not difficult to ridicule its eccentricities, highlight its hypocrisies, and berate its lethargy. Who can deny that much of this 'ecclesiological iconoclasm' is necessary? Or that much of Christendom was a 'humpty-dumpty' edifice deserving 'a great fall'? 'Uprooting' trees not planted by the Father (Matt. 15:13) is necessary work and I have done my fair share of demolition and site clearance! The Church is 'always reforming' and in need of prophets still. But if 'tearing down' and 'uprooting' are *prophetic work*, 'planting' and 'building' are *apostolic work* and these are *much harder tasks to accomplish*. It is these tasks that raise the question: 'Who is equal to them?' Thankfully, the very era that calls for the more demanding and constructive tasks of church planting and building up of new covenant communities is also the era in which the resources for that ministry are available as never before.

So, what is the new covenant and its ministry? The very word 'covenant' evokes the bittersweet memories of the larger story of God's commitment through Moses to call a people into covenant with Himself. Israel's Old Testament story essentially revolves around the twin poles of Exodus, the beginning, and Exile, the effective end of life as an independent people. As the Exodus led to the granting of the old covenant, so the Exile held out the promise of a new covenant.

Paul connects with both poles in Second Corinthians, especially in chapters 3–6. So, Paul recalls Sinai and the giving of the Law (2 Cor. 3:7–11) on the one hand; and, on the other, re-echoes the prophetic call to leave Babylonian Exile with renewed hope of the Davidic covenant (of 2 Sam. 7:14) being fulfilled (2 Cor. 6:17–18). It is into this overarching covenantal narrative of God that the Gentile believers in Corinth have been immersed through faith, baptism and rebirth with the result that the earlier, larger story becomes their own story (cf. 1 Cor. 10:1–11).

The particular phase of the big story that Paul is shadowing here is the trauma of the Babylonian Exile. He quotes directly or implicitly from the major prophets of the Exilic period – Jeremiah 31 (2 Cor. 3:6), Ezekiel 36 (2 Cor. 3:3), Isaiah 49 (2 Cor. 6:2). In fact, it is likely that the sequence followed by these prophets is being shadowed by Paul in this section of his letter: *a new covenant* (2 Cor. 3; Jer. 31) *involving a new kind of Davidic kingship construed as suffering servanthood* (2 Cor. 4; Jer. 23; Ezek. 34; Isa. 53), *which ultimately heralds a new creation* (2 Cor. 5:17).

The promise of the first three aspects, Paul believes, has been fulfilled in the death and resurrection of Jesus and the giving of the Spirit, and with them the fourth and final phase of the renewal of all things has been inaugurated. The fact that the prophets viewed the Exile as the 'death' of the old Israel and promised a renewal portrayed as a 'resurrection' suits Paul's purpose well as he makes the death and resurrection of Jesus the fulfilment of Israel's vocation and the model for Christian living and ministry. And where the old covenant was defeated by the people's deep-seated inability and unwillingness to obey God, the new covenant promises to thwart the unfaithfulness of the human partners. Radically cleansed and forgiven, changed from the inside out, Spirit-filled believers are empowered to become the kind of covenant partners God has always been seeking.

Paul's question that has been hanging in the air can now be taken up: 'who is sufficient for these things?' Who is adequate for this? The existential answer to the question is clearly stated by Michael Knowles: 'It is precisely the recognition of his own inadequacy that leads him to depend not on himself but on the God who alone raised Jesus from the dead.'[2] Or to give Paul's fuller, theological answer to the question: 'who is equal to such a task?' – those who are privileged to be *ministers of the new covenant*; they are made competent, inadequate as they are!

What is enacted in such a ministry? Jeremiah outlines *four main features* of the new way in which God will forge a covenantal relationship with His people. If we follow the prophet closely, we will – by extension – see that to be involved in a new covenant ministry will be to further the aims of these four features.

Engaged as we are in new covenant ministry we will seek to

1. Lay a foundation of forgiveness and foster the freedoms which flow from forgiveness.

'For', God promises through Jeremiah, 'I will forgive their wickedness and will remember their sins no more' (Jer. 31:34).

'For' probably implies that everything depends on this and follows from it. Knowing the God who forgives and cleanses and leaves us clean and guilt-free and uncondemned is absolutely fundamental. There can be no real freedom to live out the story of who we are unless we know and believe and feel ourselves forgiven. There is no way a community of trust and openness and love will grow unless everyone has a deep and felt sense of God's grace and mercy; only a people freed from sins and the wounds and bitterness of resentment and mistrust can become a community of forgiven forgivers. Tragically there are Christians who presume on grace and who live carelessly on the assumption that it is God's business to forgive. But this is an abuse of grace which is *tough* grace as it is *holy* love. Forgiveness is a moral miracle that must never be treated lightly. Perhaps, only those who have knelt broken and repentant can appreciate forgiving grace; only those who stand awestruck at the extravagant cost of their redemption can know the overwhelming 'joy of sins forgiven, of hell subdued, and peace with heaven' (Isaac Watts, 1614–1748).

The more the awareness of God's holy majesty and exalted transcendence informs our intimacy with God, the more it remains a key function of new covenant ministry to *foster forgiveness and the freedom it brings*. Such a ministry will practise grace and forgiveness – and bring people into an assurance of this. Still too much avowedly evangelical speech is legalistic and moralistic. It thrusts people back into their awareness of sinfulness and guilt. If we are preaching or talking or counselling grace we are preaching the gospel in everything we do – so that people are motivated to change, lifted out of themselves into the wider spaces of salvation.

When I ended my five-year stint as a 'visiting' teacher at a small but vibrant evangelical church, I suggested to the people, whom I had come to love, that they had often been disconcerted by my preaching because it had not left them *feeling bad about themselves* as their earlier tradition had sometimes done. I explained that I had not been (and am still not) interested in making anyone feel bad about themselves, nor – for that matter – in making anyone feel *good about themselves*: my intention had always been to make them *feel good about God*.

Larry Crabb's mature prayer after a long and successful ministry is one I would echo:

> I would beg God to deliver me from Calvary-denying sermons, which leave people feeling scolded and pressured and falsely hopeful because biblical principles are presented as formulas for making life work. I would plead protection from Pentecost-denying church services

where we do the Spirit's work for him with contrived worship and emotional provocation and endless programmes that substitute for community. I would ask God to never let me again preach an Eden-denying message where psychological insights replace biblical wisdom in a misguided attempt to repair emotional damage when the real problem is a serpent-inspired determination to experience life without God.[3]

Money is the hardest mountain to move in many churches. Every inducement is tried, from principles of giving, through laying down laws on tithing, to slick programmes of six steps to successful stewardship. But just here is where grace works. The charismatic churches I have ministered in have had many faults but never was there any problem raising money. Grace-filled, Spirit-motivated churches have few money problems. People who are awash with abundant grace overflow with generosity as did the Macedonians. Which is why 2 Corinthians 8–9 is classic new covenant territory and Paul's Jerusalem-bound collection an enduring and ecumenical tribute to it. The new covenant roots us in the overwhelming grace of Jesus Christ who impoverished Himself to make us rich (2 Cor. 8:9) and is loved by us and by the Father who knows a 'cheerful giver' when He sees one.

It is worth saying, too, that the inconsistencies and failures of new covenant ministry itself are covered by the same divine generosity it extends to others. As Donald Messer notes,

> this is the promise held out by the 'covenantal character of ministry … Qualitatively different from a contractual one, a covenantal relationship does not require complete satisfaction of the interests of both parties. In the death and resurrection of Jesus, God has confirmed the covenant despite the drastic contradictions of our lives. The Church is a covenantal community, and ours is a ministry of grace.[4]

A ministry of the new covenant will aim to

2. Develop a heartfelt grasp of the defining story by which we live.

This is in line with the promise God made through Jeremiah: '*I will put my law in their minds and write it on their hearts*' (Jer. 31:33b). 'Law' or 'Torah' is more than laws or commandments: it enshrines the founding stories of how the One Creator God called the patriarchs, Abraham and Isaac, Jacob and Joseph, to join His saving adventure in the world; the stories of how God invests His love and hope in a particular people's destiny, how He entrusts to them a special vocation to bring blessing to the world. The Torah tells the crucial story of how God rescued and redeemed this people from worthless lives of slavery in Egypt, how He brought them miraculously to Sinai and there forged them into His covenant partner for the sake of the world. The laws He gave were to help them define what it meant to be a people with *this story*; they were to be holy as He is holy, living out *this story and no other* on the international stage.

This was their story, this was their song; except they failed to live by this story God had scripted for them. They hankered after the stories of the pagan nations around them. Like the rest of humankind, they chose to live by their own self-made scripts. 'Sin ... is the attempt to live sui generis, to live as if we can be the authors of our own stories. Our sin is, thus, a challenge to God's authorship and a denial that we are characters in the drama of God's kingdom.'5

How will God cause them to live by the story? God will change the human heart – says Ezekiel: 'I will give you a new heart and put a new spirit in you; I will remove from you your heart of stone and give you a heart of flesh. And I will put my Spirit in you and move you to follow my decrees ...' (Ezek. 36:26–27). God will put the God-glorifying, identity-shaping story right inside them – says Jeremiah: 'I will put my defining story in their minds and write it on their hearts.' In this way God's people will begin to live up to their true identity, becoming the true covenant community God desires, in distinction from the pagan cultures surrounding them. The new covenant promises not only a *heart transplant but a story transplant*.

This hopeful, prophetic vision is regarded by the apostles as fulfilled and made effective for us through Jesus (whose death as a sin offering achieved what the Law could not) and the gift of the Holy Spirit (who enables us to fulfil the just requirements of the Law). So Christ and the Spirit displace the Torah as the motivating, enabling power within our lives as believers (Rom. 8:1–4).

This is as far removed as is possible from preaching legalism or being moralistic. Ministry helps to develop every believer's disposition to obey God through a deeper passion for and sense of the story that defines who they are. On this account, Christian ethics is not primarily about correct behaviour but about formation of character; not about making right decisions but about becoming a certain kind of person. By this account, people are changed not by moral exhortation but by transformed imagination. This is the apostolic method – as in the epistles where what we do is a lived-out response to what we 'see' of the vision of who we are in Christ. The so-called ethical sections in the latter half of the epistles are really cameos of what a Christ-like, Spirit-empowered life looks like - given the cultural and social restraints of the time; that is, they are descriptive rather than prescriptive. After being on a road of rediscovery in recent years, Larry Crabb has come to believe, as I do, that the most powerful thing we can do to help someone change is to make them the rich offer of God's transforming grace and empowerment in the new covenant. It will be a further aim of any new covenant ministry to

3. Strengthen a sense of identity and community in belonging to God and His people.

This is in line with God's promise: 'I will be their God, and they will be my people' (Jer. 31:33b). Part of this aspect of the task of new covenant ministry is to stimulate a sense of deep security in God.

'*I will be your God and you will be my people*' is a version of the classic covenant formula which so regularly summed up Israel's covenant relationship with God. It was emphasised at the beginning of her history (Exod. 6:7; Lev. 26:12; Deut. 29:12–13), reiterated in the covenant of kingship (2 Sam. 7:24) and is held out as part of the eschatological hope of the Exilic prophets (Jer. 24:7; 30:22; 31:1,31; Ezek. 14:11; 37:27). Paul develops this aspect of the ministry of the new covenant in 2 Corinthians 6:16–18 by conflating Leviticus 26:12 with Ezekiel 37:27. He adds to it a citation from Isaiah (Isa. 52:11) where again the context is the prophetic call to the exiles to leave their unbelieving Babylonian neighbours and separate themselves from Babylonian values and standards.

To minister the new covenant – and, in particular, to stimulate a deep sense of security in God, is not to create a user-friendly comfort zone.

It involves a strong cultural challenge which urges a break with the dominant 'Babylonian' culture-system.

Paul adds to the equation 2 Samuel 7:14 which is the key passage where God establishes covenant with David and the Davidic kingship. The special 'father–son' relationship promised to David is after all only a narrowing and focusing of the wider, national 'God–people' relationship. Now by including Isaiah 43:6 Paul democratises the kingly covenant. Here are pictured the sons and daughters of the king, living out the covenant story of God and His kingdom in a distinctive way within a godless culture.

The only way such a community will be formed over time is to tell and retell the one continuous covenantal story of God. This is what Paul is doing here: not simply offering an arbitrary selection of 'proof texts' but pressing the Corinthians – Gentiles as they were – back into the shape of the one covenant story that actually defines who and what they are: namely, the people who belong to and confess *this* God, the God who in Christ is their Father and to whose covenant family they now belong.

Finally, in applying the fourth feature of Jeremiah's promise, a new covenant ministry aims to

4. Deepen and widen the experience and implications of knowing God.

God promises through Jeremiah that 'No longer will a man teach his neighbour, or a man his brother, saying, "Know the LORD," because they will all know me, from the least of them to the greatest' (Jer. 31:34). It will be the task of a new covenant ministry to encourage people to look for God to act, and to expect to experience God for themselves. Paul consistently prays that the churches in his care may know God in a deeper way (Eph. 1:17ff.; Col. 1:9ff.).

The implications of 'knowing God' are intensely practical. In Jeremiah 'knowing God' is knowing a God who practises social justice: 'Thus says the LORD: Let not the wise man boast in his wisdom, let not the mighty man boast in his might, let not the rich man boast in his riches, but let him who boasts boast in this, that he understands and knows me, that I am the LORD who practises steadfast love, justice, and righteousness in the earth. For in these things I delight' (Jer. 9:23–24; cf. 2 Cor. 10:17, ESV).

By this account, 'knowing the Lord' is not some mystical or super-spiritual experience but is a knowing of the Lord as He dispenses *kindness*, executes *justice* and practises *righteousness*. Knowing such a God will, inevitably, in Paul's view, transform your attitudes to money and status, affect your relationships, and turn your heart to delight in what God delights in – social justice and concern for the poor and needy. It is knowing *this God and enacting this theology* that calls forth and shares in the joyful delight and pleasure of God. This is the promise of the new covenant 'heart to know me' (Jer. 26:4; 31:31ff.) whose fulfilment in Christ by the Spirit shapes the whole of Paul's vision of ministry (2 Cor. 3:3ff.).

In the new covenant, the knowledge of the glory of this God is known in the face of Jesus Christ. The ministry of the new covenant is called to do theology and do it well.

Too much popular Christian thinking – as at Corinth – is still dominated by concepts of God that are at best philosophical, at worst frankly pagan. Paul uses a military analogy drawn from siege-warfare to attack the way in which his opponents have misconstrued the nature of God. 'For though we live in the world, we do not wage war as the world does. The weapons we fight with are not the weapons of the world. On the contrary, they have divine power to demolish strongholds. We demolish arguments and every pretension that sets itself up against the knowledge of God, and we take captive every thought to … Christ' (2 Cor. 10:3–5). Earlier we said that in contrast to Jeremiah, Paul, as a minister of the new covenant, was more concerned with building than with tearing down. But this is the exception.

> A great deal of theology has been held captive by concepts of God that need to be exposed as idols in this sense. The insidiousness and falsehood of such concepts go very deep, and the task of discerning and combating them is well described by Paul as a military campaign.[6]

Speculative thinking, however trendy, that floats free of prophetic scripture and apostolic testimony must be captured and made to submit to the cruciform shape of the gospel. The incarnation and the cross must more radically affect our view of God.

The 'culture wars' we are so eager to engage in will be lost before we start if the weapons of our warfare are carnal and worldly. The battle to be fought on every hand, outside and inside the Church, is essentially a theological one. Before we win culture wars we must wage theological war against all those concepts of God that fail to stand the scrutiny of the cross. It is part of the theological ministry of the new covenant to lay siege to such constructs and to bring them down.

To put this in more explicitly experiential terms: in the last analysis, knowledge of God in a new covenant context is an empty formula unless it demonstrates complete reliance on the *ministry of the Holy Spirit* (2 Cor. 3:8). It is from God's Spirit that our 'competence comes'; by God's Spirit we establish the status and experience of new covenant membership (2 Cor. 1:21–22); and it is by God's Spirit that we are empowered in the ministry of righteousness that replaces condemnation and death with justification and life (2 Cor. 3:9), reinstates us in righteous relationship with God and, on one reading of the text, even begins to replicate in us the covenant faithfulness of God Himself (2 Cor. 5:21).

The Spirit opens up the possibility of breaking old deadlocks and lowering long-set barriers – so bringing peace with God and reordering to broken personalities and relationships. It is the resources of the Spirit of God that give hope to new covenant ministers otherwise only too painfully aware of their own limitations. Apart from Him I can do nothing. But, as Larry Crabb has come freshly to appreciate:

> ... if I abide in Christ, if I present myself before God's Spirit for searching and filling, if I study and ponder the Scriptures and live my life in brokenness before a grace-dispensing community, I can transcend my inadequacy. I can find myself as I worship. I can struggle on behalf of others with the energy of Christ powerfully working in me.[7]

Our current cultural condition, postmodern or otherwise, has been characterised by its:

- *Lack of a big story that gives meaning and coherence to life*: the earlier, seemingly world-defining stories of the Enlightenment – the autonomy of science, the belief in inevitable progress, international Marxism – have let us down or proved unable to answer our deepest longings.
- *Loss of any true sense of identity*: which is why, it is suggested, people

change their persona so often like chameleons with all the attendant neuroses that ensue; why they are scared of commitment and avoid vows that will demand they be faithful over time.

- *Loss of any definable community*: with the breakdown of the older groupings of family, and tribe and town.
- *Desire for experiences, sensations, intimacy*: even in spiritual matters.
- *Despair over dysfunctional relationships*: which have caused so much pain leaving so many young people with cynicism about the possibility of truly loving relationships, with a carefree attitude to casual sex but, at the same time, with a deep longing for genuine relationship.

Our postmodern world, however we style it, is especially ready for the ministry of new covenant and reconciliation. What the new covenant ministry offers is an account of the Big True Story by which to make credible and saving sense of all reality. Here, with the people created by this story, you can rediscover your true identity as a unique individual made in the image of God, whose potential is capable of redemption. Here is an authentic though imperfect but welcoming community in which all are learning the new skills of forgiveness and truth-telling and holiness. Here among this people can be found a remedy for shame and guilt. Here, energies are released to repair trust in relationship by experiencing the unswerving love of a gracious God and an unqualified acceptance from His people.

Faithfully ministering all this is a tall order that seems to expose our ineptness. But we need not be intimidated. Instead, each of us may agree with Crabb when he says, 'I have learned that an awareness of inadequacy is neither a curse to lift nor a disorder to cure. It is a gift to be received, a gift that if properly used can make me powerful and strong and clear and wise.'[8] Thanks be to God who *has so empowered us with His Spirit that being inadequate need not stop us being competent.* As for me, like Larry Crabb, I would want to minister

> *in the spirit of the New Covenant,* inviting ... everyone in the congregation to see the heart of God revealed in the cross of Christ. I would encourage them to interpret all of life's hardships not as problems to fix or struggles to relieve or pain to deaden, but as important elements in a larger story that all God's children long to

tell. I would urge them to accept wherever they are on the journey, whether happy or miserable, as the place where God will meet them, where He loves them, where He will continue to work in them. And I would offer my own life as a growing, struggling, sometimes painfully unattractive example of what doing that might mean.[9]

Michael Knowles more soberly sums up the antithesis: 'Paul is simultaneously inadequate and adequate: inadequate because of the overwhelming theological and pastoral responsibilities that such ministry entails, and adequate because he is merely responding to divine initiative and a specific divine commissioning conveyed by the Spirit of God.'[10] Like Paul, as we enter more and more deeply into this paradox, we may be 'very bold' believing that 'nothing holds us back' (2 Cor 3:12, *The Message*). And the *newness* of the *new* covenant must not be underestimated for it shares – albeit provisionally – in *new creation*.

New covenant ministry is called to plant and nurture, to found and build up, communities of faith which represent this new reality and constitute a sneak preview of God's future. Who is equal to this task? But the newness works for us and in us to create new possibilities where none seemed to exist; new powers when strength is spent, new wisdom when at our wits' end. So the question as to 'Who is equal to the task?' can be answered by *the competent 'inadequates' whose competence is newly minted by the Holy Spirit and is freshly available from Him alone.*

WOUNDED HEALERS

9

*Praise be to the God and Father of our Lord Jesus Christ, the
Father of compassion and the God of all comfort, who comforts
us in all our troubles, so that we can comfort those in any trouble
with the comfort we ourselves have received from God ... If we
are distressed, it is for your comfort and salvation; if we are
comforted, it is for your comfort. (2 Corinthians 1:3–6)*

It was the late Henri Nouwen who made memorable the image of the
pastoral minister as the 'the wounded healer'. His reflections have made
an indelible mark on the subsequent discussion about the nature of
Christian ministry. In the introduction to his small book bearing this
title, Nouwen wrote: 'Thus nothing can be written about ministry
without a deeper understanding of the ways in which the minister can
make his own wounds available as a source of healing.'[1]

In the intervening decades since the publication of Nouwen's work,
the ethos of the Western world – it could be argued – has become even
more introspective and self-absorbed. For this reason, Nouwen's stance
might be easily caricatured as conceding too much to an increasingly
therapeutic culture. Perhaps anticipating such criticism, Nouwen sought
to make clear what was involved in the insight he was offering:

> For the minister is called to recognise the sufferings of his time in
> his own heart and make that recognition the starting point of his
> service. Whenever he tries to enter into a dislocated world, relate to
> a convulsive generation, or speak to a dying man, his service will not
> be *perceived as authentic until it comes from a heart wounded by the
> suffering of which he speaks.*[2]

This observation surely still carries weight. In addition, it is worth
reminding ourselves that Nouwen's book is largely a reflection on

119

the changing cultural scene of the day (the 1970s) and how Christian ministry might react. Christian pastoral practice, Nouwen urges, should respond not by uncritically accepting such change but by 'contemplating' it with a discerning eye which sees beneath the surface needs of its generation. 'In this way, the contemplative can be a leader for a convulsive generation because he can break the vicious circle of immediate needs asking for immediate satisfaction.'[3] Far from being a chaplain to the culture, the Christian minister who is a 'critical contemplative will be a revolutionary in the most real sense'.

This is well said, but the suspicion lingers that the 'wounded healer' concept contributes to the creation of an Oprah-Winfrey-type mentality. Is it really intended to encourage that 'baring of the soul' by pastoral leaders that is the peculiarly public and Protestant form of the confessional? Popular evangelicalism rates high on the cringe-factor count. Just ask generations of manse-kids whose growing pains are exposed to a smug, raised-eyebrowed congregation, in Daddy's stock of sermon illustrations: '*You're* a celebrity pastor; get *me* out of here.' Public soul-baring to induce sympathy or evoke pity is indeed pitiful. Nouwen was too shrewd an observer of human foibles not to know this. He recognised the danger of the image of 'wounded healer' being misused to defend 'a form of spiritual exhibitionism'.[4] Rather, he argued, one's own wounds become an occasion of healing for others only as they are shown to arise from the 'depths of the human condition'.[5]

Donald Messer suggests ways of being a 'wounded healer'.
1. To be a wounded healer, one must ... *affirm and accept one's own history.*
'Along with happiness of life come heartaches; with triumphs and success come temptations and scars. All of us limp through life crippled by certain weaknesses and handicapped by various tragedies.'

In this sense, Paul surely does affirm his own life story from his regularly reiterated Damascus Road testimony through to the 'hardship lists' where he acknowledges his own weaknesses – whether endemic or inflicted. Though 'crippled' might do less than justice to Paul's grace-given tenacity and resilience, Messer's verdict holds true in Paul's case that people 'seek out persons who have known pain, tragedy, and brokenness but who have moved beyond bitterness, despair and hopelessness'.[6]

2. As wounded healers, we *can empathise with those who suffer.* Jeremiah entered into the pathos of God over God's people so that the prophet's tears seem indistinguishable from God's (cf. Jer. 8:22; 9:1). Even more so does Paul participate in the pressures and pain of Christ's Body, the Church. If this is true, then maybe our hurts can be the hope of healing for others, our scars can become our credentials for ministry, and our wounds can be the point of grafting new life onto others.

3. Wounded healers know that in their own struggle for wholeness and holiness and healing they are *sustained only by the grace of God in Christ* (1 Cor. 15:9–10; 2 Cor. 12:9). Again the subsequent usage in pastoral circles of Nouwen's image of the 'wounded healer' has been recently criticised for having been too often 'disconnected from the pattern of Christ's dying and rising'.[7] This can result – as we have noted earlier – in pastors flaunting their own pain in self-serving ways, which, in turn, may encourage people to wallow in their own weaknesses in an abject and dispirited loss of faith.

There may indeed be some congregations that do not feel that they are getting their money's worth if they do not make the pastor's life a misery. But such ecclesiological pathology does not deserve to be pandered to by pastoral self-pity. Nor should it be allowed to attract *into* ministry especially needy souls whose sense of self-worth can only be satisfied by the congregation's approval or applause. We all like to be appreciated and encouragement is a primary Christian virtue often meagrely dispensed in many Church circles. But may we be spared the verdict of the boy who said to his parents, 'You know, the trouble with our new pastor is that he needs us to love him so much we can't see God anymore.'[8]

These are points well taken. But the answer, I suspect, is not to discard the 'wounded healer' image but to return it to the rootage Nouwen surely intended it to have: namely, woundedness as a shaping of faithful ministry patterned on the dying-rising Jesus. Wounds are not enough; we must 'place our wounds into the wounds of Christ'.[9] Only then do our weaknesses and wounds have any chance of becoming strangely meaningful, personally bearable, and pastorally productive.

Comforted comforter

Paul testifies to the way the ministry of the wounded healer works early in the second letter to the Corinthians (1:3–11).

Paul begins his letter with a fulsome 'blessing' or eulogy (*eulogētos*) which is in the classic Jewish *berakah* tradition. His celebration of God as the 'Father of mercies' or 'of compassion' is rooted in the Old Testament (cf. Exod. 34:6; Psa. 25:6; 69:16). It was freshly minted for Paul in his own 'conversion' where he 'received mercy' which shaped his subsequent apostolic career as a model recipient of divine grace (1 Tim.1:12–17). All of which leads him to praise God as the 'God of all comfort' (*paraklēsēs*), an epithet which sums up the entire Isaianic hope of the Messianic age of salvation whose keynote is 'Comfort, comfort my people' (Is 40:1; cf. 49:13; 51:3,12,19; 52:9; 61:2; 66:13). This saving consolation, while strategic and wide ranging, is felt at an intensely practical and personal level, as Paul now makes clear.

What Paul hopes to see emerge in Corinth (1:4–7) is what Donald Messer aptly terms a 'community of the compassionate'. In Paul's engagement with the Corinthian believers a marvellous 'ecology of comfort' has been operating. In this life-support relationship, God comforts Paul, and he in turn comforts the Corinthians with the comfort he has received. Recalling this dynamic mutuality of consolation will enable Paul to interpret his own afflictions sacramentally, and leads him to expect further prayerful aid from the Church (cf. 1:11).

Paul is, of course, writing partly in his own defence, since the negative experiences he has had, which some are tending to despise, are turning out to be the very means of grace to them.

Paul elaborates on the affliction he faced in vivid language: 'under great pressure, far beyond our ability to endure, so that we despaired even of life ... in our hearts we felt the sentence of death' (1:8–9). What is Paul referring to? The commentators offer a range of options.

Is he recalling *persecution* or the city-wide commotion at Ephesus (Acts 19–20), as Paul Barnett and James Scott suggest? Or is Linda Belleville right in raising the possibility of a reference to a literal legal edict, a kind of *fatwa* issued against Paul and his team? Others, however, argue that the word used here, *apokrima* (1:9), is not about being judicially sentenced to death but occurs in secular Greek in the sense of 'decree, verdict, decision' which, they emphasise, Paul says is *within himself.* So Ben Witherington interprets verses 8 and 9 as more likely to be illness, while Tom Wright feels that the extreme language suggests a nervous breakdown. A.E. Harvey suggests that this traumatic illness affected Paul's whole approach to ministry, and especially his relations with the Corinthians – as reflected in this letter. Harvey quotes Karl Barth as describing Second Corinthians as *'that long drawn out harassed groan'*.[10] Harvey suggests that like all 'near-death' experiences it may have led to loss of independence (hence Paul's need for others); to social rebuff and discouragement (especially for Paul from his 'success-mode' critics); and to aspersions being cast on his work and ministry (thus putting him at an economic disadvantage since only the rich could then afford to be ill) which threatened his own self-esteem as a chosen agent of God.

Whatever the particulars, it is clear that Paul has learned to view his sufferings in a new way so as to extract meaning from them. He has been given grace and insight to enable him to integrate his afflictions into his understanding of his vocation.

a) Only in this way – this 'near-death-sentence' way – can a more profound fellowship with Christ in His sufferings be realised which in turn is the source of His comfort of others (1:5).
b) Only in this way can dependence on God be developed. Paul's afflictions trigger a certain spiritual logic: they happened so 'that we might not rely on ourselves but on God' (1:9). We are reminded of the opportunity made available often only by severe trouble to trust in God alone.
c) Only in this way – through near-death experiences perhaps – can we come to appreciate a God 'who raises the dead' (1:9c). Resurrection is the standard measure of God's power in the New Testament, as the Exodus was in the Old Testament. It is this same God who raised Jesus who will raise us and who, even now, we may dare to believe, continuously 'raises' us up by infusion of recreative energies.

So, strangely, is created a fellowship of mutual support: as Paul sets his hope on this God so the Corinthians support him with their prayers

(1:10–11). In this way Paul's own sufferings and rescue in response to the prayers of God's people then redound to the praise and glory of God as blessing overspills to others. By the unfathomable wisdom that remakes us in the midst of what would destroy us, the new covenant community is built up.

At this point, it may be worth noting *the correspondence between Paul and Jeremiah* which I am sure Paul was aware of in writing this letter.

Three points may be made.

Firstly, as noted earlier, Paul relates his ministry to that of Jeremiah in explicit terminology derived from the prophet of '*tearing down and uprooting, planting and building up*' (see Jer. 1:10; 18:7–10). Significantly, the two positive metaphors of building and planting are joined to the promise of God giving His people a new heart to know Him (Jer. 24:7); and are central to the whole ethos of the new covenant (Jer. 31:4,27–28). Paul makes the connection explicit in talking of his own apostolic task (2 Cor. 10:8; 13:10). Paul regards himself as an ambassador of that new covenant, which it was Jeremiah's joy to promise; this new covenant ministry is evidently the 'building up' part of the prophetic vision which Paul now sees operating on the other side of the 'uprooting and tearing down' of Exile fulfilled in the cross. Paul's ministry is to build up new covenant communities.

Secondly, although Paul's 'boasting' is a reluctant use of a contemporary rhetorical device employed ironically to 'commend' his own ministry, it is also a key theme of Jeremiah. Jeremiah 9:23–24, which downplays all other boasting save in God Himself, is one of Paul's favourite citations. He exploits it to cut his opponents down to size, comparing their false 'boasting' with his own 'boasting' in God's wisdom and power and glory (cf. 10:17–18).

Thirdly, Paul may have modelled his willingness to open his heart and share his catalogues of hardships and sufferings on the so-called '*confessions*' of Jeremiah. It is in these passages of self-disclosure that Jeremiah tells his own story of pain and rejection, exposes his own vulnerability and victimhood, and shares his self-doubt and internal anguish in staying faithful to the calling of God. Like Jeremiah, Paul indulges in this counter-intuitive fusion of 'confessions' and 'boasting' in order to magnify dependence on God for status, honour and vindication and thus to undermine opponents.

In Ben Witherington's words,

> it is very believable that Paul not only saw himself in the suffering figure of Jeremiah who was rejected by his fellow Jews, but also saw his often controverted and rejected ministry efforts reflected in the word of affirmation from the Lord in Jeremiah 7:25 … In Jeremiah he had a model of persistence and faithfulness even in the midst of rejection, suffering and tragedy.[11]

Conquering captives

Second Corinthians 2:14–17 offers us an even stranger paradox about ministry.

A Roman 'triumph' was the triumphal procession of a conquering general at the head of his victorious army, trailing in its wake, at the tag end of the parade, the captured and condemned prisoners of war. Popular preaching has often over-glamorised the picture Paul is painting here. Stirring sermons have been preached based on this text on how God 'causes' us to triumph in the pursuit of the 'overcoming life'. But there are no easy victories here. Recent evangelical scholarship has questioned this over-simplistic interpretation and even concluded that it is linguistically impossible.[12]

There is victory here but it is not of a 'triumphalist' kind. The 'triumph' is deeper, subtler and altogether more paradoxical. So what is Paul driving at? The picture is clearly of a Roman general's triumphal procession celebrating victory in battle. But how does it apply to Paul and to the nature of Christian ministry? Where does Paul place himself in the parade? Not at the head of the procession which is reserved for God and Christ; nor, in fact, in the main body of the victorious army – but, almost certainly, among the captured slaves bringing up the rear of the procession who are being humiliatingly displayed to the mocking crowds and who are on their way to certain death!

So, as Ben Witherington states, Paul 'is not saying that he is being led around in triumph, but rather like the captives in a triumphal process, he is being rudely treated while in the service of God'.[13] This view is strengthened if we note the parallel with Paul's earlier 'hardship list': 'For I think that God has exhibited us apostles as last of all, like men sentenced to death ...' (1 Cor. 4:9, ESV).

In Scott Hafemann's view, therefore, 2:14 can only mean: 'I am being led to death as a slave in God's victory parade.' This surely calls into question all superficial 'triumphalism' in the Church – the kind of mood and stance perhaps represented by those Paul later ironically dubbed 'super-apostles'. Such people evidently regarded 'triumph in Christ' as blazing a trail of undimmed success, sensational miracles and personal stardom satisfactory to the ego! James Scott speculates about whether we can hear even fainter but intriguing 'inter-textual echoes' in the picture. He suggests that the image of a Roman triumphal procession connects in Paul's mind with a powerful Old Testament and Jewish idea – that of God's chariot-throne (*merkabah*). The mobility of God's chariot-throne was revealed to Ezekiel beside the Chebar Canal (1:4–28; 10:1–22; 43:1–4).

More particularly Paul may have had in mind a strong Jewish tradition that pictured God descending to Sinai in His chariot-throne (*merkabah*) and ascending again to His holy sanctuary. Psalm 68:17–18 is a key commentary on this. In Jewish tradition this was elaborated so that Moses himself ascended to the Holy Sanctuary, took captive the Torah, and gave it as a gift to Israel (and the world).

Now Paul elsewhere exploits the Psalm 68 section for his purposes in talking about the authority of ministry (Eph. 4:8ff.). So Scott suggests that here in 2 Corinthians 2:14 it may well be that Paul is turning this tradition on its head by putting himself in the place of the captive while at the same time asserting that, like Moses, he is an agent of revelation. Through his apostolic ministry the knowledge of God is spread abroad (2:14). This may refer first of all to Paul's Damascus Road experience (as in 4:4–6). It may also be the first place in 2 Corinthians where he compares himself to Moses. The 'before God' (2:17) invites comparison with Moses who saw God 'face to face'. But the 'always' (2:14) may refer to ongoing revelatory experiences (as in 12:1-6).[14] Scott's view may be over-elaborate but if true at all, it serves only to deepen the paradox of Paul's ministry coming through personal weakness and suffering.

More cautiously, Paul Barnett sums up: '... that God leads Paul in triumph is a paradox. It is at the same time both triumphal [God is the leader] and anti-triumphal ["led in triumph" means suffering].' He continues, 'Set against the barely escaped deadly perils in Asia (1:8–10), the writing of the emotion-wrought, now lost (?) letter (2:4) and the deep disappointment in Troas (2:12–13), Paul gives thanks to God that, despite everything, he leads his minister, Paul, in triumph.'[15] Here is the secret of how to be a successful failure! This is the paradox of power in weakness, victory through death, a triumphal procession in which one is a captured slave. All of which may help to explain the double-edged effect of ministry which spreads everywhere the fragrance of the knowledge of God as the aroma of life or death (2:14–16). This imagery perhaps refers to the practice of sprinkling spices in front of Roman triumphal processions or more generally to incense offered in sacrifice. Either way, the stark challenge of such ministry is stressed as a scent of life or as the stench of death that rises up from the sacrificial offering of ministry that in preaching and practice and pastoral care exemplifies the dying and rising of Jesus. Anything less than this sells people short, offers truth diluted to meet superficial needs or, like watered-down wine, deliberately reduces the gospel to make it more acceptable to cultural tastes (2:17).

Without over-exploiting the metaphor Paul employs here it is worth noting that the Roman 'Triumph' was an obvious parade of the empire's power, a flaunting of its victories, an advertising of its dominance. But, as ever, the Empire of God constitutes a dramatic and paradoxical reversal of the status quo. Only by being soundly defeated, enslaved by another Lord, and led to share His death, do the servants of God's kingdom triumph and enjoy resurrection, exaltation and honour.

Only in this way can we be agents of the unadulterated truth, the reality of who is really 'Lord', and bear witness in word and deed to the strange victory that subverts all the pretentious claims of empire.

We are more than conquerors precisely through being conquered.

All that we have discussed so far is heady stuff. Paul's 'hardship lists' seem a million miles away from the seldom-disturbed routines of pastoral ministry – at least in a comfortable Western environment. And although our pressures probably bear no direct comparison with Paul's flesh and blood trials, except by analogy, we must, I am sure, explore the analogies and translate them into contemporary terms.

To be involved in Christian ministry today is to lay oneself open to the pressures of church work, pastoral challenges that tax our wisdom and patience, and incessant demands on our time and energy. Then there is the unvoiced but steady drip-drip of societal disdain for our role, the indifference even of the people we care for to what matters most to us, the factional infighting and political power-games that so bedevil church life as they do all other human institutions. And what of loneliness, stress on marriage, disappointments that threaten to plunge us into disillusionment, and the trivialisation of our gifts and calling that aggravates the open wound of unfulfilled potential? And now, as then, all such confessions of negativity can be totted up in some fanciful *God TV* world as a sign of lack of faith or of being off the pace.

> With Jesus as C.E.O. as a dominant Christological orientation of our time, what is to prevent the capitalistic, consumer-driven, felt-needs driven church from desiring and selecting its minister to function partly as … master of ceremonies and entertainer … and partly as a Wal-Mart-style manager and motivator, with the goal of happier, greater, bigger, and more?[16]

But maybe yours is not a 'pile 'em high; sell 'em cheap' ecclesiology. You do not serve in a mega-church. Your church is more a specialist antique dealer where tradition is valued and faithfully cherished by a loyal band of devotees, or an unpretentious but valued corner shop that is open all hours to its regulars for daily bread and daily news. You may never have heard of the concept of a 'philosophy of ministry'. Then encouragement is right here at hand in the apostolic testimony.

The point is not whether our trials are major or minor, glamorous or mundane. We start from the conviction that all our attempts to represent God are an impossible task – whether speaking faithfully for God, modelling discipleship for others, or changing people. '… who is equal to such a task?' (2:16b). Only the wounded healers in Christ who rely wholly on the Holy Spirit.

Whether our hardships are intense or merely irritating, they need not debilitate us if we follow Paul in seeking to interpret them theologically. Far from inhibiting his ministry or disqualifying him from exercising it, Paul turns his trials into authenticating signs of his calling. He does this by linking his afflictions to a theology in which God's power is perfected through weakness in the counter-intuitive story of the dying-rising Jesus. A gracious synergy occurs between what Paul believes and what happens to him. Here emerges a 'lived theology'. It is not that we possess a rigid, preconceived or remotely academic theological system into which the facts of life are forced to fit. Nor is the opposite the case so that our theology is derived directly from our experience. Rather, that experience is the proving ground for faith and the articulation of what a theology of the cross and resurrection really means.

So the ministry of the wounded healer, in so far as Paul is our guide, is to interpret the congregation's experience for them theologically so that they can find God in it; to articulate the robustness of faith-under-pressure so that people achieve a tougher, more realistic trust in God. In this way we may school others in how to live well, and – perhaps above all – how to die well, which, as Karl Barth said, was the chief end of ministry. Our pastoral task, in Michael Knowles' words, is to 'exemplify the process by which followers of Jesus make coherent sense of experience in light of Christian faith, and make sense of Christian faith in light of experience'.[17]

This helps to explain why Paul's 'hardship lists', while graphic, are in fact described in quite generalised terms and are sparing of gory detail. It is noticeable, too, that he almost invariably recounts these 'lists' in the first person plural ('we') in a self-deprecating and inclusive way. Where he speaks of his own exclusive experience he does so in a curiously circumlocutory way ('I know a man who ...', 12:1–5) much as Jesus, for far larger reasons, spoke of Himself in the third person as 'the Son of Man'. What is paramount for Paul in rehearsing his troubles is the overriding theological and pastoral benefits to be gained from them. This is as sobering as it is hopeful. But it is hopeful nonetheless.

Knowles helpfully suggests that Paul's own understanding has developed since he wrote the first letter to the Corinthians. Whereas in the 'hardship lists' of 1 Corinthians 4:7–13 the emphasis appears to be on the cross, in the afflictions mentioned in 2 Corinthians 1:8–11 it seems to be on 'God, who raises the dead' and who can deliver us again in the future. In which case, our unanswered prayers may be the occasion for receiving unexpected and exceptional grace; our 'near-death' experiences may prove 'near-resurrection' experiences.

And, as for me, my response to my 'fatal' frustrations and 'terminal' irritation, may well be to fall about laughing!

10
TREASURE IN CLAY POTS

But we have this treasure in jars of clay to show that this all-surpassing power is from God and not from us. (2 Corinthians 4:7)

In 1948, an Arab boy chasing his goat to the back of a cave on the edge of the Dead Sea found 'treasure' concealed in some tall clay jars. It had been there a long time. As the Roman–Jewish War of AD 70–73 came to its bitter climax, the community of pious Jews at Qumran stored their precious manuscript copies of Old Testament texts and in-house monastic rules in large storage pots and hid them away for safekeeping in the deep caves cut out of the hillside above their settlement. When, some nineteen centuries later, the ancient documents started appearing for sale in local markets, experts began to take notice and soon realised that in these Dead Sea Scrolls they had discovered 'buried treasure' that would transform our understanding of the Jewish world into which Jesus was born. If with parchments and pots how much more with the new covenant and the people to whom it is entrusted.

I spoke to Lesslie Newbigin only once and that briefly. When I met him at a 'Gospel and Culture' conference at which he was a brilliant keynote speaker, the renowned missiologist was already an old man. What he said when I thanked him for his published work was gracious. But what I remember most were his face and his feet. His weather-beaten face radiated with an inner glow; his feet were shod in ancient, well-worn, cracked leather boots which I suspect had survived long years of hard service in India. In that moment Newbigin, already one of my theological heroes, instinctively exemplified for me something of the essence of authentic Christian ministry as Paul described it when he said: 'Though outwardly we are wasting away, yet inwardly we are being renewed day by day' (2 Cor. 4:16). My instinct, if accurate, and Paul's insight, are grounded in Paul's basic image of Christian ministry as carrying *'treasure in jars of clay to show that this all-surpassing power is from God and not from us'* (2 Cor. 4:7). As Martin Luther said in the sixty-second Thesis, 'the true treasure of the Church is the holy Gospel of the glory and grace of God'. This is the priceless new covenant message and ministry entrusted to all who stand in some measure in the apostolic succession.

As for the 'clay pots', they allude to the small pottery jars which contained the flame of first-century oil lamps. Homely and common, cheap and cheerful, fragile and 'unadorned', they represent our basic humanness and especially symbolise the inherent and acquired weakness of our 'ordinary lives' (*The Message*). But the 'outward appearance cannot be taken as a sure guide to the inner contents: rather the outward container must be judged by what it holds'[1]. It is precisely this human frailty that offsets to best advantage the 'all-surpassing power of God' and the priceless value of the gospel.

It is useful here to notice a general comparison that may be made between the two Corinthian letters. Paul's conviction (1 Cor. 1:25ff.) that the *'foolishness of God is wiser than man's wisdom'* in a sense sums up First Corinthians which is concerned chiefly with the issue of *spiritual wisdom*. His further statement that 'the *weakness* of God is stronger than man's strength' sums up Second Corinthians, which is perhaps more chiefly concerned with the issue of *power*.

It is this counter-intuitive secret of Christian ministry which flows out of the 'treasure in clay pots' image that Paul goes on to explore in the poetic paradoxes that follow 4:7–11. By this inverted theo-logic, the scars incurred in Christian service are 'on every side' and 'always' badges of honour: 'hard pressed' by intense demands but 'not crushed' by unbearable pressure; 'perplexed', often at a loss, not knowing all the answers but not needing to know all the answers, and so 'baffled to fight better'; hemmed in by hostile forces like a hunted prey yet not abandoned by God; damaged but not destroyed.

As before, Paul can make sense of his adversities and understand the mystery of his own resilience only by reference to his union with Christ. The cruciform narrative of Jesus gives meaning to our ministry for 'We always carry around in our body the death of Jesus, so that the life of Jesus may also be revealed in our body. For we who are alive are always being given over to death for Jesus' sake, so that his life may be revealed in our mortal body. So then, death is at work in us, but life is at work in you' (4:10–12). Henri Nouwen comments,

> To be a living reminder of Jesus Christ … means to reveal the connections between our small sufferings and the great story of God's suffering in Jesus Christ, between our little life and the great life of God with us … By connecting the human story with the story of the suffering servant, we rescue history from fatalistic *chronos* into *kairos*, from a series of randomly organised incidents into a constant opportunity to explore God's work in our lives.[2]

For Paul, the adversities viewed by some in the Corinthian church as inconsistent with the Spirit-filled life of victory and the ministry of grace are recalibrated by the cross into means of showing the power of God made effective through human weakness.

In 6:1–13 Paul augments his argument with a further catalogue of trials. It is as *un*modern a CV as you could find! The gospel promises no immunity from trouble. Adversities are not incompatible with living in the era of unprecedented divine favour which is the Messianic age of salvation (6:2); 'in great endurance' (6:4b) includes and sums up the reaction to all the specified trials that follow. Three triads, characterised by the preposition 'in' (en) spell out the list.

Firstly, in 'troubles', or 'afflictions' whether from outside forces or inner anxieties (cf. 7:5); 'in hardships' (*anankais*) necessarily incurred by, but defiantly overridden by, his God-given obligation (*anank*) to preach the gospel (1 Cor. 9:16); in 'distresses', those calamitous tight spots in which our scope is limited and narrowed which prove so vexing for expansive souls – all these sum up how in 'hard times, tough times, bad times' (*The Message*), Paul and his team have paid the price of bringing the gospel to a hostile culture.

Secondly, 'in beatings, imprisonments and riots' – a list on which 11:23–25 is a commentary – measures the social hostility faced by the servants of Christ whose message threatens the political powers-that-be. In the modern Western world, at least, we may have had for a long time to psychologise these trials, though Christians in other parts of the world will not have. In post-Christendom Europe, indifference rather than hostility may currently be our fate, but for the immediate future, who knows? In any event, cruciform people have surely been forewarned not to settle for a quiet life.

The third triad features 'hard work, [and] sleepless nights' (6:5b) both no doubt a harsh reality for Paul as he laboured at his tentmaking day job and burnt the midnight oil in prayer and pastoral concern. As for 'hunger', it may be voluntarily undertaken for the purposes of fasting or – more likely – may refer to the random irregularity of meals while on the move (cf. 11:27) or forgone in the interest of not wishing to be a burden to his hosts (cf. 11:7,9; 12:13).

Next, Paul maps out an eightfold path to enlightened and transparent ministry all sourced by the Holy Spirit (6:6–7). Purity and perception, patience and kindness characterise Paul's relationships and attitudes to others. The Holy Spirit inspires sincere love, effective communication of the Word of truth (probably a reference to the gospel itself, cf. Col. 1:6), and arms him with a righteous character that serves to commend him (the right hand of offence) and to defend him (the left hand) whether he is treated honourably or shamefully, whether praised or blamed.

In other words, the solid virtues evident in Paul's ministry show him to be no less Spirit-driven, no less charismatic than the showboating sections of the Corinthian church. The Spirit has proved well able to sustain him in an honour–shame culture. He can hold his head high whatever comes his way because he is looking beyond the social ethos for his approval ratings. In vivid and memorable antitheses (6:8–10), the apostle testifies to a life which by the Spirit's power enables him to live life 'against the grain'. Deemed to be a poseur, he is in fact the genuine article, the real deal, unhung in the empire's 'Hall of Fame' but known and valued by God. All of which conforms to the cruciform pattern of his life with Christ in which deadly things are dealt to him but through which he shares the resurrection surprise – '*behold*, we live'! (6:9, ESV).

So he is startled by a sweet and sudden joy in the midst of grieving; he is amazed to discover how running on empty he fills others up. Possessing nothing of worldly securities, he is astonished at the freedom this brings him. So he throws his empty hands wide to the world as if he owned it all and discovers that in a real sense he does and that since he is God's, all things are his (cf. 1 Cor. 3:21–22).

Power through weakness

These are the paradoxes of ministry as worked out in Paul's life and we need to appreciate that they still apply to Christian ministry today. 'It is remarkable how deeply God is involved in the *contingent* events of history.'[3] The word 'contingent' means 'dependent upon events, accidents, conditions, and reactions'. 'The crucifixion was contingent upon what people did to the "Son of God". Paul's ministry is contingent upon the varied responses to his message, and the spread of the Gospel is inseparable from appeals, decisions, encounters and sufferings.'[4]

The cruciform paradox of Easter becomes the governing paradigm for us. How the gospel works is how Christian ministry in service to that gospel also works. In the words of Frances Young and David Ford: 'Paul's more specific word for a key feature of this contingency is "*weakness*".' If one's idea of God's power united to knowledge is that it should be able to bring about its purpose with maximum results and minimum vulnerability then Paul would call that *kata sarka* – according to the flesh – the kind of worldly notions of power held by his opponents (chapters 10–12). 'Paul's gospel relates power with weakness. Rather, both are re-interpreted through the crucifixion and resurrection of Jesus.'[5]

Faced with the daunting task of being the first to bring the gospel to the seething and corrupt port of Corinth, unsure of his reception, Paul had felt naturally apprehensive so that he came to them, he confesses, 'in weakness and fear, and with much trembling' and in need of direct reassurance from the Lord (1 Cor 2:3; cf. Acts 18:9–10).

In Paul's case, 'weakness' included physical assault and its after-effects. It also included the pain of being misunderstood, of motives misread, of integrity maligned (cf. 2 Cor. 1:12–2:13) – all of which added to the emotional vulnerability of an 'openhearted' man (2:4; 6:11–13). On top of this was the social stigma weighing heavily on Paul of being regarded as an oddball who was out of step with social mores. His bodily presence was deemed to be 'weak' and 'his speech of no account' (10:10, ESV). Paul was not a superhero in any conventional sense.

Christian ministry – as anyone knows who attempts to practise it – is not carried out six feet above contradiction, conflict or concern. Ministry is subject to contingency and contingency involves the passive tense as well as the active tense, what happens to us as well as what is done by us. But our ministry is grounded in God's sovereignty which embraces this contingency in the incarnation and crucifixion. Believing this, we may rejoice to discover the tough grace that God's power does not always operate now directly to provoke events but God works contingently through events, through seeming reverses and obstacles to His will, encountered in the rough and tumble of the historical process. His direct invasions only serve to endorse His incremental workings. *So the resurrection does not cancel out the cross but serves to endorse the rightness of a seemingly all-wrong contingent event.*

So we speak of the 'passive' endurance of suffering by the Lord Jesus as His active redemptive achievement. The direct intrusion of Easter Day makes this more, not less, visible. So power is not that which sweeps aside all obstacles to its aims – including suffering – but that which achieves its full potential, its *'being made perfect', through weakness* (12:9). This, says Scott Hafemann, is the 'high point of his argument in this passage and … a summary of the theological substructure of 2 Corinthians as a whole'.[6]

Which brings us to Paul's *'thorn in the flesh'* (11:16–12:10). From the irony of being 'too weak' to arm-wrestle with the overbearing personalities in Corinth to the real hardships encountered in apostolic travels, Paul wryly observes that 'Who is weak, and I do not feel weak?' (11:21, 22–29). He concludes, 'If I must boast, I will boast of … my weakness' (v.30). Even recalling an elevated, spiritual, almost mystical, experience further reminds him of the 'thorn in … [the] flesh' that kept his feet on the ground and saved him from being over-elated (12:1–9). Was the 'thorn' a disability like deteriorating eyesight (cf. Gal. 4:13–15; 6:11), or an especially vicious opponent? No one is sure, and perhaps just as well. At the same time Paul describes his 'affliction' as a 'messenger of Satan'. Pastoral theologian, Andrew Purves, not prone, one assumes, to flights of fancy in this area, agrees that 'the passage raises a profound and troubling issue: Satan is after God's own, seeks to bring us down, rendering us faithless' (cf. 2 Cor. 2:11). In his own prolonged bout of cancer, Purves says, through some kind of visionary experience, he came to realise that his illness was 'an attack of evil' but that Christ had the victory. 'One thing I know for sure', he concludes, that the only hope for faith and ministry is to 'follow where Paul would take me: "My grace is sufficient for you, for power is made perfect in weakness".'[7]

Remarkably, Paul testifies that the 'thorn was *given me*' so that whatever it was, the original grace was in his receiving it as a gift from the Lord at all. Fortunately, as Douglas John Hall observes, we do not know what it was. 'I say "fortunately"', he footnotes, 'because Paul's point would be lost if the problems to which he alludes were narrowly defined. *Whatever* his (or our) particular "thorn", what it betokens is a lack of self-sufficiency which makes the human open to undeserved and unearnable grace.'[8]

Contingency is a smooth word for a raw and rugged reality. Paul's hardship lists are not contrived for effect like deliberately distressed jeans. Rather he enters into the paradoxical amalgam of antagonism and healing characteristic of the Easter event itself: unutterable and unrepeatable words heard, together with unanswered prayers offered (three times, like Jesus Himself); divine revelation subverting Satanic attack; extreme human weakness the occasion for sufficient and compensatory divine grace. Paul speaks like this in order to reconfigure the Corinthians' criteria of ministry along cruciform lines. To do so 'required him to use irony, parody, invective, and paradox to make clear to his converts this message: *Things are not what they seem*'.[9]

Setting this in the wider context of Paul's discussion shows us something of the true nature of spiritual authority in which God's strength is made perfect in our weakness.

Firstly, authority is a *gift of God's grace,* a God-given charisma of the Holy Spirit (10:8). Grace means favour and empowerment and has three implications:

- grace *authorises* and gives freedom to minister according to one's giftedness; it energises and makes for enthusiastic serving that brings 'job satisfaction';
- grace *assigns* a sphere of service (10:13) which sets limits to what one is expected to do. It restricts one's area of influence but stops us overreaching ourselves or getting dangerously out of our depth. It means of course that we must learn to need others and to work alongside them with the grace-gifts they are given. This does not stunt growth because by grace our sphere can be expanded (10:15; cf. Rom. 12:3–6);
- grace makes us *accountable.* It implies that we are entrusted with authority and a role and are 'stewards of that ministry' (1 Cor. 4:1, ESV) and are answerable for its faithful deployment.

Secondly, authority is *embodied.*

Paul's is an incarnational spirituality, an incarnational ministry, and therefore an embodied authority (10:9–11; 11:27–28; 12:6). Which means that we recognise the fragility of the 'clay pot' which holds the treasure; we respect the humanness and human frailty of God's people and their leaders. We are not God and we are not blamed for not being God. We may apply this sensitivity both to our people and to ourselves. It follows that authority is *vulnerable* – not only in its recognition of its own humanness but in not relying on external validation (10:17–18). Paul did not exercise his authority overbearingly or manipulatively or seductively – we were too 'weak' for that (11:18–21). There is no sleight of hand here, no smoke and mirrors (cf. 4:1–2) – Paul is able to say that what you see is what you get (12:6).

The advantages here are obvious. If we face *criticism* it need not destroy us, for our self-esteem is in being loved by God. *Popularity,* if it comes to us, need not corrupt us as long as we practise tough love (11:10–11). We can renounce all underhand methods of getting our way, all control freakery, and all evasions of leadership initiatives. We may even risk – as Paul did – playing the fool (though knowing when to do this requires subtle wisdom; Proverbs 26:5 rather than Proverbs 26:4!).

Thirdly, and to sum up where our discussion has taken us, strength-in-weakness authority is thus *accredited by afflictions*, validated by adversity as highlighted in the keynote statement: 'Therefore I will boast all the more gladly of my weaknesses, so that the power of Christ may rest upon me. For the sake of Christ, then, I am content with weaknesses, insults, hardships, persecutions, and calamities. *For when I am weak, then I am strong*' (12:9–10, ESV). Some 'contentment'! But what else can 'clay pot' stewards of the treasure do than interpret their 'weakness' not primarily as physical or moral or mental frailty but as vulnerable dependence on God's grace?

Such authority is nothing else but the *authority of the cruciform gospel* itself. Which is why the integrity of the gospel matters so much to Paul (11:4,7). Serious implications follow this conviction.

- *If it doesn't take the cross and resurrection of Jesus to achieve the aims we have in ministering to people, then we are not being faithful to the gospel but are plying some more self-help.*
- *It means that we must trust the gospel to evoke the responses it deserves and effect the transformation it promises.*

So much of the Church's nervous search for new methods and its nail-biting obsession with being relevant merely reveals a startling and shameful lack of confidence in the gospel to be the power of God unto salvation.

Finally, what follows from all the above is that true spiritual authority which demonstrates strength-in-weakness will be *Christlike in its methods*: I entreat you 'by the meekness and gentleness of Christ' (10:1, ESV). Seeming bold at a distance and being humble when close up is not a mark of insincerity or inconsistency but of a genuine attempt to woo his readers over. Paul is not fighting with worldly weapons. The fact that he pours out his concern in letters to the Church implies a reluctance to pressurise his hearers into submission to his personality. In fact Paul both plays down the impressiveness of his own personality, as if to say 'What are you afraid of?' and, at the same time, warns them not to assume that his letter carries more weight than his presence will and so his arrival can be shrugged off (10:9–10).

Pastoral letter-writing assumes the power of appeal and persuasion and argument, rather than hectoring and bullying, as the way to assert his authority. Paul's authority is employed not to crush people but to demolish arguments raised against the knowledge of God (10:1ff.); it is asserted not in order to put people down but to build them up; not to keep pulling them up by the roots to see if they are growing but to plant and water and to feed their vitality into fruitfulness. This is surely the Jesus way, the cruciform way.

> The form of ministry and the kind of ministers that we are and are becoming show whether or not it is the theology of the cross which informs and forms us. 'Ministry is theology's polygraph, its infallible lie-detecting test, revealing the truth of what the church believes and the identity of whom she worships – the God of the cross or the idols of the cultural idolatry.[10]

In Tim Savage's words, 'As a minister of the gospel of the crucified Christ, and as one called to serve in an age dominated by a self-exalting outlook, the apostle Paul has little option but to respond to his worldly critics: *"when I am weak, then I am strong"*'.[11]

No, things are not what they seem. Don't disdain the clay pots. Don't ever underestimate the weather-beaten face and the old cracked boots.

11
UNDIMINISHED FLAMES

*Therefore, since through God's mercy we have this ministry,
we do not lose heart … Therefore we do not lose heart.*
(2 Corinthians 4:1,16)

An *energy crisis* is perhaps the most immediate threat to our Western standard of living. Will our supplies of gas be cut off by the Russians or whoever currently controls them? Will fresh Middle East turmoil drive up the cost of oil? Will electricity prices as a result become prohibitive? Or will we simply exhaust the earth's fund of fossils fuels? Which ever way it comes, what we fear is a *power failure*.

Without in the slightest minimising these challenges or conceding that the gospel has nothing to say about them, I mention them as a way of asking, by analogy, *whether or not* an equivalent '*energy crisis*' lies at the heart of the pressure Paul is feeling at this point in his ministry and which, by his own testimony, he is withstanding.

It is noteworthy that what brackets this part of Paul's magnificent testimony to the gospel and its ministry is the phrase 'Therefore … we do not lose heart' (4:1; see also 4:16). This repeated statement forms an *inclusio* for the whole section (4:1–18) and acts, I believe, as an interpretive key to the personal and pastoral challenges underlying it. In writing openly to the Corinthians, Paul faces up to the reality of what Christian ministry costs us in human terms. In this section of his argument, he particularly addresses the issue of discouragement, or – to use business jargon – 'burnout'.

John Sanford, in a helpful analysis, rehearses some of the down-to-earth reasons for 'burnout' in Christian ministry.[1]

1. *The job of ministry is never finished.*
All life is a journey and we can, at best, help people on their way. The satisfaction of a product made, a room decorated, a lawn mown is not found in Christian ministry itself. We may preside at the wedding successfully but whether the marriage will work is beyond our powers. People often move on so that our input into their lives is partial and temporary. Too often in ministry, like teachers, we are in the sowing rather than the reaping business. And since our ceaselessly creative God enjoys a 'day off', we might indulge in the luxurious necessity of keeping a regular Sabbath.

2. *The ministering person cannot ever be sure that his or her work is yielding any useful results.*
We may never know how effective – in the long term – our ministry has been. Ministering to people rarely comes into any quantifiable category. There always remains someone else who might have been, perhaps should have been, visited; something else one wished one had said – or, perhaps, not said; more prayer that could have been prayed. In which case, stop what you're doing and mow the lawn or decorate the lounge or paint a picture.

3. *The work of ministry is usually repetitive.*
The same round of activities can tax the most eager soul. The same faces, presenting the same old problems, the same irritating personality traits surfacing. But compared to the checkout assistant at the supermarket dulled by tedium, or the elderly shelf-filler in Sainsbury's – or even the overtired surgeon who says 'not another appendix' – how does our task look? In our case there really is merit in resigning, or taking a vacation from this particular sort of ministry, or going on a course to learn more about what concerns us in ministry.

4. *Ministry faces the pressure of other people's expectations all the time – some realistic, some not.*
People join churches expecting them to be perfect: the worship sublime, the preaching superb, and the pastoral care divine! Failure on the part of pastoral workers to be a cross between the Angel Gabriel, Mother Teresa and General Patton leaves a lot of desires unfulfilled. In which case learn to say 'no' as well as 'yes' by remembering that Jesus was the

servant not of the people but of His Father. He was able to walk away from promising situations in order to do something else in the Father's will (Luke 4:42–44; John 6:15).

5. *Working with needy people drains the energy – psychic, emotional, spiritual, physical – of the one ministering.*
People in pain are not always pleasant to be with. 'Why do you want to be a counsellor, pastor, cell-group leader, youth worker?' 'Because I like working with people.' 'Have you *met* people?' There are all kinds of reasons why some people cannot be helped. They merely act as a drain with no plug to all our efforts to help. Some are 'clinging vines', tenaciously dependent on us or on the Church with no intention or strength to stand on their own feet or take responsibility for their own lives. Watch such people that they don't drain *you*! Henri Nouwen's advice is wise and well worth taking to take to heart: 'The words of Jesus: "It is for your good that I leave" should be part of every pastoral call we make. We have to learn to leave so that the Holy Spirit can come.'[2]

6. *Some people simply want 'stroking' or are seeking attention* and can waste your time by testing your patience and discernment. Some merely want us to 'rubber stamp' everything they are feeling or have already decided for themselves. Jesus refused to tick other people's boxes at the asking; He refused to arbitrate on terms set up by others or for a third party, or dole out advice on demand (cf. Luke 12:13–15).

7. *Ministry in any public or official form at all necessarily means that you function behind a 'persona'.*
Though often inevitable, this can lead to us becoming unreal, losing our humanity, and repressing our own legitimate feelings. The role we have to play – that we have to *force ourselves* to play when the phone goes late at night or when we are tired and had promised ourselves some special time – is not *in itself* bad or hypocritical. In other spheres it would be termed, legitimately, 'professionalism'. But if we never de-role, never take the mask off, then we are in danger of 'burnout' or of confusing a Messianic anointing with a Messianic complex.

8. *The ministering person may become discouraged by failure.*
The gap between vision and actuality, ideal and reality, is always there and seems to stretch us across it. Methodist bishop and theologian

William Willimon tells of asking a distinguished neurosurgeon half in jest: 'Why are all the brain surgeons I know such strange people?' 'What do you expect?' she replied: 'About 90% of the work we do is either standing by and watching nature take its course or else a total failure. Some days I do nothing but stand by helplessly and watch people die. That does something to a person.'[3] We too do a lot of standing by watching as marriages fail, as prayers for healing go unanswered, as enthusiasm wanes, as old self-destructive habits reappear. That can be terribly depressing!

So, how can we combat discouragement in ministry and avoid 'burnout'? I want to suggest that the most important step we can take is *to change the categories in which we consider it*. This is not to minimise how tired we can become, how stressed we get in ministering to others. It is not to overlook the way our time is eaten up by the needs of others, how caring drains our nervous and spiritual powers, and exhausts our spiritual resources. But William Willimon is right, I believe, in concluding that the real cause of 'burnout' in ministry is *not* that we *lack resources for the task, but that we lose track of the reasons why we do it.*
The problem is not so much that we lack strength or reach the bottom of our energy levels, but that we suffer a breakdown of our sense of purpose and hope. In other words, the problem is *not loss of energy, but loss of meaning.*

This, I suggest, is borne out by further reflection on Paul's own testimony.
There can be no doubt as to Paul's expenditure of *physical energy* nor do the 'hardship lists' conceal the physical effects of his apostolic career to date. The 'wounded healer' has been beaten, flogged, stoned and left for dead; he has been shipwrecked, exposed to extremes of heat and cold, been constantly on the move, known sleepless nights and food deprivation (2 Cor. 11:23–29). But it does not seem to have been physical tiredness that has in any way deterred Paul.
Is the danger loss of *moral energy* – a failure of courage or determination? Hardly, for Paul shows no sign of any loss of nerve and reasserts the boldness that characterises him (2 Cor. 3:12).
The draining, also, of *emotional energy* taxes even the most ardent doer of good but there appears to be 'compassion-fatigue' in Paul whose

144

affections remain at full stretch and whose joy is undiminished (2 Cor. 6:11–13; 7:3).

As for falling levels of *mental energy*, a mind becoming dulled or bored, again this seems not to be case here either, as Paul argues for the gospel and its ministry with sharpness and passion. In short, there is no evidence that Paul is, or has been, on the brink of psychological power failure.

Changing the categories in which we consider 'losing heart' means that the problem is presented *not as loss of energy, but as loss of meaning.* 'Burnout', then, can be a misnomer as if our problem were merely a loss of energy or power; 'blackout' might be better, suggesting not only loss of power but loss of light, the loss of meaning and purpose. As Willimon observes, 'Burnout … dissipation of energy and commitment, are matters more of distress than stress. A lack of meaning rather than a lack of energy.'[4]

It is this concern which underlies Paul's richly textured exposition of the gospel and its ministry in 2 Corinthians 4:1–18. Commenting on this passage, Tom Wright summarises that concern:

> Paul had every reason to lose heart. There he was at Ephesus, all the news was bad, God had seemed to have abandoned him, most of his friends were forsaking him, the churches where he had worked hardest had turned round and blown a raspberry at him, and he was ready to quit. Perhaps he thought bitterly of retiring back to Tarsus and writing a few books in his old age, complaining about how tough life was. God could finish the job.[5]

Why did Paul *not* lose heart?

The reasons Paul gives can help us – in our measure and on our scale – to avoid 'burnout' and to refuse to give up.

We will not lose heart if we …
1. Remember what kind of ministry it is we have (4:1)
What is *'this ministry'*? It is the ministry of the *new covenant*. A calling and work has been given to us that eclipses the greatest glories of Moses,

that speaks and lives out of the unspeakable grace of being forgiven and gifted with the precious gift of God's own Holy Spirit. What prophets longed to see and visionaries dreamed of in their wildest dreams, you have been privileged to see and know and learn and become a part of. It is entirely 'through God's mercy' that anyone shares in this ministry. Pursue Paul to the last days of his ministry and ask why he does what he does and why he suffers for who he is and what he does, and he will reply because 'I was shown mercy ... I was shown mercy' (1 Tim. 1:13,16). Paul's early record as a killer of Christians could have crippled him in ministry but not even bitter memories can dispirit the ministry that grace sustains as effectively as it once saved. Why would anyone give themselves wholeheartedly to the service of God? Why be a non-conformist to this world's values and spend your life for others? Why surrender control of your own destiny to the mysterious will of God? Paul's only answer would be: because the human heart has been invaded and captivated 'by the mercies of God ...' (Rom. 12:1, ESV).

This is part of the insufficiency which we gladly confess of ourselves (2 Cor. 3:6); this is a crucial aspect of the 'we do not preach ourselves' (2 Cor. 4:5). Effective new covenant ministry does not depend on our skills or resources, but rests entirely on God's gracious supply. If we were to ask Paul, at any juncture, why he is what he is, he would answer: '... by the grace of God I am what I am' (1 Cor. 15:10). The ministry of the new covenant far outstrips in privilege and significance even the prestigious ministries of patriarchs and prophets under the old covenant. No one loses heart who shares with Paul the 'stimulus and exhilaration' of making known Christ as the mediator of the new and far better covenant.[6]

We will not lose heart if we ...
2. *Renounce deception and distortion of the Word of God* (4:2)
The repudiation of all alien ways of making the gospel work in others' lives is necessary for several reasons. For a start, we can be hugely discouraged by those who do adopt such methods and who seem to have achieved far more success by doing so than we have by not doing so. Whether charlatans intentionally deceiving people with their semblance of superior spirituality, or celebrity performers who are giving large doses of what people want, or whether just 'lucky' in being in the right

time and place to achieve a spurious fame, these 'super-apostles' (as Paul termed them in his day) vex our peace of mind. It is hard for us not to feel put in the shade. In which case we either wear ourselves out with anger or jealousy, or become thoroughly dispirited and so lose heart.

The only antidote is, with Paul, to renew one's own original commitment not to use shameful and deceptive ways and to resist the comparison with any who do. It may be true for you, as Michael Esses once said,

> God will wrap you in a jealous love and will put on you demands of obedience that will not allow you to do things which he seems to let other good people do. Other Christians may push themselves forward, pull wires, and work schemes to carry out their plans; but you cannot. And if you attempt to, you will meet with such failure and rebuke from the Lord as to make you sorely penitent. Others can brag on their work, on their success; but the Holy Spirit will not allow you to do any such thing. And if you begin it, he will lead you into some deep mortification that will make you despise yourself and all your good works.[7]

I have had cause to return to these severe but wise words many times since I first came across them nearly thirty years ago.

For his part, Paul will not lose heart and compromise his integrity but renews his rejection of all underhand methods of ministry. In any case, we can afford to forgo clever tricks, phoney methods, psychobabble, undigested therapeutic theories; we can trust to honesty and being true to God's Word. We can avoid manipulating people into change. False methods are actually much more tiring than telling the truth. Simulation and intrigue are more wearing on the spirit. The word Paul uses – *panourgia* – means literally 'every work', perhaps suggesting the thought of 'anything will do as long as the job gets done' or 'the end justifies the means'. On the contrary, new covenant ministry frees to *practise truth-telling*! Truth is not something we believe in but live. Truthfulness is our story, it is the air we breathe; any other way we suffocate. It is perhaps a lifetime's task to allow the scalpel of the truthful word to peel back the layers of self-deception in us all. As C.S. Lewis said in *The Great Divorce*, 'Reality is harsh to the feet of shadows'. To face reality and practise truthfulness calls for a courage to be open that only the mercy of God and a community of forgiven forgivers can cultivate. But we will not lose heart if we do.

We will not lose heart if we …
3. *Face up to the reality of evil in ourselves and in the world* (4:3–4)
Paul knows the difficulties he faces in presenting the gospel in a climate where speaking the truth is a lost language. He knows too that the hardness of the task is not due to any deficiency in the message, nor even in the messengers. The minds of his hearers are 'veiled' by an unwillingness to 'turn to the Lord' which brings the shutters down (cf. 2 Cor. 3:16). Tragically, at this point, the Corinthian Christians are in danger of behaving as unbelievers themselves. The unrepentant heart is resistant to appeals that rely only on human communication skills or a persuasive personality. Closed minds can be prised open only by the plain setting forth of truth. Heavily fortified ideas and entrenched attitudes can be stormed and taken only by spiritual weapons (2 Cor. 10:5). Darkness can be dispelled only by the light of the gospel shining in the heart (2 Cor. 4:4–6).

We might wish it otherwise but there is a force out there combating our best efforts. We will minister without illusions. There are no easy fixes. A sentimental refusal to acknowledge what we're up against will surely wear us down. We speak truth to power – and powerful self-interest – and only the victory of the cross can give us success. Only as we rely on divine revelation can we bring people to faith. Only the Holy Spirit can open blind eyes and set the captive free.

We will not lose heart if we …
4. *Remember the majesty of the One we are serving* (4:4–6)
Don't invert this or you will soon get discouraged. If we are in Christian ministry for our own ego we will self-destruct or else leave a trail of bruised reeds behind us. But 'we do not preach ourselves' – with God's true servant there is no self-promotion any more than there is any self-denigration. You have the highest dignity of serving the Servant-King, the Lord of lords of whom it was envisioned: 'A bruised reed he will not break, and a smouldering wick he will not snuff out … he will not falter or be discouraged until he establishes justice on the earth' (Isa. 42:3–4). Servanthood, mysteriously and miraculously, will not break

down or burn out; precisely because it does not promote itself or serve its own interests or succumb to the needs of the people. In this spirit a new covenant ministry is the people's servant only in so far as it is first the Lord's servant (2 Cor. 4:5).

Only in this perspective can so much of the mundane work of ministry be sustained with an unflagging devotion. Many of us might agree with William Willimon's observation that 'people appear to burn out in the church not necessarily because they are overworked, but because they are overburdened with the trivial and the unimportant'.[8] How true!

Having jettisoned whatever we can of the seemingly pointless burdens heaped on us, there remain countless and unavoidable minor duties which we can turn into meaningful ministry only by relating them to the majesty of the Lord we serve. And if this is true of the apparently insignificant details of the work of ministry, how much more does it need to be true when we ponder the magnitude of the task?

The scale of need and the scope of ministry can overwhelm us. As Jeremiah was told when burdened with the pressures of ministry, 'If you have raced with men on foot and they have worn you out, how can you compete with horses? If you stumble in safe country, how will you manage in the thickets by the Jordan?' (Jer. 12:5). I remember as a young pastor the immense relief I felt when I woke up one morning and decided to resign as Saviour of the World.

All leadership is submission to His Lordship. Ray Anderson suggests we do well to distinguish between being 'called to the ministry' and 'called to follow Jesus into ministry'.[9] It was along these lines, as I recall, that Mother Teresa usually answered those who asked about her call to come to Calcutta: 'I didn't feel called to come to Calcutta,' she replied, 'I followed Jesus and he led me here.' Which is why she showed herself willing to expend so much on so few (cf. 2 Cor. 8:9).

All of which means to *live in the light of and for the sake of the glory we have glimpsed* (4:6). That glorious light which first dazzled Paul on the Damascus Road for ever blinded him to his own vision of his future career. Yet, now, as a minister of the new covenant, Paul deems his ministry more glorious than even that of Moses (3:7–18). In contrast to the activity of the 'god of this age' whose demonic aim is to blind and deceive (4:4), the laser light of the knowledge of the true God – focused in the gospel – shines in our hearts to illuminate the face of Jesus Christ for us: the human, suffering, dying, risen, exalted face of Him whom we call 'Lord'. In David Ford's words:

> Paul 'sums up his whole gospel ("this treasure") as having the face of Christ shining in our hearts … All that goes on in our hearts is before this face. Jesus Christ is the focus of our core community … But to concentrate on the face of Jesus Christ is to find our boundaries shifting and expanding as we slowly "grasp what is the breadth and length and height and depth of Christ's love". This is someone whose hospitality is universal – face by face by face. To be before his face is to find that he is looking with love on all sorts of unexpected, marginalised, or, to us, disagreeable people, as well as on us.'[10]

Paul's opponents preach 'another Jesus' (2 Cor. 11:4) – one he doesn't recognise – because their approach to ministry involves assertiveness, competitive boasting and self-exalting behaviour, which speaks volumes for 'their Jesus'. But new covenant ministry is gripped by an intense '*kurios*ity' – an endless fascination with discovering how to do the *Lord's* work, the *Lord's* way, in the *Lord's* strength, and for the *Lord's* glory. To do so is to accept the role of suffering servanthood – to relish the treasure in earthen vessels so that the light can shine.

We will not lose heart if we …
5. *Recognise our humanness, and own our human limitations* (4:7)
Servant ministry relishes the treasure while at the same time being acutely aware of the earthen vessel that contains it. We are, in our mortality, old clay pots. We may be finest porcelain in God's eyes, but from the inside out it feels like being a polystyrene cup. Marva Dawn is a much-appreciated writer and thinker in contemporary Evangelicalism. With several postgraduate degrees and at least one PhD, she is one of our brightest minds, an adjunct professor at Regent College, Vancouver, who at the same time teaches children with sweetness and truth. Deserted by her first husband and now recently remarried, she gives seminars for young people on sexuality. Her books on the gospel and culture are shrewdly prophetic yet she also writes

moving biblical devotional material. Her two books on worship have been groundbreaking and widely discussed. She is undoubtedly one of God's gifts to the contemporary Church.

Why mention her here? Well, to give honour where honour is due but also because she exemplifies for me the paradox of treasure in clay jars. She argues passionately that the contemporary Church too often in its worship trivialises suffering and the pain of the world by glossing it over with glib and happy songs that produce only warm fuzzy feelings that soon fade away. Marva Dawn has earned the right to say this, as her testimony may make clear.

> I don't write as a mere observer. I have struggled with health complications ever since the measles virus destroyed my pancreas when I was a teenager. This has led to blindness in one eye from retinal bleeding (I was totally blind for seven months); kidney disease (mine function less than 20%); nerve dysfunction in my legs and digestive processes. I also seem to be a magnet for collecting rare disorders and other maladies – a dentist pulled the wrong tooth (complicating my jaw breakdown); sudden deafness syndrome impaired one ear; an intussusception strangled fifteen inches of my intestine, which turned gangrenous, and its removal led to problematic scar tissue; breast cancer led to a mastectomy and extremely deleterious chemotherapy; arthritis afflicts my hands; demineralising of the upper torso leads to severe pain. Also a doctor's misdiagnosis of a foot problem led to a shattered foot, a rebuilding after a year in casts, then a broken leg that healed crooked, so now I wear a leg brace. Frequently I get wounds inside that brace, so I spend plenty of time on crutches or in a wheel chair. And those are just the most noticeable physical afflictions.

She has earned the right, wouldn't you agree, to say: 'Suffering has also made me realise how much our churches fail to be genuine, caring communities that are different from our technicized, consumerist, narcissistic world'?[11] Acknowledging our own human fragilities, rather than being a negative factor we expend energy bemoaning, might just become, as it did with Paul, a positive sign of a realistic self-assessment that better allows God's light to shine and God's power to be seen through us.

It follows that we will not lose heart if we ...

6. *Accept the paradoxical nature of Christian existence* (4:8–9)

That power at work which is not from us (4:7b) becomes the dynamic of our whole life and ministry. The 'not from us' encapsulates all those times when to everyone's amazement, including our own, we have overcome the odds stacked against us. Taken to the edge so many times 'but not' cast down, faith holds out for what is resurrectable. At times of severe stress, we sense that survival is all we can hope for. But what's wrong with 'being a survivor'? Survivors of a plague or persecution are the stock of the future. Much less dramatic as our pressures no doubt are, our own history with God can surely bear witness to something strangely unquenchable and startlingly irrepressible. The ability to bounce back, to get up again, to brush ourselves down and start again is captured well by Paul in these vivid antitheses which are considered in context elsewhere in this book. Suffice it to say, here, that they testify to the remarkable reversals of mood the Spirit can work in us. They remind us to be open to the unexpected intervention of God that can pull us back from losing heart.

I was waiting with 400 pastors and wives who had gathered on the tropical island of Langkawi from all over Malaysia for a Leadership Conference sponsored by CWR. I was the supporting speaker to Selwyn Hughes who was on first and whom the audience had patently come to hear. In the expectant buzz before the session started, all my doubts as to the value of my life and ministry seemed to flash before me and I wondered what I was doing there and with what justification. At that moment, a delegate seated in front of me turned round, introduced himself, and told me that words I had spoken in New Zealand fifteen years earlier changed his life and kept him in ministry. He even reeled off the outline of the sermon I had preached!

I recount this incident not because such divine 'coincidences' habitually happen to me, but because I have known enough of them to urge you to be open to the surprising intrusions of grace. There is a certain divine humour in this, I think, as if God is teasing us out of taking ourselves too seriously. That day, it certainly brought a wry smile to my face and silent thanks in my heart to a God who knows us better than we know ourselves. It was my 'unknown yet well known' moment (cf. 6:9) which brought encouragement to a fainthearted conference speaker a long way from home.

We will not lose heart if we ...
7. *Realise that to be a Christian – and to be a Christian in ministry even more so – is to be prepared to live a sacramental life* (4:10–12)
Glory through shame, light out of darkness, power through weakness – this pattern of being and living and ministering now intensifies into the *life-through-death dynamic* which Paul speaks of here. In a sacramental way, Paul's dying brings life to others. To be 'weak in [Christ]' (13:4) is to be incorporated into Christ's death-resurrection so as to share in His unself-serving, servant-like, God-glorifying faith and, at the same time, to do so in the power of the new age. This is what it means to live out a larger story than our self-made, self-protective one; we are called to live out the dying-rising pattern of the Jesus story, because in baptism His story has become ours. 'Death in us, life in you' constitutes what Stephen Kraftchick calls the 'apostolic medium'. In this way, 'the function of the Christ as a bringer of life through death is mapped onto Paul's own activity ... For, in the apostle, the embodied nature of God's redemptive power – strength in weakness, life in death, light from darkness – is revealed' (4:10–12).[12]

Yes, it does tire us to minister to people. We feel life draining out of us. There is a real expenditure of our life – a kind of dying in us – that life can flow to other people. Death to our natural life squeezes the resurrection life of Jesus out of us. This leaves open the important question of how we replenish our life-resources in Christ. But however weary we become, we will not ultimately lose heart, and throw in the towel, if we remember that by our baptism we are enlisted in the sacramental lifestyle of Jesus. We become in His hands broken bread and poured out wine for others.

We will not lose heart if we ...
8. *Replenish our life-energy at its central source and imbibe the Spirit of the psalmist of the Scriptures and of Jesus Himself* (4:13)
All three may be in view here. Plunging deep into Scripture with the aid of the Holy Spirit we not only come up with new thoughts, but in doing so – to change the metaphor – we connect with the same Spirit of faith which

lay behind its original inspiration. We pick up, as it were, the psalmist's 'spirit of faith'; his determination in the face of adversity is transmitted to us as through God's powerful Word to strengthen our faith.

We lose heart only when we seek alternative artificial stimulants. This is unlikely to be alcohol – though there is a salutary warning in the story of the many leading healing evangelists of the 1950s and 1960s who took to the bottle to help them cope with the incessant pressures of maintaining their 'anointed' persona during long and demanding itinerant ministry. More likely, the artificial stimulant will be another round of church initiatives, a rebranded programme, some fresh attraction to excite the punters and to keep them on their toes.[13] This is almost always self-defeating, and a recipe for the kind of 'emotional hangover' which many Corinthian-type churches now suffer from. The Corinthians' confusion stemmed from disconnecting the Spirit from the cross. In the light of this, Tim Savage takes 'that same spirit of faith' of 4:13 to be neither that of the psalmist nor the Corinthians but the same spirit of faith shown by Jesus in submitting to suffering and death. It is the Spirit of God who conforms Paul to the Christ-shaped way of living and dying.[14] Infused with His 'same' Spirit we will surely not lose heart.

We will not lose heart if we …
9. *Maintain our perspective, and live for the long term* (4:16–18)
The story is told of the student who wrote home to her God-fearing parents as follows:

> Dear Mum and Dad,
> I have so much to tell you. Because of the fire in my dorm set off by the student riots, I experienced temporary lung damage and had to go into hospital. While I was there, I fell in love with an orderly, and we have moved in together. I dropped out of school when I found out I was pregnant, and he got fired because of his drinking, so we're going to move to Alaska. We might get married after the birth of the baby …
> Signed … your loving daughter
> … PS None of the above really happened, but I did flunk my chemistry class and I wanted you to keep it in perspective.

We will not lose heart so long as we maintain *our perspective on present reality.* '*Though outwardly we are wasting away, yet inwardly we are being renewed day by day*' (4:16). God does not look on the outward appearance but on the heart. The 'world' – more often than not – takes a cosmetic view of things: a superficial judgment, which even the Corinthian believers share when relapsing into a carnal, worldly frame of mind. Only the reality of 'new creation' gives us a new angle of vision to see things differently (5:16–17). Only through 'eyes that have become young with eternity' – as Tom Torrance said of John of the Apocalypse[15] – can we see the world *now for what it really is* and see our increasingly fragile, crumbling clay pot selves paradoxically resisting the law of entropy by spiritual renewal. God seldom lets us see the success of our ministry, concluded Oswald Chambers – which was certainly true in his case. But we dare to believe that what we are and do – however simply and poorly – in His service, in the ministry of the new covenant

- has lasting consequences
- partakes of a glory that can never fade, and
- forges covenant restoration and healing that cannot be undone.

Mysteriously, against the odds, despite all outward appearances, and despite our fears and misgivings, we *are* being inwardly renewed, our congregations *are* benefiting, grace *is* spreading to more and more people, and praise *continues* to overflow to God (4:15).

'*Therefore we do not lose heart …*' We are sustained by our *perspective on the future*. 'For our light and momentary troubles are achieving for us an eternal glory that far outweighs them all' (4:17). What a challenge this is to a contemporary Church culture which is very much preoccupied with the here and now, impatient of otherworldliness, and intensely pragmatic in its concerns. To such a mindset, Martyn Lloyd-Jones typically poses the question:

> How do I keep myself going? What is it that enables me to live? Am I living in the hope that something wonderful will happen, and that all our troubles will be banished and all will be well in a year's time, or two years', or perhaps ten years' time? Am I still clinging to something that is going to happen in this life and in this world for my happiness? If I am, then according to the New Testament, I am worldly minded, I am carnally minded.[16]

This is tough talk, and I am not sure I can take it: look to the unseen not the seen; walk by faith not sight; look to the real inner person as God sees it, not to the external image by which the world judges us; look to the eternal, not the immediate and temporal. It can all be made to sound too easy – put like that.

We know only too well the daily visibility of the world which we inhabit and with which we have a love–hate relationship; the undeniable – sometimes blissful, sometimes painful – reminders in our own bodies of our human constitution; the stress caused by responsibility, pressures, trials, ill-health or persecution; all this seems to outweigh the future glory we are set to inherit. Even the staggering beauty and bountiful joys of this old creation can dull our appetite for the splendours of the new world coming. We need Paul's inspired testimony and that of the 'cloud of witnesses'.

In the late seventeenth century, a young Huguenot girl named Mary Durant was urged by the authorities to repudiate the Protestant 'heresy'. When she refused to recant, she was thrown into a tower with thirty other women and incarcerated for thirty-eight years! She and the other women scratched on the walls of their prison the word *'resistez'*, still to be seen to this day. Karl Olsen, who tells her story, wonders at the resistance of a young woman as time withers her and her prospects, and she passes into middle and old age. Struggling to come to terms with such steadfastness, Olsen's verdict leaps off the page: 'We cannot understand a faith which is not nourished by the *temporal* hope that tomorrow things will get better.'[17] But if every least thing you and I do by grace is *shot through with meaning*, it can only be, in the end, for the very good reason 'that the one who raised the Lord Jesus from the dead will also raise us with Jesus and present us ... in his presence' (4:14). 'Therefore we do not lose heart' (4:16).

Finally, we will not lose heart if we ...
10. *Rely utterly on God the Holy Spirit*
Loss of meaning, it has been argued, is our danger, not loss of energy. How could it be otherwise, since the 'ministry of the new covenant' is a ministry of the *Holy Spirit, who is God*? Throughout the Bible, from creation to new creation, the Spirit is synonymous with God's *power*.

Invisible as the wind, the Spirit is known by His effects, and made real among us by His manifestations. Every form in which the Spirit manifests Himself – whether storm wind, or oil, or fire – is not just for display, as if heaven's special effects department were showing off.

But the signs and the symbols that attach to them are marks of a real impartation of spiritual, moral and emotional energy. The Spirit creates freedom and an increasing appreciation of what is glorious; the Spirit makes us competent with resources we do not supply; the Spirit writes our ministry in people's hearts in ways that, much to our surprise, transform their lives; the Spirit enables weak vessels to display the power of God; the Spirit connects us to the God of resurrection so that mysteriously and inwardly we grow stronger even as to the watching world we grow older.

'Therefore we do not lose heart.'

> 'All that is gold does not glitter,
> Not all those who wander are lost;
> The old that is strong does not wither,
> Deep roots are not reached by the frost.
> From the ashes a fire shall be woken,
> A light from the shadows shall spring;
> Renewed shall be blade that was broken,
> The crownless again shall be king.'

Aragorn's Song from J.R.R. Tolkien's *Lord of the Rings*[18]

SECTION 3

An angle of vision that is ...
... CULTURALLY CRITICAL

'You know that those who are considered rulers of the Gentiles lord it over them, and their great ones exercise authority over them. But it shall not be so among you ...' (Mark 10:42–43, ESV)

12

IDOLATROUS RELEVANCE

(Jeremiah 23:1–40)

Futurology is a growth industry in contemporary Church circles. By which I do not mean the 'end times' variety – though heaven knows there's a surfeit of that around – but of the '*now* times' kind with which the Church is also currently awash. I have stopped trying to keep up with the endless publications that analyse the crisis of the Church as it threatens to be swept aside by postmodernity. Some of this reportage is frankly depressing, especially of the statistical kind which seems driven by the 'fear factor' into demanding that unless the Church 'do this or that' it will die out in a generation. Some of this doom and gloom strikes me as almost humanistic in giving so little deference to the notion that the Church is God's doing, and something Christ is building.

Elsewhere among the plethora of advice on offer is much that I find stimulating and insightful; I am all for encouraging what's emerging, allowing room for alternatives, and facilitating the flow of new forms of liquid Church. The creativity and ingenuity of a new generation of missionally minded Christian thinkers is to be admired. My chief worry for them is that they seem almost *too* concerned that the Church should not appear to the world in a negative light, a little *too* anxious to be thought well of by society's avant-garde.[1] But, often as the adage goes, when all is said and done, often more is said than done. Prognosis is not inevitably prophetic. Pundits are not the same as prophets. Jeremiah helps us to 'taste the difference'.

Jeremiah lived through critical times in Israel. In fact such times usually evoke the prophetic word. The major 'outbreaks' of prophetic activity in the Old Testament cluster around the twin traumas of the Assyrian invasion in the eighth century BC and the Babylonian Exile in the sixth century. Located at the time of the latter crisis, Jeremiah ministered, as we do still, in a marketplace of ideas and competing truth-claims. Sadly, some of the most vociferous competing truth-claims were being made in Yahweh's name. Jeremiah does not regard these other voices as acceptable alternative versions of God's truth, nor as making a contribution to the debate. He denounces them and exposes their futility. Almost invariably these false voices tried to soften the message and massage the nation's ego and that of the leadership by soft-pedalling on God's demands. In fact in some cases these rival spokesmen had become so identified with the culture of their day that they shared its lax moral standards and corrupt practices (Jer. 23:10). Even supposedly prophetic and priestly servants of God's people had become almost indistinguishable from the permissive society around them, living as loosely and immorally as everyone else (23:14).

These apparent servants of God had 'gone native', and had assimilated the *laissez faire* attitudes towards sexual purity that were acceptable in a fashionable society already compromised by the overt and casual sexuality associated with Baalism (23:13).

Jeremiah is the original member of God's 'awkward squad'. From the roots of his vocation he is an 'against' sort of person (Jer. 1:19). He was not minded to seek the 'feel-good' factor but to tell the truth as God showed it to him – albeit with tears – but without reduction. His ministry was *culturally critical in two senses*. His message was unseasonable, sounded unreasonable and was decidedly unpopular. But by being unfashionable, Jeremiah's ministry brought Judah to a critical moment in her history, to a moment of crisis, an hour of decision, a day of judgment.

At the heart of the conflict between Jeremiah and the 'false prophets', as he designated them, is the big issue: 'How does God evaluate His people's current situation and what is He saying to them at this time?' Jeremiah is warning of God's reluctant but relentless judgment on the persistent sin of His own people and of the upcoming disaster of invasion and coming Exile. But what of the other so-called prophets? 'They keep saying to those who despise me ... "You will have *peace* ..."' (23:17). That this is the contentious issue is borne out elsewhere in the Exilic prophets (see Jer. 6:14; 8:11; cf. Ezek. 13:10,16). Why is this so? Why are the 'prophets' who are castigated by Jeremiah and Ezekiel so fixated on this peace message? The answer is apparent: because that is *what the people wanted to hear*. I was told as a small child that if I went to the beach at Southsea and picked up a seashell and held it to my ear, I would hear the roaring of the sea. Even so, in John Oman's classic words, 'The false prophet is a shell gathering up and echoing the temper of the age; the true prophet is no echo of the moods and passions of his age, but a living voice declaring what is its true lesson.'[2] Such 'echoing' voices treat the crisis of God's people lightly or superficially; they 'dress the wound of [God's] people as though it were not serious' (Jer. 6:14; 8:11). As if applying a sticking plaster to a broken limb, they practise cosmetic therapy rather than radical surgery. So superficial is their diagnosis and treatment that God despairs for lack of a true physician and asks: 'Is there no doctor in God's house?' Is there no healing 'balm in Gilead?' (Jer. 8:22). Is there only a falsely prophetic placebo? Is there no one who can truly diagnose the people's condition and prescribe a genuine remedy? But those who unrepentantly refuse to acknowledge that they are sick have no need of a doctor.

I want to connect this misguided concern to say what the people want to hear – an issue which lies at the heart of the conflict between Jeremiah and these false prophets – to what Os Guinness calls the '*idol of relevance*'. 'Relevance', in the strict sense of the term, is of course a good thing; the relating of God's eternal truth 'to a matter or situation in hand in a pertinent and appropriate way ...' But the point of contention here is not the pertinence of the people of God to their own day and generation. In this sense the Church becomes anachronistic only if it totally jettisons the divine revelation and indwelling which are its *raison d'être*. The Church has always grasped the daily newspaper in one hand and the enduring good news in the other. As I was urged as a young pastor, 'read *The Times*, and preach the Eternities'.

The point at issue is the Church's anxious, almost obsessive concern with keeping pace with supposedly changing trends in society. But cultural fashions are a fast-moving target. Absorbed with hitting these targets, we rapidly become twitchy and neurotic. Os Guinness lays out the charge in typically pungent style.

> By our uncritical pursuit of relevance we have actually courted irrelevance; by our breathless chase after relevance without matching commitment to faithfulness, we have become not only unfaithful but irrelevant; by our determined efforts to redefine ourselves in ways that are more compelling to the modern world than are faithful to Christ, we have lost not only our identity but our authority and our relevance. Our crying need is to be faithful as well as relevant.[3]

Guinness goes on '... it is time to challenge the *idol of relevance*, to work out what it means to be faithful as well as relevant, and so to become truly relevant without ever ending up as *trendy, trivial, and unfaithful*'. Note the words 'trendy, trivial, and unfaithful'. Nothing is more relevant to the world and its needs than the God who made the world and the salvation He makes for it. We do not have to try to make God relevant; the more one thinks about it the more ludicrous the notion appears.

Of course, postmodern Christians are under no obligation to immortalise out-of-date extra-biblical methods, nor to perpetuate obsolete extra-biblical terminology. We have no vested interest in dead traditionalism or outmoded institutions. But serious concerns can be raised about current attempts to retranslate our message to fit in with so-called postmodern culture. So much of our energy is expended on the need to understand and connect with the outlook of postmodern people – all of which is well and good if we are to 'understand the times in which we live and know what God's people should do'. But such attempts are self-defeating if, at the same time, we remain entirely uncritical of contemporary culture, if we stay so moonstruck about postmodern culture's power and fascination that it is we – on the Church's side – who have to do all the adapting and changing.

Dietrich Bonhoeffer features often in this book because he is rightly regarded as one of the great heroes of modern Christianity, and because he is one of mine too. As a young Lutheran pastor and theological teacher, he was the catalyst for a small and brave band of believers who stood out against the Nazis in 1930s Germany. Eventually, through assisting his brother-in-law, he was implicated in the plot to assassinate Hitler in 1944 and was murdered by the Nazis in Flossenburg Camp within sound of the artillery fire of the advancing American armies. But Bonhoeffer's chief conflict was not directly with the Nazis but with the Church in Germany which was increasingly accommodating itself to the new mood in the nation. It began to go along with the increasingly strident emphasis on being Germanic and nationalistic. It connived with the government's increasing anti-Semitism, repudiating the Jewish roots of the gospel. In this it was reaping the bitter fruit of decades of the 'false prophets' of theological liberalism who had evacuated Jesus of His Jewishness in favour of viewing Him as a pale, Enlightenment moral teacher. So the German Christians bowed to the will of the people in wanting strong government that would restore pride and success to the nation. They said what the people wanted to hear; they spoke 'peace, peace' when there was no peace – certainly none of the kind God wanted to establish. But to Bonhoeffer and other fellow-prophetic voices in the wilderness, such attempts to conform the Church and its message to the current trends and mood of the nation were fatal to the gospel.

While at the small dissenting seminary he founded at Finkenwalde in 1936, he wrote this, ostensibly about biblical interpretation: 'Either the biblical message must justify itself in the present age – and must therefore show itself capable of interpretation - or *the present age must justify itself before the biblical message and therefore the message must become real ...*'[4]

Can Christianity make itself real to us, just as we are, asks Bonhoeffer, or must it be interpreted in such a way that it fits contemporary demands? If the later is the case, then, says Bonhoeffer, 'the biblical message is passed through the sieve of man's own knowledge – what will not get through is scorned and tossed away ...' So, warned Bonhoeffer, 'where the question of relevance becomes the theme of theology, we can be certain that the cause has already been betrayed and sold out ... The question of *relevance* all too easily acquires a false emphasis and displaces the question of *fact*. What is the sense in talking about presentation when we cannot even feel completely sure about what we are presenting?'[5] Bonhoeffer rightly reminds us that a thirsty person will always choose to drink fresh water from any container, however unsuitable. Better to take trouble to get the water pure than to try to drink polluted water out of a smart glass. 'Anyone who is really thirsty', says Bonhoeffer, 'has always found living water in the Bible itself or in a sermon *in fact* based on the Bible, even if it were a little out-of-date.' It is a sign of faith's decadence if the clamour for relevance becomes too loud.

So, Bonhoeffer argued, 'The intention should be not to justify Christianity in this present age, but *to justify the present age before the Christian message.*'[6] The reason for this is that relevance is a reflex of the message rather than the messenger. 'True relevance', Bonhoeffer insists, 'lies in this question of the fact [of the Christian message]. It is felt of the *fact itself* that where it is really expressed it is in itself completely and utterly relevant; it therefore needs no other special act of interpretation, because the interpretation is achieved in the fact itself.' He concludes: 'The relevant is not where the present age announces its claim before Christ, but where the present age stands before the claims of Christ, for the concept of the present age is determined not by a temporal definition but by the Word of Christ as the Word of God.'[7]
While Bonhoeffer spoke his prophetic words, Germans – including, no doubt, many Christians – were dizzy with the hopes raised by the new dawn of National Socialism, numbed by the hedonism of the thirties, flooding the nightspots of Berlin and other cities, jitterbugging their way to judgment and dancing to disaster. All this is uncannily reminiscent of what Jeremiah warns are the effects of such false prophecy which tells people what they want to hear.

The first effect immediately stands out from the text. False prophecy and teaching, which pursues the 'idol of relevance' and tells people only what they want to hear, almost always raises false hopes and breeds complacency: 'Do not listen to what the prophets are prophesying to you; they fill you with false hopes' (Jer. 23:16). In an idolatrous quest for relevance the false prophets are raising false hopes by promising 'peace' when there is to be no peace. By contrast, Jeremiah, by warning of impending judgment, risks being parodied as a miserable pessimist or prophet-past-his-sell-by-date, a grumpy old dinosaur of a preacher. After disaster has struck, he writes a famous letter to the exiles (Jer. 29).

The letter is remarkable for many reasons – not least because the prophet urges the exiles in Babylon to settle down for the long haul. He urges them not to listen to those who tell them what they want to hear – that they will be coming home soon (Jer. 29: 8). There will be no quick fix for God's people; no short cuts to revival; no immediate return to the land but a seventy-year exile which will give ample opportunity for a long-term and distinctive revival of covenant living. And – we might add – time enough for building a godly community under the tough conditions of exile, which the prophets were unable to persuade the people to do when the going was easier and God's people could call the shots in their own land! This too is a parable for Church in our time.

There are situations – and Jeremiah's day was one of them – when as T.S. Eliot put it, 'I said to my soul, be still, And wait without hope, for hope would be hope for the wrong thing; wait without love, for love would be love of the wrong thing; there is yet faith, but the faith and the love and the hope are all in the waiting ...' ('East Coker').

So these rival teachers spread complacency ('No harm will come to [us]', 23:17b) rather than alertness, sensitivity, and readiness to respond to God. This breeds a spiritual apathy which misreads the signs of the times (23:20b), or that fails to acknowledge that God has purposes to accomplish which He is intent on fulfilling.
So timing is all in prophecy (cf. 1 Chron. 12:32). 'Peace, peace' was surely part of God's covenanted promise: but *not here and not now* in this situation of blithe unbelief and complacent presumption. Right word, wrong time!

Contrary to the standard perception, Jeremiah is not one long 'jeremiad'. In fact, he offers some of the most stunning promises of hope to be found in the whole of the Old Testament. But the hope he brings is of a salvation which lies on the other side of judgment, a hope of salvation in which God's 'no' must be felt before God's 'yes' can be embraced. It is a hope in which salvation lies on the other side of Exile and humiliation, on the other side of a dying and rising experience. Jeremiah is not optimistic but he is hopeful. As Stanley Hauerwas has it, 'Optimism is hope without truth'. So we do well to resist the pressure that is a potentially idolatrous clamour to accommodate the gospel to prevailing thought forms; to bend the message to the capacity of the current mindset or trim the demands of the gospel to the sensitivities of our postmodern culture. So desperate may we become to translate the message into, or style our worship upon, the therapeutic currency of our day that we may – albeit unwittingly – sell out the gospel and dilute the very message we are seeking to get across. Beware of the seductive voices which urge us to make the gospel more palatable or to increase its appeal or to make it more user-friendly. In the words of the influential sociologist of religion, Peter Berger:

> ... the various efforts by Christians to accommodate to the 'wisdom of the world' in this situation become a difficult, frantic, and more than a little ridiculous affair. Each time that one has, after an enormous effort, that culture turns around and changes. W.R. Inge, the Anglican theologian put it thus: 'He who would marry the spirit of the age soon finds himself a widower.'[8]

Berger reinforces the view that Christians are too eager to adjust to the passing moment. The 'wisdom of the world' – as Berger styles it – 'has a sociological address' so that in every accommodation to it Christians will be '"relevant" in one very specific social setting and "irrelevant" in another. As a consequence, recent theology is well populated with bewildered and understandably resentful widowers.'[9]

At the heart of the conflict then between Jeremiah and these other voices claiming to speak for God is whether what is being said is what the people want to hear or what God wants to say.

The question at stake as Jeremiah poses it is who has truly 'stood in the council of the LORD?' (Jer. 23:18,22, ESV). This is the characteristic picture in the prophetic texts of God's Privy Council where God's special confidants share His secret (cf. Psa. 25:14). This council is pictured as the sphere in which true prophets heard God speak His strategy for history (cf. Isa. 6:1ff.; cf. Micaiah in 1 Kings 22:19). Jeremiah's rivals have not stood there – he has.

- As a result, they have not been sent or authorised or commissioned by God. Jeremiah has (23:21–22, cf. 1:5ff.).
- They speak visions and dreams *concocted in their own minds* from

their own speculation or the second-hand *borrowings* of likeminded others (23:16,26,30).

Their failure is not a failure of biblical knowledge or cleverness or sociological acumen but a failure to maintain humble relationship and close communion with God.

Now, Jeremiah seems not, in any way, self-satisfied or smugly proud to be right where others are wrong; rather, he says, 'My heart is broken within me; all my bones tremble' (23:9).
And this in two senses:

Firstly, Jeremiah is emotionally and spiritually shattered by the word he has to bring from God. The prophet is stunned and shaken by the severe message God is bringing through him. Like a drunken man, he is intoxicated by God's *'holy words'* (Jer. 23:9c). God's words destabilise him and knock him off balance. Do we, for our part, know anything of this extraordinary sensitivity felt by Jeremiah to the holiness of God's words?

Furthermore, such is the effect of taking seriously that what is being heard and handled are 'holy' words – words that come white-hot from the fire of God's burning holiness – that Jeremiah is horrified that other so-called prophets treat God's word with such disrespect. It grieves him deeply that the prophetic office has been so corrupted by the court prophets of his day (23:9). He grieves because he knows that 'ideas have consequences'. He grieves because he knows that when falsehood is proclaimed instead of truth it pollutes society with ungodliness (23:15).

All this is to say that the most serious damage done by false prophecy and teaching is to our understanding of God. True theology is its first victim and theology matters. Jeremiah is profoundly affected by the dishonour being brought to God and to God's name.

Anyone who has truly 'stood in the council of the LORD' (Jer. 23:22, ESV) becomes a thoroughly God-centred, God-obsessed person. Jeremiah indicts the false prophets and the devotion they inspire for *radically misrepresenting God.*

1. To uncritically pursue the 'idol of relevance' is to *seriously underplay the wildness of God.* The presumption in knowing God belies the failure

to draw near enough to God to realise that God cannot be domesticated. It is a shock in every generation for God's people to have to reckon again with the sheer wildness of God – a God of holy anger as well as holy love, a God who is not only a gentle breeze of benevolence but a storm wind of reality (23:19). But how edgy this makes us and how tempted we are to make God more palatable to unregenerate tastes!

I recall Richard Niebuhr's famous mid-twentieth-century indictment of theological liberalism – that it represented 'a God without wrath who brought men without sin into a kingdom without judgment by the ministrations of a Christ without a cross'. Desperate to get a hearing, it is tempting for us to soften God's image, to give Him a postmodern makeover, to make Him more user-friendly. But as with C.S. Lewis' Aslan, he's good, but he's not tame. And God will often take us by storm. Whether in judgment or in mercy, the whirlwind of God's Spirit blows where it wills. 'This is something' – as Mark Buchanan puts it – that 'we cannot work for, work up, predict, direct. It doesn't slot neatly into a program. You just hear it coming and fling yourself headlong into the hurricane.'[10]

2. Uncritically pursuing the 'idol of relevance' *risks putting our agenda before God's* (23:20b). Jeremiah is bringing an intrusive word that cuts through what people want to hear to tell them what God wants to say. They fail to 'discern the times'; *now* is not the time for the 'peace' they expect and assume God will maintain; *now* is the time for judgment to begin with the household of God. Earlier, Jeremiah had recorded the people as saying: 'The harvest is past, the summer has ended, and we are not saved' (Jer. 8:20).

This popular view seems to suggest that God is tied to special times and seasons when He can be presumed on to save: that 'salvation time' may be drawing to a close and God had better hurry up not to miss our deadlines or fail to fit in with our expectations. But God has an altogether larger and longer-term agenda than our blinkered self-interest will allow. God will deal firmly not least with his own people 'until he fully accomplishes the purposes of his heart' (23:20b).

What matters prophetically are not our plans and purposes and how we can fit God into them to make us happier or more successful; what matters most are *God and His plans and purposes of redemption* and how we can fit in with them and co-operate with Him for the success He wants to achieve. And what matters prophetically is whether we can discern how those long-term strategies of God impinge upon us in the here and now – in our day and generation. As the apostle Paul said of King David: after he 'had served God's purpose in his own generation, he fell asleep' (Acts 13:36). He did not fall asleep during it! The flattering prophets who oppose Jeremiah breed a spiritual dullness which misreads the signs of the times (23:20b): that fails to acknowledge that God has purposes to accomplish which He is intent on fulfilling – and some of that is to be worked out *now – in this generation.*

3. Pursuing the 'idol of relevance' risks *presuming on God's presence and availability.* The theology of the rival prophets is seriously askew, causing God to protest: 'Am I only a God nearby ... and not a God far away?' (23:23–24). What a failure of theology this is: to use technical terms it confuses God's *transcendence and His immanence.* It is to lose a sense of God's otherness and majesty by allowing it to be swallowed by an overemphasis on God's closeness and availability.

The Temple officials were more prone to this mistake for, after all, had not God promised to be present with His people at all times? Does not God pledge His presence whenever we worship? Perhaps, but this assumption that God is guaranteed to turn up (in this case in the Temple) and could be presumed upon to insulate the worshippers from judgment was what lay behind Jeremiah's scorching earlier critique of the Temple and its worship (Jer.7). The prophet had previously noted with dismay the people's stereotypical affirmation: 'Is the LORD not in Zion? Is her King no longer here?' (8:19b). This reflects the complacent presumption critiqued by Jeremiah which assumes that God is always available when God's people gather together to worship in Zion. It is as if it is God's business to be here when we need Him, to be present as promised, to turn up when we name His name in the arranged place.

Those who mouth 'the Temple of the Lord ... the Temple of the Lord ...' as a kind of mantra to ward off bad news were in for a big shock. Yes, says Jeremiah, God is pleased to dwell in Zion and to focus His holy presence in the Temple. But this does not mean that God comes under our control so that we can switch Him off and on at our convenience.

However close God comes to us, He remains the God He always is. His coming near us doesn't diminish His holiness or transcendent glory.

We cannot manage God. As Rowan Williams who was there at the Twin Towers rightly said the day after 9/11, 'God is useless'. The archbishop was criticised and misunderstood for this. But he was right. God is *with us* at such times but he is use-less in the sense that He is not to be 'used' as and when we see fit. We cannot domesticate God. When He draws near (in gracious immanence) He does not stop being wholly God (in holy transcendence). We cannot box God in or – as is the danger in our day – make Him cosily familiar so that we seek warm and sensuous feelings in our worship of Him, and confuse His closeness with a God-is-my-girlfriend kind of intimacy.

4. Pursuing the 'idol of relevance' leads to terrible *neglect of God's name* (Jer. 23:27). What does Jeremiah mean by this?

God's name stands for all that God has shown of His character, His will and His way – and the emphasis is on what *God* has chosen to make known about Godself. Knowing God's name – from Moses and the burning bush onwards – is to be taught *by God* something of God's own nature and heart. To forget God's name, then, is to turn your back on God's own self-revelation. Then, what God has revealed about Himself lies neglected and overlooked, perhaps regarded as irrelevant to contemporary needs and ill-suited to current tastes. The tendency is to fill the gap, as the false prophets were doing, and to set our ideas about what God should be like and how God should behave above what He has revealed about Himself in word and deed. This is the classic failure of liberal theology to which popular evangelicalism is prone. This impulse, for example, largely drives the current attacks from within evangelicalism on the reformed doctrine of the substitutionary atonement – not because of greater exegetical insight into the apostolic testimony but on the grounds that it offends postmodern sensitivities and upsets feminist theologians who caricature it as a form of cosmic child abuse.

Forgetting the past in the sense of not being hamstrung by it is one thing; it is quite another to seek to erase the past by obliterating the God-given, historic truth handed down to us as sacred trust. It is instructive to note that when Jeremiah first counters the 'easy peace' message of his rivals he does so by urging respect for the past: 'Stand at the crossroads and look; ask for the ancient paths, ask where the good way is, and walk in it, and you will find rest for your souls' (Jer. 6:16). The 'good way' is not necessarily the novel way; the search for a peaceful fit with culture may deny us the true peace of mind and heart that a return to our roots might give us. An obsessive pursuit of relevance can become an insatiable quest for novelty, an almost adolescent striving after 'up-to-dateness' that is self-defeating. Such a quest produces the very opposite of the desired effect. Rather than making our peace with contemporary culture, it creates dispeace, as everyone gets caught up in a restless rush to keep up with the times. Paradoxically, the authentic peace more often comes through humble, but intentional, cultural dissonance.

Jeremiah warns, therefore, against disdain for the ancient paths. Too often they are seen not as God-given, biblically-shaped, 'tried and tested' patterns and practices handed down to us, but as outmoded relics of a forgotten past.

Christendom is now the latest dumping ground for whatever grates on postmodern sensitivities. But contemptuous disdain for tradition is a dangerous drug. It will not let you go until you have sawn off the very branch you are sitting on which only yesterday seemed an audacious perch to be on. All that follows is another round of the kind of Church splits and factional schisms that are less a sign of bold innovation than of sad repetition of what is deep in our fissiparous Protestant genes. Restoration movements, however God-initiated, should be wary of such historical amnesia. I have done my time as an iconoclast, and can proudly boast the scars. But the 'idol of relevance' ought not to be spared our attention. Jeremiah himself was called to 'uproot and tear down' (Jer. 1:10). But he also anticipated the new time coming when God's priority would be planting and building which, as far as we are concerned, is more sophisticated work.

Jeremiah could differentiate between the undergrowth obscuring the ancient paths and the ancient paths themselves. As a true prophet, he promises good in God's future while at the same time recalling God's people to old truth and earlier practices which need to be restored and reinstated, not consigned to the ecclesiastical rubbish heap. *Tradition* is often confused with *traditionalism*. Worth noting is the oft-quoted remark by the eminent Church historian, Jaroslav Pelikan, to the effect that *'traditionalism is the dead faith of the living; tradition is the living faith of the dead'*.[11] Tradition, as Chesterton often said, is simply the extension of the franchise to the departed, a 'democracy of the dead', as well as the living 'communion of the saints'. 'Tradition', said Pelikan,

> lives in conversation with the past, while remembering we are where and when we are and that it is we who have to decide. Traditionalism supposes that nothing should ever be done for the first time, so that all that is needed to solve any problem is to arrive at the supposedly unanimous testimony of the homogenised tradition.[12]

To repeat what we said earlier, ultimately, our failure here is the failure to accept that our first priority for which prayer sets the tone is: *'hallowed be Your name'*; and, having said it, to bow to God's own historic self-revelation, foundationally in Scripture, and providentially, in a history from which – for all its blemishes and betrayals – the Spirit of truth has not been altogether absent. Not even to attempt to grapple with this is to dishonour God's name.

5. Pursuing the 'idolatrous relevance' *risks playing fast and loose with God's 'holy words'* (23:28–29). This is where Jeremiah's prophetic concern starts, in being discomfited by God's 'holy words' (23:9). For the true prophet – and for a genuinely prophetic people – who have humbly stood in the council of the Lord, God's words are 'holy words', to be taken with utmost seriousness.

• God's words are not 'straw' but 'grain'.
God's word does not come as straw to feather our nests and to make us more comfortable; God's word is not straw on which to make a bed of false assurance. God's word comes to us as genuine wholegrain 'grain' – finest wheat – to feed us with truth and to nourish us continually on a diet of God.

• God's words are not hot air but 'fire'.
Here is precisely the difference between the phoney prophets and Jeremiah: 'The prophets are but wind and the word is not in them ... [but] I will make my words in your mouth a fire and these people the

173

wood it consumes' (Jer. 5:13–14). The false prophets are all 'air' (*ruach*) and no substance with no substantial word from God. They offer a tepid moralism or bland advice or puffed-up charismatic hype. But the true prophetic word is a divine flame that ignites a passionate love for God. The true prophetic word confronts the 'idol of relevance' with the stunning reality that God is not cool and will never be cool – God is a consuming fire.

• God's words are not a rubber stamp but a 'hammer'.
God's word does not come as a rubber stamp to give God's unconditional endorsement to whatever we think is in our best interests. It does not come softly-softly but as 'a hammer' to demolish our doubts and smash to pieces our complacency and unbelief, and to nail our self-life to the cross which is our only hope (Jer. 23:28–29).

God's word is an incisive word – it cuts across the grain of our cultural correctness, pierces to the heart, awakens the conscience, dazzles the imagination, stimulates the mind, galvanises the will. What is characteristic of biblical preaching is that it *does* something, it is impactful, it provokes a reaction, evokes a response.

6. Those who uncritically pursue the 'idol of relevance' *tend to reduce God's word to clichés or sound bites* (23:33–40). Here Jeremiah has a play on words: ironically playing with the two variant meanings of the Hebrew word *massa* – which can mean either 'oracle', the speech of a prophet, or 'burden'.

So, in receiving an 'oracle' from the Lord, a prophet is said to be carrying the 'burden of the Lord'. So glibly are the false prophets dispensing prophetic words that the phrase 'the burden of the Lord' has become in their mouths a popular cliché. Again the people want to hear from the popular prophets what they want to hear – and so they keep asking: 'Where is the burden of the Lord?' We like what we are hearing, give us another one: 'Where is the burden of the Lord?' And God has had enough and interrupts. 'Since you're asking,' says the Lord, '"Where is the burden of the Lord?", I'll tell you – you are! You are the biggest burden I've got at present … and if you go on like this I will lift you up and carry you off to Babylon out of my presence.' God will not have His holy words reduced to glib clichés or slogans.

Not even for the sake of making the message more immediately relevant or easily understood will God have His holy words trivialised into five steps or ten principles for easy listening. He would rather we were overwhelmed with the glory of the inconceivable, with the grace of His indescribable gift, than succumb to the clichéd sound bites of the superficial.

7. And, finally, those who pursue the 'idol of relevance' *much prefer 'reckless' words to risky action* (Jer. 23:32). Talk is cheap and reckless words cost little.

By contrast, recall the story told in Jeremiah 32. Now, there is generally respect for a man who puts his money where his mouth is. But what are we to make of a prophet who invests in land ownership at a time when his land is about to be overrun by an invading army? Granted it might be available at a knock-down price, but what is it worth anyway given that the land-grabbing Babylonians are on the horizon? But precisely in these circumstances Jeremiah is told (and in fact pre-warned of the deal, 32:6-7) to take up his redemption rights on a piece of land near Anathoth and to buy the field from his relative (Jer. 32:8-11). Jeremiah duly does so and the deal is signed, sealed, witnessed to, and the deeds deposited with Baruch for safekeeping.

This is nothing less than a bold and extraordinary act of faith; an act of faith in defiance of the prevailing advice and in the teeth of all evidence to the contrary.

It is an act of faith in God's future. It is faith in future grace, as John Piper calls it.

Jeremiah's symbolic action is a pledge of God's faithfulness that will one day see 'fields bought and sold again' on the other side of Exile (32:42-44). Maybe sensing the temerity and enormity of what he has done, Jeremiah turns to the Lord in a memorable prayer (Jer. 32:17-25) in which the key affirmation is, 'Nothing is too hard for you' (32:17b). God matches the prophet's conviction when He responds to the prayer with a rhetorical question begging the answer 'no'; 'Is anything too hard for me?' 'No.' Nothing is 'too hard' for or nothing is 'impossible' to the Lord, and He will do it (Jer. 32:27).

The false prophets are reckless when it comes to speechmaking; but they play safe when action is called for. Unlike the false prophets,

Jeremiah puts his money where his mouth is and invests by faith in God's impossible future.

So Bonhoeffer caught the last boat to sail from New York back to Germany in August 1939 because he said: 'I shall have no right to participate in the reconstruction of Christian life in Germany after the war if I do not share the trials of this time with my people.'

So on 1 December 1955 Rosa Parks, a humble and unknown seamstress in Montgomery, Alabama, refused to give up her seat on a bus to a white passenger and move to the back of the bus – so sparking the civil rights movement.

Eugene Peterson sums up well:

> Jeremiah knew that buying the field looked impractical and foolish. It was against history, against reason, against public opinion. But he didn't buy the field on the advice of his broker, but by the leading of God. He was not planning a retirement cabin on the property; he was witnessing an involvement in the continuity of God's promises.[13]

So we may sum up this critique in Peterson's paraphrase of God's counsel to Jeremiah: 'Let your words change them; don't change your words to suit them' (15:19, *The Message*).

It was the late Henri Nouwen who pointed out that Jesus' first temptation was to be relevant by turning stones into bread. But you recall – Jesus counters the temptation precisely by reaffirming His commitment to live by every word that proceeds from the mouth of God. 'I am deeply convinced', said Nouwen, 'that the Christian leader of the future is called to be completely irrelevant and so stand in this world with nothing to offer but his own vulnerable self.'[14]

Christian ministry today faces the perennial pressure to make something happen, to make things work, to make a mark on our generation; feeling this, it is tempting to jettison all the cargo to lighten the ship. But as Nouwen suggests, 'feeling irrelevant may bring us closer to the real needs of a dysfunctional world and enable us to enter into deep solidarity with the anguish of all who feel irrelevant to life as others know it'.

If Jesus was as wary of crowds and as anxious to avoid popular acclaim as the Gospels tell us, we can afford to be wary too. When crowds flock to Him, drawn to His fame and healing powers, He leaves suddenly for the next village, pleading urgent kingdom business (Luke 4:43). When He turns a small boy's lunch into bread for the hungry multitudes, the crowds clamour to make Him king – by popular vote. In each case, by giving them what they wanted He could have short-circuited the cross and sold His Saviourhood cheap. But He consistently refused to allow them to define His Messiahship for Him, to succumb to the pressure of their needs, or adapt to the language of their discourse, or conform His ministry to their tastes, or expectations.

Jesus distanced Himself from the crowds even as He had compassion on them, lest they squeezed Him into their mould and made of Him the Messiah they wanted and assumed He should be. In the end, He wept over Jerusalem because it did not know the things that truly make for peace. Easter only confirmed this.

If the cross is utterly foolish and unreasonable to the Greeks and a scandalous stumbling block to Jews, subverting the world's wisdom; if the cruciform Lordship of Jesus offends the arrogant, autonomous, self-defined rationalists; and if the crucified Messiahship of Jesus redefines all notions of what kind of power rules the world – then we should scarcely wonder that it might ruffle a few postmodern feathers.

Why then, as Richard Lischer ponders, do we 'heartily accept the world's definition of "the world" and humbly try to accommodate the gospel to it, as if the cross and resurrection have not deranged the old world and started a new one'?[15]

If the resurrection is what the apostles say it is, then as the late Lesslie Newbigin said, it cannot be made relevant to any culture's understanding of the world, precisely because it is the starting point for a whole new way of understanding the world – given only by revelation through the gospel by the Spirit to those who lay their minds, their wills, their pride in the dust and surrender.

Christian ministry that has the courage to forgo idolatrous relevance will not lose out. God is not locked into His people's past, however much He has created it. Jeremiah himself was a prophet of amazing new things. 'So then, the days are coming,' declares the LORD, 'when people will no longer say, "As surely as the LORD lives, who brought the Israelites up out of Egypt," but they will say, "As surely as the LORD lives, who brought the descendants of Israel up out of the land of the north and out of all the countries where he had banished them." Then they will live in their own land' (Jer. 23:7–8).

For Israel, the extraordinary events of the Exodus were foundational. But even these will be eclipsed by the new things God will do in the return from Exile. If that glorious past is transcended and fresh expressions of faith arise it will not be because God's people have discarded their past but because God brings fresh experiences of His future into the present.

The 'eternal world', P.T. Forsyth asserted, 'from which Christ came is contemporary with every age. To every age it is equally near, and it is equally authoritative. It is never antiquated in its final principles and powers. The only preaching which is up to date for every time is the preaching of this eternity which is opened to us in the Bible alone.'

No one need fear not being on the cutting edge by staying faithful to that.
Repudiate the idolatrous devotion to relevance, and feel again the impact of God's word of faith that moves mountains. As Alexander Solzhenitsyn says: 'It is infinitely difficult to begin when mere words must remove a great block of inert matter. But there is no other way if none of the material strength is on your side. *And a shout in the mountains has been known to start an avalanche.*'[16]

13
PROPHETIC UNTIMELINESS

(Jeremiah 8; 15; 20; 36)

Of all the ways in which Jeremiah may be distinguished from the other so-called prophets claiming to be speaking in God's name, by far the most crucial is this: they are telling people what they want to hear; Jeremiah is saying what God wants said.

On the one hand are spokesmen who – using Os Guinness's terminology – are pursuing the 'idol of relevance'. Jeremiah, on the other hand, is practising what Guinness calls 'prophetic untimeliness'.[1] By this is meant speech that is 'timely' in being *exactly what the moment needs to hear* – but is 'untimely' in *not being an echo of what people are thinking and feeling or want to hear*. This speech is enacted by faithful and risky prophetic deeds that plant the flag of God's future.

The prophetic ministry is an invasive claim of God, inserted into this cultural era, this generation, often in defiance of what Guinness terms the 'unholy trinity of the powerful, the practical, and the profitable'.[2] Now, the methods of receiving a prophetic word appeared the same: the false prophets employed dreams and visions as did Jeremiah. But for them dreams and visions were the source of their ideas whereas, with Jeremiah, they were merely the channel for ideas and words. In short, they had not stood where Jeremiah had stood – in the council of the Lord (Jer. 23:18,22). They had their 'ear to the ground', as it were, picking up the reverberations of popular opinion. Jeremiah, on the other hand, had his 'head in the clouds', because he is tuned in to God's point of view.

The first aspect of *prophetic untimeliness* I want to draw attention to is what I want to describe as *untimely prophetic emotions.*

One great sign of the difference between Jeremiah and his rivals is the way in which Jeremiah becomes emotionally entangled with the word God gives him (eg Jer. 23:9). As we noted in the previous chapter, Jeremiah is emotionally shaken by the severity of God's 'holy words' (23:9c). These 'holy words' come from the searing centre of God's holy heart and Jeremiah is appalled that prophets and people treat God's word with such disrespect. If prophetic untimeliness entails being at odds with popular culture, it means for Jeremiah being *emotionally 'out of sync'* with the prevailing mood. Standing in 'the council of the Lord', Jeremiah not only hears and sees what God is saying and doing but is drawn close to God's heart and begins to *feel* something of what God is feeling. The prophet emotionally identifies with God's word.

It is this experience which is at the root of Jeremiah's so-called 'confessions' – those passages of the book where he shares his anguish over the prophetic task. These 'confessions' or 'lamentations' are often put down to Jeremiah's melancholic temperament or depressive nature, as if all can be explained by the fact that he was a cup's half-empty sort of person. Now, no one would label Jeremiah sanguine. But, for me, simplistic psychological explanations for Jeremiah's emotional turmoil do not fit the bill: rather, his deep feelings appear to be evoked by his passionate involvement with God's word.

a) With untimely prophetic emotions, Jeremiah *feels God's grief over His people's sin* (8:18–9:1). As the prophet more deeply absorbs God's word, what God is feeling and what Jeremiah is feeling become so intertwined that it is difficult, from the text, to distinguish the one from the other. Is the sorrow that makes the heart faint felt by God or His prophet (8:18)? To the people's two questions (8:19bc, 'Is the LORD not in Zion? Is the King no longer there?') God replies with His own: 'Why have they provoked me …?' (8:19c). The people's complacent claim on God's promptness – 'Harvest is past … and we are not saved' – evokes anguish in God's heart. He is crushed in their being crushed and bewails with horror the lack of a healer. Pain overflows in tears (8:21–9:1). If Jeremiah is speaking *for* God and feeling *with* God then we know that the *poetry of pathos* – in

Brueggemann's words – *'penetrates God's heart'.*[3]
So the contrast is set up in 8:18–21 between an unfeeling people caught up in the pretence of going through the motions of worship, and the pathos of a God who is really hurting. While their praise rolls on, they seem to have no idea how deeply they have wounded God or affronted Him, or how bitterly God is grieving over them. God's people are sick to death of Him and, as a result, are sick unto death: 'Is there a balm in Gilead?' Is there a doctor in the house of the Lord? (8:22). Apparently there is no one to heal the wound of God's people. God weeps bitterly over the land (9:10); He looks for others to join Him in His sorrow (9:17) who will, in turn, teach others how to lament (9:20). Meanwhile, only Jeremiah shares the lonely grief of God.

b) With untimely prophetic emotions, Jeremiah *experiences the bitter-sweet taste of prophetic ministry* (15:15–21). Jeremiah's heartfelt anguish is but an echo of the pathos of God. Jeremiah's emotional turmoil deepens the more he talks to God. He protests that he has not resisted his prophetic vocation. He has taken God's word to heart. He has relished God's words and delighted in them (Jer. 15:16). Jeremiah has fed on every word that has proceeded from the mouth of God; he has consumed God's truth and found in it an emotional and spiritual satisfaction beyond anything that could be experienced in the surrounding culture. *A prophetic people feel untimely emotions.* Their joy is too fierce and exalted and intense for an over-satiated society which has lost its spiritual and emotional taste buds, and suffers terminal blandness and boredom. Jeremiah's delight in God's truth is too deep for his contemporaries to fathom, and too rich for palates spoiled by spiritual junk food. Yet for Jeremiah, God's words are bitter-sweet words since God is now saying judgment!
His social exclusion, alienation and loneliness is a direct result of his faithful attendance on Yahweh, with whom he has kept company. He has stood apart from the 'party crowd' (15:17, *The Message*) whose false joy, phoney hilarity and flip jokiness is hollow and empty. His prophetic vocation has given him a counter-cultural emotional oddness. All bearers of God's prophetic word are destined to be different and must dare to be emotionally out of sync with the prevailing mood.

God then warns Jeremiah himself of the solemn responsibility of handling God's holy words – 'if you utter worthy, not worthless, words, you will be my spokesman' (15:19a). It is as if – at this point – Jeremiah represents 'Israel' in his solitary person and faces the issue: will you live by every word that proceeds from my mouth alone?

Jeremiah is to do the opposite of what the false prophets were doing: 'Let this people turn to you, but you must not turn to them' (15:19c) – 'Let your words change them; Don't change your words to suit them' (*The Message*).

c) With untimely prophetic emotions, Jeremiah *feels what the people do not feel – a sense of sin* (17:9).

Judah's sin has been inscribed 'on the tablets of their hearts' (17:1). This is an ironic antithesis to the promised new covenant when it is God's torah that will be written on the heart (Jer. 31:33). Such sin is publicly placarded on the altar, to recall the public apostasy at the shrines and altars of Baal (Jer. 17:1–2). But the trouble is a 'heart' one. Only God knows our hearts. The 'heart is deceitful above all things' (17:9) – where the word 'deceitful' is derived from a word which means 'Jacoblike', again a deeply ironic connection with the duplicitous founder of the nation. The false teachers and prophets encourage God's people to discard as outmoded a sense of the innate sinfulness of the human condition (8:12, 'they do not even know how to blush'). But Jeremiah has been brought to realise that 'the heart is deceitful above all things'.

I am convinced Jeremiah came to this not because he was a melancholic or of a depressive cast of mind but because as a prophet of God he had come to appreciate the rock-bottom reality of the sinfulness of the human condition. Speaking with a pastor who had had a moral failure many years ago and had long ago been restored to fruitful ministry, I was told that though he was sure he had been forgiven and welcomed back by grace the deep sense of shame had never left him. And he had come to see that this deep and dark sense of sadness and shame was *not* something for which he needed counselling to be healed from in order to feel better about himself. Rather, he had come to see that through his own failure and humiliation, he had in fact hit the bedrock reality of what he was and what we all are – sinners before a holy God. He believed that this was something that rightly was never meant to go away. It remained, as in Jeremiah, 'an incurable wound' (15:18).

What he felt at depth was not abnormal but normal, not unhealthy but healthy. But if Christian ministry fudges this to spare people's finer feelings, then it sells grace cheap and robs the guilty of the true self-awareness that induces deep God-centred humility and trust.

d) With untimely prophetic emotions, Jeremiah *feels the scorn and hostility of unbelief against God* (20:7-9). This is an excruciating part of Jeremiah's story, described by Brueggemann as Jeremiah's 'most pathos-filled complaint'.[4] Jeremiah feels the fierce antipathy of unbelief to the word of God and the ridicule, mockery and insults it attracts (20:7b-8b). So later, Jesus warned His disciples that the world will hate them! God's word is an invasive word. It breaks through our defences and lays claim to territory in ourselves we proudly thought we had the sole rights to occupy. It exposes us to forces and feelings beyond our control so that we become emotionally involved with God and His message. It arouses hostility equally as it attracts faith.

This is the price of prophethood and nothing good comes from soft-talking the fact that Jeremiah is paying it.

Jeremiah feels he has been made a laughing stock and he blames God: 'You seduced me ... overpowered me' (see 20:7a). The word used here is a shocking one: it can even be translated 'you raped me' – 'Lord, You forced this word on me and pushed me into being a prophet; You were too strong for me.' Put more positively though no less passionately, God's word is a fire in him that cannot be damped down (20:9). God's word is an inner compulsion that grips him and overrides his own painful efforts at resistance with an overwhelming force that must out.

So Jeremiah is seized by a piercing joy, and a burst of praise surges up in the middle of his lament (20:13). No sooner has Jeremiah broken through to praise than he lapses back into complaint. How to explain these extremes of feeling? Is he an unstable personality? Perhaps. But these extremes of praise and self-hatred do serve a real purpose. They are like deliberate exaggeration – as if the prophetic script is written in especially large letters so no one will miss the point – as if to say, *'Think big things of God; think little of yourself.'* Think highly of God in every way, and if cursing yourself is going a bit far then, at least, let it give us a sense of proportion about ourselves: 'For by the grace given to me I say to every one of you: Do not think of yourself more highly than you ought, but rather think of yourself with sober judgment, in accordance with the measure of faith God has given you' (Rom. 12:3). A bit of charismatic humility might be in order.

Jeremiah feels himself emotionally entangled in a relationship that hurts him enough to make him want to break it off. At the same time, he is gripped by a word and a promise so fierce and strong that he is painfully unable to do so. Such are untimely prophetic emotions. Dietrich Bonhoeffer comments on 'Blessed are they that mourn':

> By 'mourning' Jesus means refusing to be in tune with the world or to accommodate oneself to its standards. Such men mourn for the world, for its guilt, its fate and its fortune. While the world keeps holiday they stand aside, and while the world sings 'Gather ye rosebuds while ye may', they mourn ... They see that for all the jollity on board, the ship is beginning to sink ... Nobody loves his fellowmen better than a disciple, nobody understands his fellowmen better than the Christian fellowship, and that very love impels them to stand aside and mourn.

Bonhoeffer adds, of such prophetic disciples,

> sorrow cannot tire them or wear them down, it cannot embitter them or cause them to break down under the strain; far from it, for they bear their sorrow in the strength of him who bears them up, who bore the whole suffering of the world upon the cross. They stand as the bearers of sorrow in the fellowship of the crucified; they stand as strangers in the world in the power of him who was such a stranger to the world that it crucified him ...[5]

Pope Benedict, in an interview some years ago, recalled that the Early Church Fathers 'considered "insensitiveness", that is, the inability to mourn (to be contrite), to be the real disease of the pagan world'.[6]

'To what can I compare this generation? They are like children ... calling out to others: "We played the flute for you, and you did not dance; we sang a dirge, and you did not mourn"' (Matt. 11:17). The unrepentant world always sings out of tune with the key melody of the kingdom of God. But disciples '... *will weep and mourn while the world rejoices*' (John 16:20). This is prophetic untimeliness. A prophetic people is always emotionally out of sync with an unbelieving generation: when it laments, we rejoice; when it celebrates, we grieve. Do not try to imitate either; we cannot win. The world knows nothing of our grief, nor of our joy. And it all has to do with *our reaction to the word of God.*

And it is in the reaction to the prophetic word of God that we see the *effects of prophetic untimeliness.*

Three stories illustrate this.

Two of the stories come from Jeremiah's lifetime. One shapes his whole outlook. The other, in which he was the significant player, demonstrates the impact of his prophetic ministry.

Story one concerns Josiah, king of Judah. Josiah lived from 639–609 BC and was killed at Megiddo trying to block Pharaoh Neco II from helping the remnant of the Assyrians against the Babylonians, the rising superpower of the Middle East. The year is about 622 BC. Josiah has been king for eight years. It is, as they say, a 'defining moment' (see 2 Chron. 34). The old book, the book of the Torah, God's Word and charter for Israel's national existence, has been long neglected. It was gathering dust who knew where. Business as usual is the order of the day. The big item on the political agenda at court today, surprise, surprise, is the economy.

Money makes things happen and there is a rising feel-good factor in Josiah's kingdom. The money under discussion on this particular day is needed to pay for a massive job creation scheme in Jerusalem, the repair of the Temple. Builders, joiners, carpenters, stonemasons and innumerable contract craftsmen are all beavering away on this exciting new project. They even have 'music while they work' (2 Chron. 35:15). The usual army of technical boffins are on hand too (34:13): surveyors, architects, planners, officials and gatekeepers – all with hard hats and wearing the right security passes – together with countless civil servants, accountants, secretaries and scribes and mysterious apparatchiks, all on the payroll, and all there to supervise everyone else and to keep everything in line and on schedule.

But then something happens that changes everything. '*While they were bringing out the money that had been taken into the temple of the LORD,*

Hilkiah the priest found the Book of the Law that had been given through Moses' (2 Chron. 34:14–18). This was most likely to have been the book of Deuteronomy, or a version of it. Shored up in some old plasterwork that had been dislodged, there it is, the old book. Curiosity soon leads to consternation. This is a Bible Discovery day. This is revolution pressing at the palace gates; this is reformation hammering on the Temple door; this is a virus on the Internet; this is dynamite in the cellars of parliament; this pulls the plug on the whole show; this a 9/11-kind of day. 'Stop,' says Josiah, 'stop everything!' and the machinery of building and politics and commerce winds down to a halt, the lights go out, the music fades away, leaving only a shocked and stunned silence.

No one dares to make a move. Except one: we had better consult this old book, God's book.

When they do, they find they have been building the nation without listening to God, ordering their homes without finding out God's way, raising their families and running businesses without reference to God's instruction. They discover that they have been trying to play the human game without bothering to look up the divine rules of the game.

To his credit, Josiah is devastated to realise how much the nation has missed: *'When the king heard the words of the Law, he tore his robes'* (2 Chron. 34:19). The king tears his robes as a symbol of his abject grief, deep humiliation and heartfelt repentance. Immediately the prophetess Huldah is summoned (34:22–28), who confirms the significance of the discovery and warns of the coming judgment which Josiah will be spared because of his humble and repentant reaction to finding the book. Josiah then reads all the words of the book of the covenant to the people and leads them in a renewed covenant commitment to the Lord to live life and run the nation in accordance with God's Word (34:30). What a moment of discovery this was. Finding 'God's Book', king and people find God again. Josiah discovers in one defining moment that *God must have the first word on everything*!

Story two concerns Jehoiakim, Josiah's son. The story is told in Jeremiah 36 and vividly presents to us another 'defining moment'. The time is sixteen years later; and Josiah's son, Jehoiakim, is king. 605 BC was a critical year in world history.

John Goldingay likens it to 1812, or 1939, or 1989; in this year at the famous Battle of Carchemish, the Egyptians were defeated by the Babylonians in the first great triumph for Nebuchadnezzar.

Jeremiah, prophet of the Lord, receives word from God telling him to write down on scrolls all that he has so far prophesied (Jer. 36:2–3). So, the nation will have one last chance to hear and respond to God's word. Baruch, Jeremiah's faithful secretary and PA, is told to take down Jeremiah's prophecies as they are dictated to him, and to do so with care and precision with a view to their being read aloud to the people. 'Perhaps ...' the text says wistfully, 'Perhaps they will ... turn from [their] wicked ways' (36:7). Some months later, his scribal task completed, Baruch goes to the Temple and reads the scrolls of Jeremiah's prophecies to the crowd who have been assembled for a national fast day (Jer. 36:10). *The first audience then, for God's prophetic word, is 'all the people'.* Micaiah, a government official, alarmed to hear this, rushes off to tell the king's advisors, spin doctors and assorted attendants.

Audience two for God's prophetic word is, therefore, Jehoiakim's 'think tank' (Jer. 36:13–15). The 'think tank' is terrified and looking 'at each other in fear' decide 'We must ... [tell] the king' (36:16). 'Where did you get this stuff, Baruch? It's dynamite! Who wrote this, you or Jeremiah?' (see 36:17). It was a joint effort, says Baruch, but they are all the prophet's words. 'You and Jeremiah had better make yourselves scarce,'! say the king's council'. And Baruch and Jeremiah go into hiding.

Audience three for God's prophetic word is now the king himself (Jer. 36:20–26). Jehudi reads the scroll to the king. God calls on king and people to repent and believe and live in covenant faithfulness again. God issues His judgment on self-seeking and power-grabbing kings like Jehoiakim. This is prophecy straight from the hip – not what the king is used to hearing or wants to hear. Here is no official whitewash, no PR gloss, no bland internal memo, no government spin, no bureaucratic gobbledygook, no political doublespeak – this is the truth from the mouth of the living God. This is why I love God's Word: it's all truth and therefore it's all good news. Even the disclosure of how much God loathes sin and warns judgment on it is good news. Here at last is someone who tells us the truth about our human condition.

But Jehoiakim can't see it. It is a crucial 'moment of truth' – a moment when suddenly and dramatically one is face to face with stark reality. Such moments are often moments of decision. And his response is fatal. It being wintertime, an open fire is blazing in the king's chamber. Arrogantly, as Jehudi reads the scroll, the enraged and rattled king takes out a knife and, as the scroll unfolds, cuts off great chunks of the prophetic scroll and hurls them into the fire. The text tellingly records: 'The king and all his attendants … showed no fear, nor did they tear their clothes' (Jer. 36:24). The contrast with his father Josiah's reaction is striking. When Josiah discovered God's Word he humbled himself and tore his clothes. Jehoiakim refuses to humble himself before God's Word and *instead of tearing his robes, tears up the scroll.*

But Jehoiakim has one lesson to learn that he cannot avoid. You cannot cut God off in mid-speech. How does God react to the king's arrogance? Is he silenced? No, of course not. God says to Jeremiah: 'Take another scroll and write on it all the words that were on the first scroll' (36:28). 'Take another scroll' – how significant. Take 'another scroll' because 'God's word cannot be destroyed, silenced, banned or drowned because it will keep resurfacing'.[7] In Walter Brueggemann's words, 'God is not deterred in the least by the king's refusal. *God is a scroll maker and will continue to make scrolls.*'[8] So Jeremiah dictates everything again to Baruch, and – with an irony to be relished – 'many similar words were *added* to them' (Jer. 36:32). The attempt to cut God's Word short fails and God's Word returns topped up with additional truth!
Jehoiakim discovers one thing: *that God always has the last word.*

God's word prophetically spoken and faithfully recorded outlives any shredder. God's word can never be deleted; God's word can never be defeated.

Josiah was a good king as kings go, committed to seeking the Lord and reforming God's people. Jehoiakim was a self-serving and arrogant king. But shockingly, neither the godly king nor the ungodly king was giving the Word of God its rightful place. Measured by this, how do today's people of God fare? In our self-satisfaction, we would not expect the 'Jehoiakim Church' to do anything other than arrogantly edit Scripture to suit its own purposes. It might not surprise us to see such a Church doing a 'scissors and paste' job on God's Word to cut out the difficult bits, to prune God's Word down into a reduced, *Reader's Digest* version, shorn of its political incorrectness and made blandly inoffensive to the chattering classes. But is the 'Josiah Church' doing any better?

Like Josiah, the evangelical–charismatic wing of the Church is concerned to update the Church and to reform the nation. It is doing many good things. Yet as it surges ahead in the 'polls', surfing a new wave of success, it seems driven by an activism that is disdainful of serious theology and thinking. In its rush to be cutting edge, it seems to be giving less and less place to the Word of God. Where is rich expository preaching any longer to be found? 'They devoted themselves to the apostles' teaching' characterised the first Church (Acts 2:42) but where in today's pared-down, fast-track Church is the apostles' teaching taught – or is it just assumed? A pastor friend of mine agreed with me about these deficiencies in the contemporary Church, but could not see where they could be made good in a way that fitted into the current programme. Fewer and fewer in ministry have a theological heritage to draw on whereas Mary and I gained our basic theological and biblical education in the normal flow of the Church's life via biblically rich teaching on Sunday morning *and* evening, and the regular Thursday evening Bible study. I am not advocating a return to outmoded forms of churchmanship, nor am I wanting to turn the clock back on all the advances made by the Holy Spirit in freeing up the Church in the last thirty years, but merely asking where the central and foundational things get done, if they get done at all. In some contemporary churches, Scripture is not even *read* publicly at all. One thankfully retreats to a cathedral Eucharist to savour the readings from Scripture, though even there the lectionary is being attenuated and reference to it, or exposition of it in the homily, is never guaranteed. The issue is serious: in Scripture we encounter the Living God and hear His voice; we enter into God's saving story and meet Jesus, the beating heart of God's book who is the Word made flesh. Time for the third story.

Story three takes us to Nazareth and the synagogue there (Luke 4:14–21). Josiah's moment of discovery of the Law, and Jehoiakim's moment of truth with the prophets, become the moment of destiny with Jesus.

Fresh from His first burst of Messianic activity, Jesus comes to His home-town synagogue at Nazareth, and there He was handed the scroll

(Luke 4:17). How significant an action that is! The invitation is *not*: share with us a few blessed thoughts, bring greetings from Your Messianic party, or news of Your recent mission. No, they handed Him the scroll with the unspoken assumption – unlock these old scrolls for us. In William Willimon's words,

> They handed him the scroll, the scripture of Israel. They do not ask Jesus: 'Tell us how it is with you'; they do not ask him to report on his days at College, to share his feelings with them. They handed him the scroll. They ask him to read. Then he interprets. Then he preaches … Watch closely as they hand him the scroll because right there in that action of handing Jesus the scroll we see a movement that is at the heart of the faith of Israel …

Willimon continues:

> There may be religions that begin with long walks in the woods, communing with nature, getting close to trees. There may be religions which begin by delving into the recesses of a person's ego, rummaging around in the psyche. Christianity is not one of those religions. Here is a people who begin with that action of taking up the scroll, being confronted with stories of God, stories that insert themselves into our accustomed ways of doing business and challenge us to change or else be out of step with the way things are now that God has entered human history.[9]

When Jesus finished reading, He rolled up the scroll, gave it back to the attendant and sat down and – Luke tells us significantly – 'The eyes of everyone in the synagogue were fastened on him' (Luke 4:20). That is exactly how it should be. He is the focus of attention because He is the sum of all the Scriptures: 'In the scroll of the book it is written of me': 'I have come to do your will, O God' (Psa. 40:6–8; Heb. 10:5–7, ESV). As Jesus discerned the Messianic role of the Son of Man as servant – indeed, a likely *suffering* servant role, mapped out in the Bible – so He shaped His life and ministry to the prophetic pattern portrayed there in the Scriptures: '… beginning with Moses and all the Prophets, he explained to them what was said in all the Scriptures concerning himself' (Luke 24:27).

He is the 'yes' and 'amen' to all the promises of God so that not one of them bypasses Him, but every one goes through Him to be transfigured and fulfilled. He is the sum of all God's revelation: 'Today [in and through me] this scripture [and all the others] is fulfilled in your hearing' (Luke 4:21). It is as if Jesus says to the contemporary Church: 'This old book of God will help you understand Me; and I will make sense of that old book. Those old prophetic scrolls will illuminate Me and I will unlock the secrets of those old prophetic scrolls.' *God's word became book, God's word became scrolls, God's Word became flesh.* God – as Josiah realised – must always have the first word. God – as Jehoiakim found out – always has the last word. But best of all – *God's first and final word is Jesus.*

Opening the scrolls speeds the momentum of God's story, and in prophetic untimeliness provokes a reaction. His prophetic time has come, and ... 'All spoke well of him and were amazed at the gracious words that came from his lips' (Luke 4:22), but when His prophetic untimeliness began to bite deep, those in the synagogue reacted furiously and drove Him to a cliff on the edge of town and were all for throwing Him over.

Amanda was a six-year-old Sunday school student, the daughter of a county sheriff. On 'Presentation Sunday' at her local church in Boulder, Colorado, she was given her very own Bible. During coffee time in the fellowship hall, a member of the church congratulated her and asked if he could see her Bible. 'OK but don't open it,' she said.

'Don't open it? But why shouldn't I open it?'

'You'll let God out.'

Open the old scrolls. Let God out!

Christian ministry that stays faithful to the written Word of God will be serious about letting the inscripturated sacred text speak for itself. Christian ministry attentive to this living voice will retain the sharpness of its prophetic calling and will be culturally critical in its deepest meaning – that of bringing the culture to a crisis of judgment and decision. Each of us engaged in Christian ministry needs to eat the Word, relish the Word, feel God's feelings, settle in for the long haul, practise righteousness, make irrational faith investments, confound the sceptics' censoring fire and republish the unexpurgated prophetic word.

Our generation needs to see the Word fulfilled in its hearing. There's no better time for us to revel in the gloriously irrelevant relevance of the Word of God; no better time to feel the impact of its prophetic untimeliness; no time like now to let God out of the old scrolls.

14
PREMATURE AMBASSADORS

We are ... Christ's ambassadors, as though God were making his
appeal through us (2 Corinthians 5:20)

The title of this chapter is taken from Richard John Neuhaus, who writes:

> we are *premature ambassadors*, having arrived at court before the sovereignty of our king has been recognised. It is awkward, of course, and our authority is very much in question. We must resist the temptation to relieve the awkwardness by accepting a lesser authority from another kingdom.[1]

Note the terms Neuhaus uses to characterise our ministry – '*premature*' and '*awkward*'. What makes Christian ministry *premature and awkward* is that we represent in word and deed a revolutionary and novel state of affairs wrought by God through the death and resurrection of Jesus. This puts us *ahead of our time and at odds with our times*.

To speak of the Church 'ahead of its time' may raise an ironic smile – since the Church is more often perceived as lagging behind the times. But it is the only conclusion the text allows us to draw. In George Weigel's words,

> Lived out in 'the world' and amid the agitation of the politics of the world, Christian hope should reflect the temporal paradox of Christian life – namely, that Christians are a people ahead of time. Christians are a people who know how the story is going to turn out; and that puts Christians in a unique position vis-à-vis the flow of history.[2]

This vision offers an intriguing, provocative, and arguably more New Testament, alternative to the five categories suggested by Richard Niebuhr in a groundbreaking work which have so dominated – and perhaps restricted – discussion about the Church's interface with culture for the past half-century and more.[3] Niebuhr's five categories were: Christ against culture, the Christ of culture, Christ above culture, Christ and culture in paradox, Christ the transformer of culture.

Commenting briefly on these, at the risk of oversimplifying Niebuhr's rich and fascinating discussion, and raising provisos to their acceptance, may set the scene for what I want to say in this chapter.

'Christ *against* culture' implies a rejection of the world as essentially evil that sets up a radical tension or mutual hostility between Church and society. At its most self-defensive, this pushes the Church into a ghetto-type mentality and encourages sectarian withdrawal from the realm of politics, arts and civic duties. There is much more to be said for this, I suspect, than Niebuhr wants to say, though he concedes that it does reflect one strain of New Testament thinking about Christians as sojourners in a foreign land.

The 'Christ *of* culture' describes too-ready an accommodation to the world's values. It evokes, taken to an extreme, the liberal equation of Christianity with what all decent people already know and aspire to. This stance strips the message of any 'news' value and tends to promote Christ as the figurehead of society and Church as its chaplain.

As for 'Christ *above* culture', this is the both/and approach, a synthesis of two realms – thinking that can be traced back to Thomas Aquinas and, beyond him, to Aristotle – in which the gospel is the fulfilment and enhancement of secular thought. So natural law is the ground of civic society and nature is supplemented by supernatural grace. This inspires an almost infinite number of variants on the 'gospel *and* ...' conjunction: the 'gospel *and* psychology', the 'gospel *and* feminism', the 'gospel *and* prosperity'; the 'gospel *and* ...' whatever is the prevailing zeitgeist. Too often, as the old adage goes, when the Church marries the spirit of the age it soon becomes a widow in the next!

'Christ and culture *in paradox*' represents a variation on the previous category in which grace does not displace law, but overrides it, and social structures are left in place as a bulwark against evil. This category has Lutheranism in its sights with its doctrine of the two kingdoms. The danger here is that faith is restricted to the realm of private, personal piety and the social realm is conceded uncritically and to other forces (as happened, it is said, with the German Christians under Nazism).

'Christ the *transformer* of culture' encapsulates an approach that believes that society is capable of being sanctified by the gospel. This is at heart a conversionist model which does not write off nature as unusable but takes sin seriously.

There is merit in all these approaches but they have rather straitjacketed the discussion and are open to criticism. No one critiqued them more persistently than the late John Yoder.[4] John Yoder's main criticism is that Niebuhr's categorisation presents far too monolithic a view of what culture is. Is there one thing called 'culture'? This query has recently gained strength in our fluid, fast-moving, late-modern, postmodern, even post-postmodern times!

In addition, Yoder argues, Niebuhr's framework clearly privileges the fifth category – the broadly Reformed approach – and is set up to lead to that conclusion. The initial sharp separation between Christ and culture implied in the headings given to the categories begs the question. This again, Yoder suggests, loads the discussion one way: to designate the world (creation) as the Father's realm apart from the Son is to cut right across the New Testament apostolic vision of Christ as ruler of the cosmos and incarnate logos. But surely, the Church can speak a prophetic word to the state on the basis of the Lordship of Christ. In his study of Yoder's thought, Craig Carter concludes,

> Thus Yoder argues, to spend one's energies in building up the church is not withdrawing from society or taking a defeatist attitude. The church is the lab for social experimentation, a pilot project, a new paradigm, a nurturing ground for countercultural values, a live alternative to a society structured around retributive sanctions.[5]

A 'Church ahead of the times' – or 'Christ ahead of the culture' – may better describe a stance that will provide us with the needed perspective from which to evaluate our culture and to discriminate what we can endorse in it and where we need to dissent from it. *Which is why 2 Corinthians 5:17 is crucial here: 'if anyone is in Christ – new creation'*. It is regrettable that the NIV introduces a verb where there is none, thus effectively overpersonalising this by translating: 'if anyone is in Christ, *he is* a new creation'. 'He is' does not appear in Paul's text.

'If anyone is in Christ, he is a new creation' – or worse, 'he is a new creature' – wrongly limits this to what sounds like a description of conversion or newbirth. The NRSV is slightly better here: 'If anyone is in Christ, *there is* a new creation.'
For the picture Paul is painting is typically larger than individual rebirth, although it includes it and is a picture of recreation on a cosmic scale. Paul is drawing again on the Exilic vision of the ultimate eschatological salvation beyond Exile for which Israel hoped and which Isaiah portrays as 'new heavens and a new earth' (Isa. 65:17–19; 66:22–23).

That Paul is drawing on the 'new Exodus' hope of the Exilic prophets is confirmed by the next phrase – 'the old has gone, the new has come' (2 Cor. 5:17b) which clearly echoes Isaiah 43:18–19 (though again the NIV inexplicably obscures this by omitting the 'behold' or 'look' in both places, in contrast to the ESV). The prophetic hope of the dawning of a new day of salvation – viewed as a renewal of God's creation – is seen by Paul as fulfilled in Jesus Christ (cf. 6:2). The old world has died and the new world has been born!

Speaking of Easter, G.K. Chesterton wrote of that garden tomb where, he said,

> the whole of that great and glorious humanity which we call antiquity was gathered up and covered over; and in that place it was buried. On the third day the friends of Christ coming at daybreak found the grave empty and the stone rolled away. In varying ways they realised the new wonder; but even they hardly realised that *the world had died in the night*. What they were looking at was *the first day of the new creation* with a new heavens and a new earth; and in the

semblance of the gardener God walked again in the garden, in the cool not of the evening but the dawn.[6]

Paul celebrates what God has accomplished through the death and resurrection of Jesus as the inauguration of a whole new realm of reality (5:17). This is an accomplished fact – the result of the initiative and action of God (5:18a). It is firmly and eternally founded on an act of reconciliation (5:18–19) achieved at the cross, where He who knew no sin was made a sin offering for us that 'in him we might become the righteousness of God' (5:21).

As a result of that 'great exchange', we receive the righteousness of God in the sense of being justified and acquiring covenant status. But at the same time, we 'become the righteousness of God' so that *we actually represent God's own integrity and covenantal commitment.* This additional point is controversial. But it makes sense to me and takes nothing away from the classic doctrine of justification by faith. It is arrived at by reading 5:21 not as an isolated atonement text hanging loose and out of place here, but as integral to Paul's claims. That Christ was made a sin offering for us is clear and wonderful. It is the balancing phrase that is not so obvious: *'that … we might become the righteousness of God'* (5:21b).

It was N.T. Wright who, to my knowledge, first proposed taking 'the righteousness of God' as carrying its full covenantal weight which has been at the forefront of Paul's mind at least since chapter 3 verse 6. He proposed we should read 5:21 as 'that we might become embodiments of the covenant faithfulness of God'.[7]

Karen Onesti and Manfred Brauch (of Eastern Baptist Theological Seminary) argue along similar lines. It is significant, they suggest, that Paul does not say: 'that we might become righteous' or 'that we might receive God's righteousness' but instead say 'that we might *become the righteousness of God'.* They recall that in the Exilic prophets, especially Isaiah 40–55 – a section of Scripture that shapes Paul's narrative thought-world here in this section of 2 Corinthians – 'righteousness' is a covenantal and relational term and is often synonymous with God's covenant faithfulness reaching out to save and restore the covenant bond. Onesti and Brauch suggest, boldly, perhaps, that 'righteousness' might be rendered *'relation-restoring love'.* 'Becoming the righteousness of God' can be construed as a compressed way of talking about believers as agents of reconciliation. 'Believers become participants in God's reconciling action, extensions of his reconciling love.'[8]

This interpretation is surely in line with what Paul is doing in context in his pastoral handling of the Corinthians, so 6:1: 'we urge you not to receive God's grace in vain.' It is also consistent with the way the Isaianic servant is portrayed as being made a covenant for the people (Isa. 42:6; 49:8b). Richard Hays has added his weight to this view. 'Paul is an ambassador for Christ announcing a new order, announcing the apocalyptic message of the reconciliation of the world by God. Those who continue to demand traditional credentials simply do not know what time it is. When a new world is bursting on the scene why look back? This eschatological transformation of the community', Hays argues,

> explains Paul's extraordinary affirmation that the purpose of God's reconciling work in Christ is 'that they might become the righteousness of God' (5:21). He does *not* say: 'that we might *know about* the righteousness of God', nor that 'we might *believe* in the righteousness of God', nor, even, that 'we might *receive* the righteousness of God'. Instead the church is to '*become* the righteousness of God': where the church embodies in its life together the world-reconciling love of Jesus Christ, the new creation is manifest. The church incarnates the righteousness of God.[9]

The liberating truth that the sinless Christ was made sin for us that we might become the righteousness of God would have had special resonance in the honour–shame society that was Corinth. In such an environment, an atonement that dealt with guilt and offered forgiveness needed also to be seen to address the issue of shame and dishonour as well. Hence Paul's emphasis on reconciliation fitted the Corinthian situation well. Mennonite theologian Norman Kraus goes so far as to say,

> In no way can *shame* be expiated through substitutionary compensation or retaliation … Only a forgiveness which covers the past and a genuine restoration of relationship can banish shame. What is needed is a restoration of communication. The rage which isolates and insulates must be overcome. Reconciliation and restoration of

mutual intimate relationship through a loving exchange is the only way to heal resentment and restore lost self-esteem.[10]

Jesus was made sin for us – the abhorrent, shameful thing itself! – so that we might become the righteousness of God; ie be restored to covenant integrity and faithfulness. To lack this sense of restored relationship in which we can now embody the covenant faithfulness of God is to receive God's grace in vain (6:1). It is to sink back, as the Corinthians were doing, into the insecurities and competitiveness and self-obsession of the honour–shame culture from which the gospel would save us (cf. 5:15). To receive God's grace in the full sense of reconciliation and restoration to the full covenant fidelity of God is to be accepted fully as His covenant partners and to be set free to be His co-workers (6:1). The cross which is that 'loving open exchange' between God and us (5:14,21) evokes a desire for a similar 'open exchange' between the reconciled – in this case, between Himself and the Corinthian believers (6:11–13; 7:2–4).

Everything flows from an act done on a world scale. God has achieved this. God has reconciled 'the world to himself in Christ, not counting men's sins against them'. To Paul – and by extension us all – is committed the ministry of reconciliation (18b) and the message of reconciliation (5:18b,19b) for which we have been made to 'become the righteousness of God' and of which we are now *ambassadors.*

The backdrop to this metaphor is possibly the world of ancient diplomacy. But just as likely, Paul has in mind Isaiah's vision of the herald of peace; whose feet are beautiful upon the mountains and who announces God's victory over Babylonian oppression (Isa. 52:7ff.). What was declared by the prophet in the face of Babylon's totalitarian claims to the contrary is now, as gospel, declared by apostles in the face of Rome's imperial idolatry and established in communities of reconciliation across the imperial world. The ministry of reconciliation is inevitably an intensely political function. It is liable to get its agents into much trouble. It is not surprising that they will feel premature and awkward, and almost inevitable that they will be regarded as a threat to the existing order of things.

We have a new mission as agents of reconciliation, ambassadors of this new kingdom of salvation, this new creation reality that has been established by Christ's death and resurrection. From this angle of vision it is possible to see that 'the church community is a sneak preview of God's ultimate redemption of the world'.[11] For this reason, the call to reconciliation is first addressed to the Church itself. Paul turns the public proclamation of the gospel into an urgent and persuasive pastoral plea: *'Be reconciled to God'* (2 Cor. 5:20).

Currently, the Corinthians are not living out the realities of the new creation. They are at odds with each other and with him, too conformist to their Greco-Roman standards and cultural values, and unfaithful to the gospel. So, the gospel of reconciliation is turned back onto the Corinthians as Paul urges them to be reconciled to the gospel, to each other in the reconciled body, and to him as its apostolic agent. They are new creation people. They need to be *re-reconciled* to God's radically new order of reality established by the cross and resurrection and tantamount to a new creation. *The Church needs to be converted before the world will be, and converted to a radical distinctiveness, to this future orientation.*

Now when public proclamation becomes pastoral persuasion, it does not soften into accommodation; reconciliation is not resignation. To be reconciled is to be reconciled to the life God has appointed for us. In particular, and in this case, as Neuhaus says, 'reconciliation means to be at peace, to be at one, with the promised new order … Being reconciled to the rule of God is quite the opposite of being resigned to things as they are.'[12] The pastoral practice of peacemaking is a priestly vocation of reconciliation in the service of a prophetic vision of the realities of the new creation. Too often in pastoral reconciliation we are merely patching people up, helping them to cope. But coping can degenerate into passivity and adjustment to the status quo. True new creation reconciliation, on the other hand, always aims at transformation.

> When we are helping people to cope by conforming rather than by transforming, when we make smooth the way of accommodation, when we relieve the tension between the actual and the real, then we have become reconcilers who have betrayed Christ's ministry of reconciliation.[13]

Rather we endeavour to help others reintegrate the disordered fragments of their lives in relationship to God and His future. To be reconciled is to be restored to relationship with God, to be realigned to His loving will and purpose. It is to be reintegrated into the big story of God that alone makes sense of our lives. So when we engage in the *ministry of reconciliation* we are doing something culturally distinctive. We are persuading people to adopt a new creation viewpoint.

We are inviting people – as Paul was inviting the Corinthians – to a totally new world-view: to look out on everything through new eyes!

How does this work? *We seek to persuade believers to see themselves in a totally new way* (5:14–15). Corinth was a self-serving society. The decline of the city-state in the Greco-Roman world saw an upsurge in individualism, the cultivation of self-sufficiency and self-worth, and a concern for status. Most of the Corinthian population was made up of freedmen, who had settled there by choice, pursuing the then equivalent of the American dream. They were an upwardly-mobile lot, self-made men, venture capitalists, fashion-conscious entrepreneurs who liked to flaunt their new-found wealth.[14] In such a culture, Christians in Corinth, or wherever, need to be reminded that they are part of the new creation order. We no longer look at ourselves in the same self-serving way since we have died with Christ (5:15). This has not demeaned us but has turned our lives upside down and given us a new direction for living '*for him who died for … [us] and was raised again*'.

To be reconciled is to be reconciled to a wholly new-creation way of evaluating oneself and the purpose and direction for living. The task of pastoral reconciliation and healing is to persuade believers in Christ to be reconciled to this new creation vocation. And not only are we changed but everything in the world looks different!

We see other people in a new way.
We no longer look at other people in the old way. Our evaluation has drastically changed: 'from now on we regard no-one from a worldly point of view' (5:16). Where '*God looks not on outward appearance but on the heart*' (see 1 Sam. 16:7), the Corinthians were judging by externals taking 'pride in what is seen rather than in what is in the heart' (5:12b). Like other parts of the Greco-Roman world, Corinth was a visual culture,

a media-obsessed, celebrity-conscious society – real Rupert Murdoch country. 'This was in fact a typical complaint against the Sophists that they were all show and no substance. They paid special attention to their clothing, appearance and to the sound of their own voices.'[15]

In an honour–shame society like Corinth Paul was being looked down on perhaps because he worked with his hands, as an artisan and tentmaker. Paul was certainly being evaluated poorly when compared to the 'super-apostles' because he exhibited weakness, suffered in his ministry, and was an 'unimpressive' figure to those 'looking only on the surface of things' (10:7,10). But this way of looking at people is entirely wrong; it has no place in the new creation. After all, the Corinthians themselves were socially not much to write home about (1 Cor. 1:26–29).

To be converted to the new creation through the reconciling work of the cross is to give up superficial criteria for evaluating people. Reconciled to God we are reconciled to each other. Racial, ethnic, tribal, gender differences no longer form a barrier to fellowship in the one new-creation community. Differences can be celebrated as diversity within the one family of God (Gal. 3:26–29). We no longer see other people as stereotypes – as mere labels: Introvert, Eldership Material, Ectomorph, Unsaved, Anorexic, Divorced, Bipolar, Single Parent, Diabetic, Tither … and so on.[16]

We no longer measure spiritual people, as the Corinthians were doing, by their outward boasting of exalted experiences; a public show of ecstatic spirituality to bolster their authority. To be reconciled is to be reconciled to a wholly new creation way of assessing people. To be an ambassador of this reconciliation is to persuade believers in the light of the new creation to be reconciled to this new way of seeing other people. We are now freed to see them as having only one 'label', a 'designer label' – 'made in God's image' – 'for whom Christ died'!

Furthermore, *We even see Jesus in a new way* (5:16b).
No longer do we view Jesus as we once might have done – and as Paul certainly once did – as just another failed Messianic pretender, but as the King of Israel and Lord of the world.

No longer do we see Jesus in consumerist terms as the Aladdin who rubs our lamp, the supplier of whatever good we feel we need for our self-advancement, but as the sovereign Lord whose grace moves us in our turn to generosity of spirit and giving of money.

This is not a kingdom of humanity with Christ to serve in it, but the kingdom of Christ with us to serve in it: 'For we do not preach ourselves, but Jesus Christ as Lord, and ourselves as your servants for Jesus' sake' (4:5). It is the staggering love of this Lord Jesus Christ that constrains Paul, hems him in to His mastering vision and motivates him with the passion for mission.

We gain a new outlook on our culture.

We embrace the paradox of a reconciled but still rebellious world. And when we hear the call to 'come out from them and be separate' repeated by the apostle as the prophets had urged it on the exiles in Babylon before (6:14–18) we do not hear it as an invitation to join a self-righteous ghetto as an exclusive bunch of weirdos. We hear it as exiles needing to break with 'Babylonian' standards and values because, like them, we are on the way home. We hear it as a call not to be unwitting pagans, unthinkingly conformed to the culture of consumerism and violence all around us. We hear it as another opportunity to gain freedom and to be transformed by the renewing of our minds, drinking in new attitudes and aspirations from the fountain of new creation, washing our habits and practices clean in the baptismal waters of His dying and rising, renewing our distinctive calling as covenant community in the Eucharistic feast.

Again we turn our faces to the glorious light of God radiant in Jesus Christ and find ourselves just a tiny bit more transformed into His likeness from one degree of glory to another. *Again we learn that the best way to serve the world is to be the Church – the Church which is the sign, herald and foretaste of the new creation.* We have a different story; we have acquired a different history and an alternative future so that we can even look death in the face and stake all on the resurrection of Jesus Christ from the dead: 'if it were not so, I would have told you'.

We are reconciled, then – and we seek to reconcile others – to the reality of the new creation which is now and not yet among us! This is something of what it means to be agents of reconciliation, 'premature ambassadors' of God's future at the court of current culture. It is to be entrusted with the ministry of reconciliation, to be made partners of the covenant faithfulness of God to see it through. So we learn to live with the 'awkwardness of being premature ambassadors' in a Church 'ahead of its time'.

Above all, we must resist relieving the awkwardness by accommodating ourselves to cultural trends.

So in your church and mine, when we listen to the Bible, our primary question should not be, 'How can we interpret the Bible in such a way that it makes sense to modern people?' but 'How can we reinterpret the Church to suit the demands of the Bible?'

> Our congregations must read scripture out of the conviction that, even as in the first centurie, the Bible is able to evoke the people it deserves.[17]

We claim to be acting and speaking on God's behalf (2 Cor. 5:20), making His appeal, raising God's voce in the courts of the Church and the world. Richard Lischer says that if there were stage directions attached to the Bible the most frequent would be 'ENTER GOD SPEAKING'.[18] We live and move and have our being by the supremely counter-intuitive action of the cross by which we are crucified to the world and the world is crucified to us. We are convinced by His 'death for all' not to live for ourselves but for Him who died and rose again and whose selfless sacrificial love constrains us and controls us and drives us on.

We are the people who have entered a new world. Things that once made no sense to us now make sense. ying to ourselves makes no sense in a culture of narcissism. Dying to ourselves hardly fits our culture of competition and ambition. 'One died for all, therefore all died.' Imagine that.[19]

And what could be more disruptive of an easy accommodation to the culture than resurrection? We tacitly accept the world's definition of "the world" and humbly try to accommodate the gospel to it, as if the cross and resurrection have not deranged the old world and started a new one. Preaching is a way of joining up with the new creation already in progress.'[20] We are the Church of the new creation 'ahead of its time'; we are ambassadors who represent a whole new realm of reality. Or as John Yoder put it, the Church is *an aftertaste of God's loving triumph on the cross and a foretaste of his ultimate loving triumph in his kingdom.*[21]

In the light of this, the keynote of the contemporary Church needs to be not 'relevance' or even 'contextualisation' but *'credibility'*.

To be a 'credible' Church means that
- Before the full results are in, we declare the outcome: Jesus is Lord.
- Before all the fighting has stopped we declare: peace has broken out.
- Before all the rebellion has ceased and before all the protagonists have surrendered their arms, we declare not the easier truth that God has reconciled Himself to the state of the world, but the defiantly unobvious truth that God has already reconciled the world to Himself.
- Before the noise of gunfire has ceased and the angry voices have died away we urge everyone to come home to a reconciled world and a reconciling God, and we act and speak this 'peace' as if it were true both to the world and to each other.

We speak and care and pastor and preach 'ahead of our time': our time is still to come. We are premature ambassadors, knocking on the doors of people's hearts with heart 'breaking' news. We announce a new creation already under way in the midst of an old world that is 'passing away'. We are moved by fear and constrained by love. The fear that moves us is not that the Church is declining and about to die but fear of final accountability, faithful to the gospel deposited with us and the stewardship of unchanging truth entrusted to us.
We are constrained by cruciform love and place ourselves at the disposal of resurrection Lordship. It is awkward and there is no guarantee of a warm reception.

I am not sanguine about the prospects for the Church in Britain: others are. As Chesterton has Our Lady say to Alfred fighting against the pagan invaders,

'I tell you naught for your comfort,
Yea, naught for your desire,
Save that the sky grows darker yet
And the sea rises higher.'

Yet strangely strengthened by this vision, Alfred is moved to give his defiant answer to the seemingly all-conquering forces of godlessness confronting him:

'That on you has fallen the shadow,
And not upon the Name;
That though we scatter and though we fly,
You are more tired of victory,
Than we are tired of shame.

'That though you hunt the Christian man
Like a hare on the hill-side,
The hare has still more heart to run
Than you have heart to ride.

'That though all lances split on you,
All swords be heaved in vain,
We have more lust again to lose
Than you to win again …

'Therefore your end is on you,
Is on you and your kings,
Not for a fire in Ely fen,
Not that your gods are nine or ten,
But because it is only Christian men
Guard even heathen things.

'For our God has blessed creation,
Calling it good. I know
What spirit with whom you blindly band
Hath blessed destruction with his hand;
Yet by God's death the stars shall stand
And the small apples grow.'[22]

As Alan Lewis wrote, 'Today must be worth living if tomorrow is worth trusting' all the more so if 'God's tomorrow has already taken up residence in humanity's today …'[23]

15
ONLY FOOLS AND MARTYRS

... receive me just as you would a fool, so that I may do a little boasting ... In Damascus the governor ... had the city ... guarded in order to arrest me. But I was lowered in a basket from a window in the wall and slipped through his hands (2 Corinthians 11:16,32–33)

The 'crown for the wall' – the *'corona muralis'* – was an honour bestowed on the first Roman soldier to scale the walls of a besieged city. Paul says that when it comes to walls he is the first over the wall to escape! Paul looks back with amusement to his rather indecorous exit from Damascus in a laundry basket as another example of the reversal of values. This is the side of Paul that critics usually overlook: Paul, in humorous, self-deprecating and highly ironic mood, 'playing the fool' in his dispute with the Corinthians. Relishing an almost clown-like instance of the paradox of victory-in-defeat, Paul declares his honour in being let down the wall for Jesus. This is the image of a real 'anti-hero' captured in a cameo from Paul's past (11:32–33, cf. Acts 9:23–25). It is on a par with a king's entry to his capital on a donkey!

But what have 'boasting', 'foolishness' and irony to do with Christian ministry? To attempt an answer, something of the cultural context needs to be sketched in.[1]

Like other Greco-Roman centres, first-century Corinth was a highly *visual* culture in which self-display was crucial to those seeking an admiring public. Achieving personal glory (*doxa*) became an acceptable goal: the word itself conveying the dual notions of visual splendour and lofty esteem. Civic life in this period was intensely competitive and people struggled to remain one-up on their peers. This was, in Tim

Savage's words, 'an era of high incentive and great accomplishment but also of anxiety and uncertainty'. Boasting was an honourable tendency; humility was scorned. There was an upsurge in *religious* interest and in salvation though a salvation that was usually viewed, in terms familiar to us today, as 'health, wealth and prosperity'. In this climate the cults were attractive because they promised 'a visible show of divinity at work'. As Tim Savage observes, 'People yearned to be thrilled by divine power and even terrified by it' and adherents of the cults 'wanted to experience that power for themselves'.[2] With little interest shown in dogma or theology, a generally tolerant attitude prevailed towards anyone who wanted to belong to several different cults at the same time. The person who advocated one religion to the exclusion of the others, however, invited ridicule and abuse. Religion, of course, provided a social context for people to eat and drink and it was often only temples that had restaurants attached.

Apart from the cults' advocacy of dance, drama, mime, and entertainment, fine culture would scarcely have flourished as it did. The Corinthians anticipated no cultural challenges from religion – 'they expected the cults to apply a transcendental stamp of approval to their lives'.[3]

Oratory was a popular 'spectator sport' though the orators were rarely highly trained and were usually happy to sacrifice truth and argument on the altar of public taste. To win applause, or gain a hearty 'bravo' from audiences wanting primarily to be amused, they 'specialised in startling effects, sensational topics, powerful deliveries'.[4] Eloquent speakers were admired not so much for their content or message as for the 'ability to project one's personality powerfully on one's hearers'[5]. 'Social ascent was the goal, boasting and self-display the means, personal power and glory the reward.'

Economically, Corinth was a boomtown, a burgeoning banking and trade centre where quick and easy money could be made and which encouraged entrepreneurial ambition. In addition, Corinth proudly hosted the Isthmian games, second only in prestige to the games held at Olympia. The biennial festival – one of which was held in AD 51 – may well have engulfed Paul in its atmosphere and hype. Not surprisingly in this *sport mad* society, with everything having a keen competitive edge, there were few prizes for coming second. This was a winner-takes-all ethos: literally – and metaphorically – a gladiatorial atmosphere. Corinthian society was *cosmetic* – setting a high premium on outward appearances. Corinth was a city of beautiful people out for a good time in what was the 'entertainment capital of Greece'.

The pressure of the prevailing cultural ethos partly helps to explain the *criticism of Paul* from within the Corinthian Church – criticism along *four* main lines:

(i) They criticised Paul for *refusing to promote himself.* His opponents are always boasting about their accomplishments, but Paul is sure that 'in all this comparing and grading and competing, they quite miss the point' (2 Cor. 10:12, *The Message*). In Paul's view such 'boasting' goes beyond proper bounds, detracts from the labours of others and takes credit from others in their sphere (10:13–16).

This reflects the self-commendation and arrogance so characteristic of first-century Corinthian culture, which Paul had already warned the believers in Corinth not to become caught up with (1 Cor. 3:21; 4:7). Then, in his first letter to them, Paul had rebuked them for going beyond 'what is written' (1 Cor. 4:6) – which probably refers to the Old Testament citations made so far: 1 Corinthians 1:19 (Isa. 29:14); 1:31 (Jer. 9:23–24); 2:9 (Isa. 64:3–4); 2:16 (Isa. 40:13); 3:19 (Job 5:13); 3:20 (Psa. 94:11) – all of which in various ways counsel humility before the unfathomable wisdom of God. As Paul makes clear in the first letter, there is a 'boasting' that pertains to faith but it is 'boasting' in a superior wisdom which paradoxically makes us humble and excludes self-promotion, except about our weaknesses!

(ii) The Corinthians criticised Paul *for his unimpressive physical presence.* Measured by their standards Paul seems 'weak' (10:10). This may refer to his physical appearance – as a later document described him – 'a man little in stature, bald-headed, with crooked legs, well-born, with eyebrows meeting and a long nose' (*Acts of Paul and Thecla*). But more likely Paul 'is being faulted for his failure to impose himself violently upon the church and, specifically, to mete out punishment and discipline'.[6] To the contrary, Paul's way is the 'Jesus way' of gentleness and meekness.

(iii) The Corinthians criticised Paul for what they regarded as *his inferior speech*. Paul is disdained for refusing to indulge in the showy rhetoric and flamboyant self-serving monologues served up by the rhetoricians in seeking to dominate their audiences. They dismiss his speech as 'of no account' (ESV) while he, for his part, forswears being 'a trained speaker' (10:10; 11:6). It cannot be that Paul is not a wordsmith or that he lacks word skills, but – as in 1 Corinthians 2:1–4 – that Paul is distancing himself from arrogant as well as abusive speech. They want assertiveness and demagoguery, high falutin', rhetoric. He gives them only words of weakness and humility.[7]

(iv) The Corinthians criticise Paul for *declining their financial support*. In an honour–shame society, Paul risked offending the Corinthians by refusing their patronage, though he has accepted it elsewhere (11:7–9; 12:13–18). It was socially embarrassing for them when their prestige was bound up with an impoverished apostle. But by forgoing their support Paul aims to eliminate their self-boasting, encourage their humility, and turn their interest in the direction of giving to others more needy than themselves (cf. 6:10; 9:1–15). This is hardly guaranteed to win him friends at a superficial level but it is truly apostolic.

Our entire discussion so far confirms that what is at stake, in Tim Savage's words, is a '*conflict between two opposing perspectives: the worldly outlook of the Corinthians and Paul's own Christ-centred viewpoint*'.[8] Paul's intense debate with the Corinthians has been about what it means to be 'truly *spiritual*'. Paul comes full circle in his extant Corinthian correspondence by returning to the paradox of God's weakness being stronger than human strength, and God's foolishness being wiser than human wisdom!

Second Corinthians focuses this debate on Christian ministry and indeed on Paul's own apostleship. The letter climaxes therefore with a passionate discussion about the true style and authority of apostolic ministry. 'The fundamental problem is the Corinthians' image of Christian leadership.'[9] Paul will argue for a ministry that displays incarnational integrity. To make his case he will play the wise fool in a world gone mad. His pastoral aim is to show how to distinguish between authentic incarnational ministry and fake 'super-spiritual' ministry and how not to be intimidated by the latter!

How does Paul go about doing this? In 2 Corinthians 10–13 Paul aims at some outside preachers – with a Jewish Christian background it seems – who have come to Corinth and have made matters worse. Up to this point, the major focus of the letter has been on the Corinthians themselves; now Paul turns the heat up and confronts his opponents head on.

He identifies them with obvious sarcasm as 'super-apostles' and more bluntly as 'false' or 'pseudo-apostles' (11:5; 12:11; 11:13, *The Message*). This full-scale attack on his opponents has been preceded by an earlier sortie where he dismissed them as 'peddlers' (2:17) and he has continued to keep them in his sights all along (eg 'do we need, like some people, letters of recommendation', 3:1; cf. 4:2; 5:12; 6:3; 7:2). He has already been forced – as he sees it – to defend himself and his style of ministry against the criticisms being made of him by these 'self-styled' apostles in Corinth and, in turn, to commend his own ministry, uses typical 'hardship lists' which were a conventional form of defence (4:8–9; 6:4–10; 11:23–28).

Especially Paul seeks to demonstrate that the resurrection power of Christ is released by the Spirit through suffering, dying and death: it is evidenced in and through weakness and humility (4:10–12). He has already argued that the Corinthians need a whole new evaluation of what it means to be a spiritual minister and agent of Christ. Now 'what has been simmering on the back burner in chapters 1–9 is brought to a roaring boil in chapters 10–13'.[10]

To expose his opponents' error, Paul decides to boast. '*Boasting*' was a current social convention, referring not simply to bragging, but rather to self-promotion, or what we might now call advertising! In order to prick the bubble of conceit around his arrogant opponents, Paul reluctantly comes down to their level and indulges in his own 'boasting' (10:8). Because 'boasting' was a conventional practice in Greco-Roman society, sophisticated rules were laid down for how the exercise might be conducted. Paul's opponents are behaving like the Sophists – travelling rhetoricians, philosophers and debaters – who toured the ancient world giving pompous exhibitions of their skill in public-speaking and argumentation. Corinth – entertainment hotspot that it was – was a particularly sought-after booking.

In contrast to the Sophist-like self-promotion of his opponents, Paul engages in another category of defence defined by Plutarch and other Greek writers as *'inoffensive self-praise'*. In this latter section of the Corinthian letter, Paul basically follows the outline of what items could acceptably be included in such self-praise. Paul, however, as we shall see, does all this with heavy *irony*. In other words, he clearly aims to *parody* their self-promotion by matching it with boasting of his own. He will – as we say – 'send it up' by satirising it. Significantly, Paul goes out of his way to emphasise that his kind of 'bragging' will never go beyond justifiable limits, and will – above all – always be 'in Christ', in line with one of his favourite texts which states that he who boasts should 'boast in the Lord' (10:13–17, citing Jer. 9:22–24; cf. 1 Cor. 1:31). What, then, are the charges Paul lays against his opponents?

In 10:1–11:15, Paul's indictment of those he dubs 'super-apostles' accuses them of:

- *Reflecting worldly methods and attitudes* (10:2)

Paul's opponents are adept at using the methods of worldly wisdom: of employing a way of evaluating things that is utterly ungodly and unspiritual, and this is conditioned by their culture. It was, says Don Carson, characterised by 'human ingenuity, rhetoric, showmanship, a certain splashiness and forwardness in spiritual pretensions, charm, powerful personal charisma'.[11] Such an approach is more dangerous than a mere lifestyle choice since a surface appraisal of reality actually blocks people knowing God (10:5,7).

- *Making flashy presentations* (10:10)

The opponents appear to be impressive personalities – unlike Paul – and impressive speakers too, again unlike Paul. It would seem that then, as now, style is triumphing over content, packaging counts more than the product, and presentation matters more than truth. PR and spin are coming to mean more than honesty and openness, to the detriment of truth, discernment and the ability to evaluate competing 'wisdoms'.

- *Designing self-made standards* (10:12)

The 'super-apostles' opposing Paul have an infallible method of inflating their stature: they measure themselves by themselves! They form a self-adoring club, a magic closed circle, immune from questioning or criticism. They constitute an unaccountable mutual appreciation society, yet one within which there is a sharp sense of the pecking order!

- *Overreaching themselves* (10:13–16)

These leaders, for all their professed faith and charismatic qualities, are classic products of their times. They are cut from the same cloth as their go-getting contemporaries. They are spiritual entrepreneurs, ambitious expansionists, empire builders. Moreover, they are invaders on Paul's territory. Overreaching themselves, they arrogantly behave as if no one had ever covered their ground before. Long on hype, they are short on self-restraint. Carson comments somewhat caustically, 'Little men can be dangerous especially when they position themselves in such a way as to capture some stolen glory from great men and forge it into the bangles of self-interested leadership.'[12]

Paul's opponents are self-deceived about their importance. In fact, when we lift up our eyes to the wider world, they appear as big fish in small ponds. Small-minded men have staked their claim to the hill; Paul's eyes are on the unclimbed mountains – the regions beyond. Some boast of their 'stream' – his eyes are on the ocean. A broader vision would provide a healthy antidote to such smug self-satisfaction and petty boasting. Above all, servant ministry remains sensitive to the only approval that really counts: 'What you say about yourself means nothing in God's work. It's what God says about you that makes the difference' (10:18, *The Message*).

At this point, Paul characteristically sees beyond personalities to the bigger issue at stake: the *integrity of the gospel*. These self-promoting faith merchants are unaware that they are propagating what amounts to a *different* gospel – that is, preaching *another* Jesus and urging the reception of a *different* Spirit (11:4).

This is the most serious charge that Paul lays at the door of his opponents in Corinth, but he will not let them off the hook without one final particular criticism:

- *Being overinterested in money* (11:7–9)

'Super-apostles', it seems, never come cheap. Unlike Paul, who does not charge for his services (cf. 2:17). The 'Sophists ... aimed to collect a growing number of disciples who hung on their words and paid large sums for the privilege of sitting at their feet.'[13] Those with seemingly impressive charismatic authority always run the danger of being ruthlessly opportunistic, exploitative and manipulative. The history of my Pentecostal heritage glows with great saints – most of them, in my experience, ordinary, inconspicuous working people with a glow of holiness on their face. But they have too often been betrayed from within their own tradition by unscrupulous poseurs taking advantage of ordinary people and growing sleek on the profits (cf. 11:20). Why are otherwise good people so gullible? Why do people put up with such abusive nonsense? Sheer intimidation – no doubt – overawed by those who claim such superior spiritual status and authority based, more often than not, on visions, revelations, and supposed miracles (cf. 12:1,12). Assured by the platform personality of his or her nine visions before breakfast, harangued by those who preface everything with a testimony about how God spoke to them, appeared to them, how should anyone respond? Frankly, by *not believing them*. I don't.

Paul now goes on the offensive in what is known as Paul's 'fool's discourse', 11:16–12:10.

Paul decides to 'play the fool' to show up by ironic contrast the folly of his opponents. This is a perfect example of practising 'situational wisdom' (in the spirit of Proverbs 26:5 – 'Answer a fool according to his folly, or he will be wise in his own eyes' rather than 26:4 – 'Do not answer a fool according to his folly, or you will be like him yourself'). Paul reluctantly descends to his opponents' level in order to parody their self-promotion and thus, with heavy irony, to prick the balloon of their self-conceit. Paul rejects those who promulgate another gospel, another Jesus or another spirit. Even more he rejects those 'who do not accept *his vision of ministry, that is as cruciform, Christlike and servant-shaped*'.[14]

That Paul's boasting is ironic and tongue-in-cheek is clear from one example. Refuting the charge of lack of integrity in financial matters, and the offence of declining their patronage, he replies, 'Was it a *sin* for me to *lower myself* ... to *elevate you* by preaching the gospel of God to you free of charge? I robbed other churches by receiving support from them so as to serve you' (11:7–8). All right, Paul concedes, let's play the silly game for a while (11:16–19) but, if I am to boast, I will boast chiefly about my *weakness* (11:30; 12:5,9). So Paul indulges in his 'fool's discourse'.

a) Firstly, Paul offers as his CV a 'hardship catalogue' (11:21–33).
Drawing up a catalogue of hardships experienced in the way Paul does here was a conventional form of self-defence. But here it is in the Lord because Paul enumerates the list of afflictions and trials as evidence *for*, not against, the authentic nature of his ministry for Jesus. Here, 'catalogue' becomes litany. Paul's opponents saw 'wonders' alone as chief signs of an apostle. Paul's testimony is not short in this regard (12:12) but it is his 'weaknesses' that he reckons to be the chief signs of a charismatic, Christlike ministry. His critics evaluated his trials as contradicting his ministry; Paul saw them as confirming it.

Paul's is a thoroughly incarnational style of ministry. If this is triumphalism, then it is characterised by being 'more than conquerors' in the most adverse circumstances; if this is success then it is measured by faithfulness in afflictions; if this is 'prosperity' it is compatible with extreme deprivation. Here is no facile, macho-Christianity but a charismatic realism that is vibrant, resilient and undaunted. Such a ministry does not exploit or manipulate people but identifies with them – feeling keenly the desperation of the weak, feeling shamefully the guilt of the sinful. Paul stands alongside believers not over them (11:28–29). Defiantly, Paul pre-empts the conclusion of his argument by saying, so 'If I must boast, I will boast of the things that show my weakness' (11:30).

b) Secondly, Paul condescends to speak of his own exalted spiritual experiences (12:1–6).
What he says here is especially tongue-in-cheek because he knows that the Corinthians and his opponents have an overinflated view of the significance of such experiences. It is as if Paul is saying: 'I can match anything they can produce in their CV; I have "boldly gone" where no one else has dared to tread – even to paradise!' As we might say in today's argot: 'Been there; done that; got the T-shirt!' But nothing should detract from the seriousness of the issue. Paul's testimony and

the restraint he shows in describing it are significant, especially in the light of the Corinthians' valid but overglossed charismatic experiences. For this reason, Paul speaks of his mystical experiences reluctantly, as a fool. He has seen and heard things that were so overwhelmingly wonderful that he was forbidden to talk about them. One can imagine how critics might view this guardedness: 'Well – if you can't talk about them, maybe they don't add up to much.' One can imagine a puzzled modern observer reflecting: 'Paul, you need to sell yourself better. You are not going to sell many tapes, books and videos or attract crowds to your conferences if you refuse to cream the cake by titillating your Christian audiences with "visions and revelations" that would surely dazzle ordinary Christians into thinking that you must be exceptionally spiritual and authoritative.' But Paul has never once used this experience, and hesitates now to allude to what had happened fourteen years ago – and who has not got a more up to date testimony than that!

Once again, Paul refuses to 'boast' except of his 'weaknesses'. The norm for authentic ministry is not a 'third-heaven' mysticism but a first-earth, incarnational, cruciform lifestyle of trials which give credence to being a servant of Jesus Christ.

c) Finally, Paul explains again the paradoxical reason for boasting about his weaknesses (12:7–10).
In fact, Paul confesses, that incredible, exalted spiritual experience – still fresh in the mind – had to be paid for by a 'thorn in … [the] flesh'.

Whatever this was, it was not enough to impede his ministry even if, on one account, it perhaps impaired his appearance (some believe the 'thorn' was eye trouble, referring to Galatians 4:13,15; 6:11, but a visionary with eye trouble who can't get his prayers for healing answered can't be a very spiritual person, can he?). And Paul is quite specific that he came to understand his 'thorn' as both satanically inspired and God-given as a means of keeping him from becoming conceited – as if to underline the danger inherent in such 'out of this world' experiences. The cost though paid in unanswered prayers for healing was far more than compensated for by the gift of sufficient grace. Since his 'weaknesses' are invariably occasions for discovering afresh that grace is more than enough, he yet again repeats his determination to

216

'boast' in them. Just as the gospel light shines in earthen vessels, so the power of God is perfected in human weakness (12:10).

Paul therefore believes he displays the hallmarks of an authentic apostle since he has the scars to prove it. He does the miracles associated with the apostolic witness (12:12, cf. the accounts in Acts), but with the added mark – equally apostolic, if not more so – of perseverance. Nothing is easier than to have hyped up the expectation for the miraculous if you know you are leaving town on the next flight after the 'miracle service' is over. Sticking around might damage the PR, and force you to deal with the pastoral problems left behind in those who expected too much and were overdisappointed.

But Paul cares for the Corinthians too much to pose as a spiritual technician. He will not burden them and loves them as a father (12:14–15). He has been playing the fool but only in Christ and only to build them up (12:19). The savage irony that Paul employs in the so-called 'fool's discourse' in Second Corinthians masks a divine wisdom that aims to out-flank the Corinthians' mindset and change the way they look at Christian ministry.

So how can we sum up what wise fools look like?
Os Guinness suggests a number of ways:

• *Wise fools are full of exuberant joy and laughter.*
Twenty-two years old and the oldest son of Pietro de Bernadone, Assisi's richest cloth merchant, he was given the nickname 'Francesco', but we know him as Francis. Challenged by Jesus to renounce everything, he was promised that what he had previously abhorred would become sweet to him.

Disturbed by God one day while out riding, he came upon a leper. Fighting back his disgust and revulsion, he dismounted, kissed the leper, remounted and rode off a changed man, radiant with joy. As Os Guinness puts it in his wonderful book, *The Call*, 'Francis of Assisi had been turned upside down and become God's jester, God's juggler, God's fool' – in G.K. Chesterton's words, the 'court fool of the King of Paradise'.[15] James Houston writes:

As finite beings with infinite desires, we live comical lives full of incongruities. Perhaps God, too, is the cosmic and compassionate comedian, because if he is God, he will have the last laugh. The Christian goes about the world tongue-in-cheek, as God's clown, knowing that the mask he wears on earth, will one day become a real face in heaven. By laughter we acknowledge the human condition and seek the transcendent power of God.[16]

Only fools and martyrs relish this secret humour. With them it is only a short step from the ridiculous to the sublime. As Francis shows us – and many others since – the sublime is often best preserved, in our grimly pragmatic age, by the hilarious sense of the ridiculous that only fools and martyrs show. For one thing they show that God is not self-conscious or worried about peer pressure, not primly concerned for His image, or what people might think of Him. God's mere association with us, in fact, ought to cause Him maximum embarrassment, but He seems able to shrug it off. This is no plea for stupid irrationality, or weird eccentricity for its own sake, but for fools for Christ's sake, unashamed romantics and lovers of God, and a few more spiritual jokers in the secular pack.

Harry Blamires once told of being followed and chased by a lamb – yes, that's right, a lamb. In our day, he said, we are less likely to feel God's demand as the 'hound of heaven' breathing threateningly down our necks and more likely to feel it as an embarrassment.[17] But that is the disconcerting tenor of our message. 'To be confronted by the gospel is to be chased by a lamb and that affronts our dignity.' When a Chancellor of the Exchequer once wanted to mock the weakness of the Opposition spokesman's attack on him, he said it felt as though he had been 'savaged by a sheep'. Blamires concludes, 'The Christian's lot is to be chased by a Lamb and to be overtaken by a Lamb. It is to have one's pride and self-centredness savaged by a Lamb'. *Only fools and martyrs represent this wise folly in the world.*

• *Wise fools show the full extent of discipleship in a half-hearted world.* 'In a controlling, calculating age,' observes Os Guinness,

the world's ideal is always to be in charge, never to be caught out – in short to be 'nobody's fool'. On the contrary, say the fools for Christ, in a world gone mad through its own worldly wisdom, true wisdom is to 'go mad for God' even at the price of being hopelessly vulnerable – to be 'everybody's fools'.[18]

The German Lutheran pastor Dietrich Bonhoeffer was lecturing in the United States when World War II broke out. Friends urged him to stay, conscious of the danger he faced in returning to Germany. But Bonhoeffer wrote:

> I have had the time to think and pray about my situation and that of my nation and to have God's will for me clarified. I have come to the conclusion that I have made a mistake in coming to America. I shall have no right to participate in the reconstruction of Christian life in Germany after the war if I do not share the trials of this time with my people. Christians in Germany face the terrible alternative of either willing the defeat of their nation in order that Christian civilisation may survive, or willing the victory of their nation and thereby destroying civilisation. I know which of these alternatives I must choose, but I cannot make that decision in security.[19]

Bonhoeffer was foolish to go, absurd to renounce self-interest and to go back. But go back he did. He did not, of course, live to help reconstruct the Church after the war; he was murdered by the Nazis in Flossenburg hours before the Russians liberated the camp. But his vision and courage have impacted Christians throughout the Western world ever since, and his word and witness still contribute to the reconstruction of the Church in our time. *Only fools and martyrs know how this happens!*

- *Wise fools stand before the world as a counter-cultural sign.*

Succumbing to the same temptation as Paul's opponents, Os Guinness argues that today's Church has bought in to the culture around it. It considers its chief task to be relevant and user-friendly. 'For many Christians the Christian life is now the good life. It simply "goes better with Jesus" even if there is no God and no Resurrection. *Against such attempts the holy fools stand as a weeping road block ... Holy folly is a counter-cultural stance.*'[20]

Wise fools proclaim that God's ways are not our ways. A wise fool celebrates that God's greatest miracles are often huge jokes. Isaac was one of His most uproarious wisecracks, for the child called Isaac (which means 'laughter') wipes the grin of cynicism off unbelieving faces and replaces it with a side-splitting guffaw of amazement and faith. The tragedy is manmade; the comedy, divine.

The new birth, like the virgin birth, is hugely hilarious; the cross is a dazzling paradox, the resurrection is an enormous surprise sprung on a sceptical world; every outpouring of the Spirit leaves us full of mirth like drunken men, prolific with new songs.

Paul's fool's discourse returns us to where he began his argument with the Corinthians – the folly of the cross, which is wiser than human wisdom (1 Cor. 1:18ff.). To those who demand a demonstration of power, the gospel offers the omnipotent weakness of God; to those who demand evidence of argument, the apostolic message offers the compelling logic of redeeming love. If this is folly, it is divine folly; if this is madness, it is magnificent madness.

By now, the criteria for authentic spiritual ministry (or leadership) is surely clear. On 13 January 1522, Martin Luther wrote to his friend Philip Melancthon, warning him about the so-called 'super-spiritual prophets' arising in his time. Now in hindsight, Luther may have misread these prophetic pioneers but his advice about the tests of spiritual authenticity remains valid:

> In order to explore their individual spirit you should inquire whether they have experienced spiritual distress, and the divine birth, death and hell. If you should hear that all their experiences are pleasant, quiet, devout (as they say), and spiritual, then don't approve of them even if they should say they were caught up to the third heaven.[21]

Paul's overriding concern which has been the point at issue all along is *theological*; at stake is the irreducible understanding of God in the light of Jesus and the cross and all that this implies about Christian ministry. So Paul ends on the same note with which he began: 'For to be sure ... [Christ] was crucified in weakness, yet he lives by God's power. Likewise, we are weak in him, yet by God's power we will live with him to serve you' (2 Cor: 13:4; cf. 10:4–5). This is the paradox at the heart of the gospel and at the dynamic heart of Christian ministry

which only fools and martyrs know.
Michael Card sings God's wisdom, which is foolish to us, made known in Jesus, whose family thought He was mad ...

> When we in our foolishness thought we were wise
> he played the fool and he opened our eyes
> When we in our weakness believed we were strong
> He became helpless to show we were wrong
> And so we follow God's own fool
> For only the foolish can tell;
> Believe the unbelievable; Come be a fool as well.
>
> So come lose your life for a carpenter's son
> For a madman who died for a dream
> And you'll have the faith his first followers had
> And you'll feel the weight of the beam.
> So surrender the hunger to say you must know
> Have the courage to say I believe
> For the power of paradox opens our eyes
> And blinds those who say they can see.

'God's Own Fool'
Michael Card, used by permission

Austen Farrer says: 'He who gave himself to us first as an infant, crying in a cot, he who was hung up naked on the wood, does not stand on his own dignity. If Jesus is willing to be in us, and to let us show him to the world, it's a small thing that we should endure being fools for Christ's sake, and be shown up by the part we play.'[22]
Who is sufficient for these things? Only those wise enough to be fools for Christ's sake whose wisdom is the word of the cross and the Spirit of God.

REVIEW

16
THROUGH A GLASS, DARKLY

Now we see but a poor reflection as in a mirror; then we shall see face to face. Now I know in part; then I shall know fully, even as I am fully known. **(1 Corinthians 13:12)**

The seminar was rather ominously billed as *The Leader's Spirituality*. It was a sidebar session for ministers at a large Christian festival, and I was the guest speaker. Now you understand my using the word 'ominously'. What, I asked myself, did I know about such arcane matters and how could my presentation avoid being airbrushed beyond the bounds of good conscience? As so often in Christian ministry, you wonder how you ever agreed to do something. I decided, like the most streetwise in a rugby scrum, to get my retaliation in first.

In my experience, seminars with titles as grandiloquent as this one attract only two types of customer: those who come *warily* and those who come *wearily*. The *wary* approach such events expecting to be offered a quick-fix solution with seven easy and foolproof steps to ensuring a vibrant spiritual life. But their wariness is the result of having been disappointed before. To all such who turned up that day to hear me, I was able to promise that I aimed quite deliberately to disappoint them; in fact I guaranteed to disappoint them! The *weary* come guardedly, as I sensed they did that day, expecting another bucket-load of guilt and condemnation to be heaped on their faithful heads. I hoped to disappoint them too; it was, in fact, my specific intention to do just that. To anyone who feels either way about the matter in hand, I offer reassurance; do not worry: in the Great Prayer Marathon, I am right behind you.

The title may also give pause for thought for other reasons. 'Spirituality' is not so much a 'buzz' word as a 'fuzz' word. In common usage, it seems to refer to a bewilderingly wide range of subjective experiences, variously suggestive of the human search for identity, or meaning, or transcendence and variously expressed as mystical awareness, oneness with nature, or self-fulfilment.

The Church has often muddied the waters here by its confusion as to what 'spiritual' means: religious versus secular or mundane; non-material or incorporeal as over against physical; mystical, as having to do with the inner rather than the outer life of the believer; devotional as over against activist or even intellectual; sensational in contrast to ordinary. But Christian spirituality is the way the whole person responds to the actions of the Holy Spirit and relishes His indwelling. It would be better to come clean here and speak, as Gordon Fee has passionately insisted we should, of *Holy Spirit*uality. This is in line with the Eastern Orthodoxy tradition as represented by the great liturgical theologian, Alexander Schmemann. It is important, he writes, 'to stress that the very essence of Christian spirituality is that it concerns and embraces the whole of life ... which Paul defines as "living and walking in the Spirit"'.[1]

With this firmly in mind, I venture my personal suggestions on how as a Christian leader you may stay 'spiritual'.

Live off the capital of close encounters with God.

The pietistic tradition of a daily 'quiet time' is a noble one and serves many well. But I suspect that it is 'more honour'd in the breach than in the observance'. It fits some types of personality and temperament better than others in enabling us to maintain a healthy relationship with the Lord. The stories passed down to us of Luther or Wesley rising daily at 4am to spend hours in prayer have proved a millstone round too many necks and reflect, I suspect, a selective reading of Church History.

The more freewheeling ways in which other saints equally faithful have sustained vital union with God have been airbrushed out of the accounts by the legalistic doorkeepers of evangelical piety. I doubt that Jesus had a rigid *daily* programme of devotional discipline. Certainly He rose early to pray on occasions, especially on days of decision or in seasons of crisis. He prayed before a pressured day of ministry to the sick and needy (Mark 1:35); before choosing the Twelve (Luke 6:12); and supremely in Gethsemane, where He 'offered up prayers and petitions with loud cries and tears to the one who could save him from death' (Heb. 5:7). And who has not thrown themselves on God's mercy for help in critical times? But, for the most part, I suggest, Jesus *lived off the capital of supreme moments of disclosure.* In particular, He ministered in the good of His baptism and transfiguration. It was by John the Baptist that His emerging sense of vocation was confirmed, by the Divine Voice that His identity was secured, and by His Father's love that He was nourished in His deepest being. In that baptism, Jesus was established as God's Son and Servant King and anointed by the Spirit who empowered Him for ministry. All of which was endorsed and renewed on the Mount of Transfiguration.

Dallas Willard expresses a similar caution about *personal guidance* – almost an article of the creed in my pietistic heritage. His insight is worth quoting at length. Willard warns against a 'message-a-minute' view of our relationship with God. 'In this view', he writes,

> God is either telling you what to do at every turn of the road, or he is at least willing and available to you if only you ask him. I do not believe that either the Bible or our shared experience in the way of Christ will substantiate this picture. There is no evidence in the life of Peter or Paul for example, that they were constantly receiving communication from God.

Willard presses his case with reference to Jesus.

> The union Christ had with his Father was the greatest we can conceive of in this life, if indeed we can conceive it. Yet *there is no indication that he was constantly awash with revelation as to what he should do.* His union with the Father was so great that he was at all times obedient. Yet this obedience was something that rested in his mature will and understanding of his life before God, not on always being told 'now do this' or 'now do that' with regard to every detail of his life.[2]

As for Paul, in reaffirming his call and defending the validity of his apostleship against his critics, he invariably harks back to his Damascus

Road experience, just as the apostle Peter recalls the memory of the Transfiguration to authenticate his authority (2 Pet. 1:18). So Paul counsels Timothy: 'I give you this instruction *in keeping with the prophecies once made about you* so that by following them you may fight the good fight' (1 Tim. 1:18). The word to all engaged in Christian ministry is to live off their spiritual capital: 'reaffirm your call to ministry'. Standing in the strength of such prophecies we may remind the Lord and ourselves, 'You called me to this.'

Paul urges Timothy: 'Do not neglect your gift, which was given you through a prophetic message when the body of elders laid their hands on you' (1 Tim. 4:14). Here, a quite specific occasion is being recalled to bolster Timothy's faint heart. We may dispute what 'ordination' means or whether we should not jettison the whole concept. But rebrand this how we must, we lose an anchor in the storm when we dispense with these formative, foundational events in which the Church officially endorses our ministry. Luther often rebuked the devil in the midst of severe spiritual attack with the only weapon to hand: 'I am a baptised person.' So, with Timothy, reassert our giftedness for ministry and the Church's confirmation of it. It has not gone away; you cannot lose it. You can grow weary in well-doing; you can grow sluggish, you can unconsciously begin to withdraw from expending energy for fear of getting overtired; then remember your gifts and calling and pray with the psalmist: 'sustain me with a willing spirit'. Above all, 'fan into flame the gift of God, which is in you through the laying on of my hands. For God did not give us a spirit of timidity, but a spirit of power, of love and of self-discipline' (2 Tim. 1:6–7). Again, whatever the laying on of hands did or did not mean for you – or, indeed, whether hands were laid on you at all – *renew daily a total reliance on the Holy Spirit*. In doing so, you may, as Henri Nouwen suggests, hear the voice of the Spirit reaffirming your baptism, assuring you that you too are a beloved son, or daughter, you too are accepted – someone, remarkably, with whom, in Christ, the Father is well pleased! As Brennan Manning often says, 'Think of yourself as the one who is called "the disciple Jesus loves".' And join me in praying regularly and occasionally desperately: 'Do not … take your Holy Spirit from me' (Psa. 51:11).

Make room for mystery.

Trusting the Holy Spirit will demand at least this. Perhaps the most important thing we can learn about the New Testament view of the Holy Spirit is eschatological. It is that we live in the 'now and not yet' tension of a kingdom that has come and yet is still to come, of a Spirit who brings us rich blessings which are merely the first fruits of the final harvest, tastings of the powers of the age to come.

Our spirituality will, then, be about learning to live with a certain incompleteness and imperfection both in others and in ourselves. It will be to stay poised and alert and eager for as much of God as we can enjoy now without claiming too much or settling for too little. It is to get things in perspective. We do not see everything subject to human control but we do see the Truly Human One, Jesus, crowned with glory and honour, as the pioneer of our ultimate salvation and the standard-bearer of our restored dominion. Meanwhile, we should beware of trying to manage the mystery. The Spirit blows where He wills. Being the generous man that he was, Selwyn Hughes, as he often did in the course of our travels together, shared with me a good 'quote' he had come across: 'Mystery is not the absence of meaning but the presence of a meaning that we cannot fully comprehend.'

Reflecting critically on the tendency to opt for a less threatening God, Mark Buchanan recounts how strongly in Bible college he was taught to rail against Rudolph Bultmann's demythologisation which stripped the New Testament of its supernatural dimension. But, says Buchanan, he discovered that his evangelical training had served just as well. It achieved what he calls the 'demysterious-isation' of Scripture:

> My main interpretative task, as I understood it, was to distill from the Bible principles, technique, a series of points to ponder, or steps to take. It was to compress the infinite into the numeric, corral the miraculous into the pragmatic, tidy the messy earthiness of the Bible into a neat-edged moralism, parse its poetry into prose – or worse, propositions. In short it was to banish mystery.

How ironic, Buchanan suggests, that 'Jesus' famous statement to Nicodemus, you must be born again, has in our hands, been turned into a slogan and a formula. Out of Jesus' mouth, in Nicodemus's ear, that proclaimed a staggering mystery. It was the ultimate anti-formula.' It was, he insists, 'a description of the in-breaking and surprising move of God. This is something we can't work for, work up, predict, direct. It doesn't slot neatly into a program. You just hear it coming and fling yourself headlong into the hurricane.'[3]

From this there develops a 'working relationship' with the Holy Spirit in which our freedom of action is always a result of His Lordship, but during which it is not always easy to say of any particular action or effect either 'I did it' or 'He did it'. Study Acts 16 as a cameo of the mixing of the miraculous and the mundane. The apostolic team are 'kept by the Holy Spirit' from preaching in Asia, prevented by 'the Spirit of Jesus' from entering Bithynia, and invited in a night 'vision' by a 'man of Macedonia' (was it perchance a vision of Alexander of Macedon himself?). But at once we learn that the apostolic team themselves 'concluded' and decided on their next move, arriving where they 'expected to find a place of prayer' and are then 'invited' by Lydia to her house and 'persuaded' to stay. Was the Holy Spirit any less marvellously involved in these rational decisions and intuitively human moves than in the more obviously supernatural ones? No. This is simply an everyday sample of working where God is working, and of working with Him (see John 5). Better than straining to master what Peterson calls 'the technology of the supernatural'[4] is to stay the course as sensitive assistant to the 'senior partnership' of the Holy Spirit.

Own your own story 'warts and all'[5]
As Anne Lamott says, 'Forgiveness is giving up all hope of having a better past.'[6] The old preachers talked of the 'memory of sin in the saint'. They were referring to Paul's own testimony to Timothy that even though he was a 'blasphemer and a persecutor and a violent man' he was 'shown mercy' (1 Tim. 1:13). As one of those old preachers, William Clow, notes, 'the man who remembers with a humbling glance, the sin from which he has been delivered by Christ's cross, has the lover's desire in his thought and the lover's note in his prayers'. Forgiven much, he loves much. 'God permits us to remember our forgiven sin,' says Clow, 'only as long as they may be spurs and goads to our will, incentives to our trust, sources of love and devotion.'[7]

This is not cheap grace. This is not to lessen the heinousness of the sin that was committed or to minimise the anguish it caused to those near and far. But it is to say that prodigals – even those who make a mad, late dash into prodigality – have one thing going for them: the last pathetic shreds of self-righteousness have been torn from them and tossed aside as filthy rags. It can leave one strangely free of self-pretence and self-delusion. Isaac Bashevis Singer recounts an old rabbinic story about a pious Jew who falls into sexual sin and confesses to the rabbi: 'I have forfeited my share in the world to come.' To his surprise, the rabbi congratulates him: 'The master of the universe has plenty of paid servants, but of those who would serve him for nothing, he has hardly any at all.' Where sin abounded, grace abounded even more, and leaves us free to live the Godward life. The 'heart is deceitful above all things and desperately wicked' and there is no denying it; but grace is 'above' all things, the cross-made remedy for all that lies beneath its glory. So remember your greatest failure, your most grievous betrayal. Did you get forgiveness for it? Then remain forgiven, get over it, keep short accounts with God, and stay in the grip of grace.

To tell one's own story is to be astonished again at the blessed contradictions that constrain the narrative and give to the Christian life its peculiarly paradoxical shape. I know that paradox can sometimes be the first refuge of the lazy mind. But this is not necessarily so. For the Christian paradox is unavoidable. As I see it, paradox lies at the heart of our dying–rising Easter faith. In this strange dialectic of the gospel, even our sin and failure can be mysteriously co-opted for God's gracious purposes, and human disobedience somehow incorporated into the saving plan (eg Rom. 11:30–33). The dialectical nature of Christian existence makes our own destinies replete with mystery that we cannot always satisfactorily resolve. Take the 'once saved always saved' conundrum. Far more rigorous theological minds than mine make noble efforts at tackling the question, and it is right they should. But reflecting on one's life as an ongoing personal story helps to hold the mystery here intact. If the Bible is a textbook of theological propositions, then we must stand back as neutral observers and seek to subsume all its seemingly contradictory directives under one consistent *schema*. This may or may not be possible or satisfactory. I leave others to judge.

But my point is just this: if the Bible is actually the story of God which is still ongoing and we are here and now participating in it, then we are not in a position to stand aloof from it with lofty detachment and attempt to 'reconcile' perseverance, eternal security, conditional faith and the risk of apostasy in one remit.[8]
We are not *outside* the Bible looking in on God's story from a vantage point of supposed objectivity so that we can weigh one item against another and 'balance' them out. Rather, we *indwell* the Bible; we are *in* the story the Bible tells. And right in the thick of the story as it unfolds we hear both voices as God's, saying equally crucial things at different stages of the journey.

We only see the need to reconcile what seem conflicting voices or, indeed, to opt for one over the other if we think of ourselves as standing apart from the unfolding drama and able to offer detached comment on it. Rather, on the journey round the mountain we hear God reassuringly say, 'Do not be afraid; the road is safe; I am with you all the way; you will make it to the end' *and*, at some stage, of necessity, we need to hear God warn: 'Don't go near the edge. If you disobey Me, you will fall to your death.' I am not here attempting a philosophical answer or even venturing a theological one; but merely speaking of spirituality and of the need in owning one's own story to recognise mystery again and the joyous challenge of walking by faith not sight.

If, as I did, you can survive the headline which read, 'Vicar marries wife's sister', anything is possible. Once or twice I have been brave enough to demonstrate 'consecrated truculence' as Oswald Chambers terms it (cf. Acts 4:18–20); too often it has been the unconsecrated variety on show. I write daily Bible-reading notes but cannot quite shake off the uneasy feeling entertained in childhood that the Bible is too precious a book to be given the rushed fast-food breakfast treatment and, like a fine wine, should be saved up for special occasions.

I am predisposed to doubt. When Neil Armstrong stepped onto the moon I wondered if it had been staged in the New Mexico desert. One small step for him; one large leap for credulity. I think differently now. When President Nixon grandiosely asserted of the moon landings that this was the greatest week in the world's history since the creation I knew he was 2,000 years late. I have not changed my mind about that. Apart from the recognition that 'I used to be indecisive, but now I am not so sure', I am now more aware of the vagaries of the 'spiritual weather' and the need for the appropriate footwear along the way. Which leads to the next reflection.

Recognise that there are seasons of the soul and that the way personal spirituality works changes over time.

Jacques Ellul, the distinguished French Professor of Law and Protestant lay theologian, suggests that our relationship with God can be usefully compared to our relationship with wife or husband.[9] Loving relationships like this go through various stages, deepening and evolving in the process.

Stage 1: Love is *passion* and ecstasy, the 'explosive discovery of the other' but this cannot be maintained at its volcanic peak.

Stage 2: Love evolves into *common responsibilities* (for children, usually). Complementarity works in the totality of life. Critics see this as a decline into slippers and boredom, says Ellul. But, he suggests, we may instead see a deeper love emerging which is integrated with all aspects of living. Love becomes a shared battle for life, a battle *against* weariness and boredom. 'The acceptance of joint responsibility is the test of the veracity of love declared.'

Stage 3: Ellul calls this stage the stage of '*recognition*, the moment when one truly comes to know the other'. This is a kind of existential distancing which can go either way: either to separation or to a fresh ability to see and know the other clearly as never before and to value them in their own right.

Stage 4 is the period of *inseparability*, when we cannot think of one without the other, as love extends into deep and trusting friendship.

Stage 5, says Ellul, is union; in one sense, two people only become 'one flesh' at the end of a marriage rather than at its beginning. Is this why, curiously, some spouses end up looking physically a bit like each other? Certainly in one deep sense, we do not make love, love makes us.

Somewhat akin to Ignatian spirituality, the Protestant Ellul takes the growth of a marriage relationship as analogous to our relationship with

God, however dimly we can see how our spirituality grows.

First comes *the revelation of divine truth*, of God's love, of forgiveness effecting a new birth and empowerment (conversion and baptism with the Spirit) which penetrates my whole being. Here we are rooted and grounded in love, and know ourselves cherished and accepted at the deepest level of our personality.

Stage two sees this *deepen into responsibility*, a covenant partnership, a shared sense of mission and the tasks that must be done on the basis of that initial revelation.

This leads, thirdly, to *the recognition of 'the otherness of the other'* in His majesty and glory, so that a certain distancing or even 'remoteness' ensues and we may become discouraged by the 'lack of sustained dialogue'.

Next comes the time of *inseparability* when the Wholly Other is no nearer but I cannot think of myself without Him. It is not a question of whether I am a Christian but of what would become of me without Him. Not to have a relationship with Him has become inconceivable. If He is not there, I am not there.

The last stage is that of *union*, when I fully accept the fact that my life is in Christ and that I can only die to self because, in fact, the incarnation of Jesus Christ has achieved all that I could hope for in terms of relationship with God. And this is true, says Ellul, *'even in routine, in the silence of God, in the nongranting of prayers, in exile, for the whole history unfolds from the initial point where God was present even if only once in my life, and I have to live the rest of my life on the basis of this victory, preserving this memory that shapes my whole existence.'*

The title of this chapter, 'Through a Glass, Darkly', which is the King James Version of 1 Corinthians 13:12, is largely discounted by contemporary scholars and translators. It probably owes too much to Numbers 12:6–8 (the passage Paul is undoubtedly echoing) which contrasts the enigmatic quality of the dreams and visions ('riddles', ESV) entrusted to ordinary prophets with the personal face-to-face revelation vouchsafed to Moses. Paul would surely not allow that the new covenant ministry comes off worse by comparison with Moses.

Quite the reverse (2 Cor. 3:7–11). What has been revealed to us in the gospel is not faulty as if needing to be made reliable, nor even fuzzy as if waiting to be made clear; but it is partial, anticipating completeness in face-to-face encounter. Aware of this, we do well to hold even our firmest and most absolute convictions 'with a sense of humility and a sense of humour'.[10] 'The man who thinks he knows something does not yet know as he ought to know.' Full knowledge will finally be what it has truly, if partially, been all along – the disclosure of *love* (1 Cor. 8:2–3).

Cast your net wide when it comes to spiritual techniques and disciplines; grab anything that gives you access to God and use varied means to appropriate grace.

For what it's worth, I note that in my ministry I have used devotional stratagems that are diverse and used them sporadically. Over forty years the following have been of periodic or permanent assistance to my soul.

- The *Minister's Prayer Book* (a Lutheran publication of daily prayers and readings that helped greatly early on in my ministry) as did Donald Baillie's small book of prayers, and more recently, Phyllis Tickle's *The Divine Hours*, a manual of prayers for every day of the year.
- I once worked out a 'prayer hour' based on Dick Eastman's teaching, using the outline of the *Lord's Prayer* which served me for several years as a pattern for regular praise and prayer – and which I am thinking I need to revive and revisit.
- In some very dark months in which suicidal thoughts were dominant and I could no more read my Bible or pray than climb Everest, I fell back on the ancient practice of the Eastern Church of repeating like a mantra the *'Jesus Prayer'* ('Lord Jesus Christ, Son of God, have mercy on me – a sinner'). Sometimes hyperventilating with stress and acute anxiety, I learned to synchronise this prayer with deep breathing and, as promised on the label, it got me through.
- I have occasionally – and not as much as I would have wanted – made *solitary and silent retreat*. Once I spent three life-changing days – in part, wonderful, in part, scary – in close encounter with the Holy Spirit. On those occasions I used Henri Nouwen's marvellous

reflections on the parable of the prodigal son which were themselves based on Nouwen's meditation on Rembrandt's famous painting of the prodigal's return to the Father, which hangs in the Hermitage Gallery in St Petersburg (and a copy of which faces me when I sit at my desk).

- In recent years I have come to value *icons* for their meditative value. I was stimulated in this by a visit to the major post-communist exhibition of Russian iconography at the V&A museum in London. Like many evangelicals, I now have a copy of Rublev's 'Trinity' above my desk.

- I now rely on *liturgy* to an extent that would amaze my non-conformist forebears, startles me, and puzzles my friends. In classical liturgical structure, I find blessed relief from the tyranny of my own mood or, better still, from the emotional hype of the unrelenting cheerleaders that pass muster for worship leaders in too many churches. The Eucharist – sung wherever possible and with as much incense as allowable – sustains me on my journey. I have come to appreciate the clergy by other criteria than their charisma or personality. I increasingly value the example they set of submission to what is given to them – surely a foundational evangelical premise.

- I am far from unique in finding *music*, too, a constant stimulus. No longer the great hymns or worship songs alone but the classical choral music of the Church to which I have come as a late discoverer stumbling on buried treasure. A 'serendipity moment' several years ago led us to the St Endellion music festival in North Cornwall whose Easter and summer festivals we have frequented whenever possible. We felt it as a personal loss when its founder, the world-famous conductor Richard Hickox, died prematurely last year.

- Like many, I *read* a lot, probably too much, mostly history, political, social and military. At bedtime, I read crime thrillers on the ground that crime is boring and sends me to sleep whereas theology is stimulating and keeps me awake.

- *Poetry* regularly reasserts its attraction, especially on holiday, as it did recently when I embarked on a study of T.S. Eliot's 'Four Quartets' assisted (the purists would be horrified) by several commentaries on the text. I value R.S. Thomas a great deal. No doubt he suits my melancholic turn of mind. But his austere take on faith has helped me come to terms with the absence of God. I have come to see God's absence as the lingering of His presence that evokes a longing for Him. It is, says Thomas, an 'absence that compels me to address it without hope' but 'It is a room I enter from which someone has just gone.' 'What resource have I' asks the poet, 'other than the emptiness without him of my whole being, a vacuum he may not abhor?'[11]

- In recent years, too, *art and paintings* have become a special means of grace. Ken Gire's lovely little book *Windows of the Soul* opened my eyes to experiencing God not so much *in* paintings as *through* paintings. He showed me that great art could be sacramental as windows of the soul through which God's light and beauty flow. His book was the key that helped to make spiritual experiences out of a long-desired trip to Paris to visit the Louvre, the Musée d'Orsay, L'Orangerie and, later, to Amsterdam for the 200th anniversary of the Golden Age of Dutch painting to view the Rembrandts and Vermeers. These artistic experiences enriched our lives, and we now go regularly to the National Gallery.

- Lately, we have developed an interest in the *natural world*, or to be more modest, birds. We were encouraged by our favourite journalist Simon Barnes' delightful book *How to Be a Bad Birdwatcher* to learn to observe birds, however 'badly', and two mornings in a hide at the RSPB's Reserve at Minsmere in Suffolk only fed the bug.

- Of course I have my own favourite *'devotional' writers*, ranging from Frederick Buechner through Brennan Manning to John Piper, Eugene Peterson, Lewis Smedes, Peter Kreeft and Tom Howard, to name but a few. I seem to recall that Martyn Lloyd-Jones scorned the idea of other people doing his devotions for him! In any event, I am just as likely to be 'devotionally' awestruck with 'wonder, love and praise' when immersed in a tightly argued and intensely passionate bit of exegesis by Gordon Fee. Theology is, after all, loving God with your mind.

- Lacking a spiritual director – which I would redress if I had my time over again – I rely on *deep friendship*, especially with one dear friend with whom I check out everything I am feeling, thinking, am writing and planning to do, knowing complete confidence guards the confessions and makes possible the adventure of thought as searches after God and God's truth.

236

- Beyond all this I am conscious of engaging God in a constant conversation all day. Though whether this qualifies as 'prayer without ceasing' no one seems able or willing to say. I aspire to what John Piper relentlessly and extravagantly describes as 'the Godward life'. 'So whether you eat or drink, or whatever you do, do it all for the glory of God': all is *sacrificial* – the offering back of everything we do in praise to God for His glory; all is *sacramental* (see 1 Cor. 10:31) – the receiving of everything that is offered to us as potentially able to be a means of grace to us and glory to God.

What now, where next?

When that indomitable missionary statesman, E. Stanley Jones, explained his ability to fulfil a heavy load of engagements at the age of eighty-seven, he put it down to 'grace, grass, and gumption'. 'Gumption' in his three physical exercises before bedtime. 'Grass' he admitted he had had to change to 'cereal' because people were using the word to refer to marijuana. And 'grace'? Well, that explained everything. He writes, in his inimitable way,

> I have found to my glad surprise that Jesus Christ is energy, stimulus, and fire, but like Moses' burning bush, the bush of my body is not consumed. So his fire is not fever, his energy is not enervating, his stimulus is not just stimulating without any increase in energy. It's real and lifelong and dependable and it works. 'How long are you going to keep this up?' I am asked. I don't know, but I know one thing: I am going to go full steam ahead till the boiler bursts. And I hope my last cry will be, 'I commend my Saviour to you'.[12]

Amen to that!

Finally, come at the challenges of life and ministry from the standpoint of a deep sense of peace.

In my ministry experience I have often found myself poised between being a *rest-seeker* and *risk-taker*. I have felt this as an inner tension in which excitement is mixed with unease. There is an initial and underlying *rest* which, Jesus said, He gives to everyone who comes to

Him to be His disciple. Receiving His rest is the starting point for every move we make. Thereafter, we come at life, we approach ministry, we confront its challenges from a position of 'rest'. We gravitate to it with relief after every endeavour. The grace of 'rest' is the default position for discipleship. As Sam Wells has said in the context of discussing Christian ethics, 'if Christians have learned to take the right things for granted (discipleship), they will more readily experience God's ways with them and the world (grace)'.[13]

As we venture forth in the strength of the rest we have already *received*, we will *find* the new rest that is promised to all who take His yoke upon them and learn of Him. *Only the rest-seekers take risks: only the risk-takers find fresh rest.* Discipleship grants gracious rest as its starting point and promises rest along the way.

Maintaining our poise is difficult and often feels under threat. Losing our peace is fatal. Ministers suffer the mood swings of the Church or find themselves in the middle of the highly charged internal 'to-ing and fro-ing' of competing visions for the Church. Achieving balance here is not a matter of sitting on the fence, of attempting an indifferent neutrality that can only be a betrayal of leadership. What is called for is the kind of spiritual acumen described by Jones and Armstrong as 'counterweighting'. As they explain, 'counterweighting is not a lukewarm moderation that has nothing to offer, but rather a dynamic "centering" that tilts the scales back and forth to maintain a balance over time'.[14]

Christian ministry's task is to attend to the centralities of faith, the fulcrum of cross and resurrection. If this 'centre cannot hold', to paraphrase Yeats, then 'things fall apart' and 'mere anarchy is loosed' upon the Church and within it. If the pivotal point is secure we may risk rocking the see-saw to experience further extremes of praise and lament, contrition and celebration, than a fearful and inhibited status quo has allowed us.[15] If the fulcrum holds firm then we may enjoy, in creative tension, rest *and* risk, habit *and* initiative, order *and* freedom, tradition *and* change. When I personally sense that I have wandered to the far edge of the field to admire some exotic flowers, I retrace my steps to gospel centralities. I readjust my compass at the cross with

Peter Taylor Forsyth. I take a break from overheated spirituality by plunging into the equivalent of a cold bath with Martyn Lloyd-Jones or John Piper. And I feel all the better for it, as if I have had a short, sharp detox at a spiritual health farm.

At one friend's frequent urging, and despite repeated failure, I try to 'keep my spirit sweet'; I attempt to battle against the toxins of comparing myself with others and being jealous of them. I pray often for cleansing from the poisonous competitiveness that bedevils evangelicalism as it does every branch of the Church. 'What shall this man do, Lord?' 'It's none of your business: you follow Me.' I continue to fight the good fight of faith which, more often than not, is the fight *for* faith. In a moment of awareness, I realised why the saints of previous centuries longed so much for heaven: they longed finally to be free of the demons that haunted them, the guilt that shadowed their lives, the lustful thoughts that plagued them, and the perennial habits that still cramped them … I sing joyfully and hopefully with Isaac Watts:

Sin my worst enemy before
Shall vex my eyes and ears no more
My inward foes shall all be slain
Nor Satan break my peace again.

Isaac Watts, 1674–1748

Meanwhile, like you, I trust and travel, knowing that without Jesus I can do nothing, but that with Him it is always fruit-bearing season. By the power of the Spirit, all things are possible.

Well, there it is: *my* personal angle of vision on 'a leader's spirituality'. I hope that both the *wary*, expecting too little, and the *weary*, expecting too much laid upon them, are disappointed and maybe, along with a few others, pleasantly surprised.
From what I've learned, you can be sure that Jesus is all that He is said to be, *and more*, and that A.W. Tozer was right to say that 'the Holy Spirit lives up to the advertising'.

239

17
FACE VALUE

... the light of the gospel of the glory of Christ who is the image of God ... for God, who said 'let light shine out of darkness,' made his light shine in our hearts to give us the light of the knowledge of the glory of God in the face of Christ. But we have this treasure in jars of clay.

(2 Corinthians 4:4–7)

'*He had a face ...*'

The opening words of *The Faces of Jesus* – a collection of nearly 150 images and portraits of Jesus from across the centuries with a beautifully written commentary by the celebrated American writer, Frederick Buechner.

'*He had a face ...*'

Just four words; but for reasons I cannot adequately explain, they moved me to tears. I have loved Jesus all my life. But in that moment I could have clung to him like a sobbing child. I could have hugged him to bits like a long-lost brother returning from exile.

'*He had a face ... it was a human face ... the face of a man.*'[1]

Scholarly opinion now regards it as extremely unlikely that Paul had seen that face of Jesus prior to the Damascus Road experience. Even then – if the Acts accounts are anything to go by – Paul is reticent about what he saw. The visual and auditory are strangely blended. Paul seems primarily concerned with the voice that smote him with the realisation that in hurting Christians he was hurting Jesus; the voice that commanded him and recommissioned him. In fact, the light that shines there in full brilliance like the sun at full noonday strength dazzles and blinds him before it enlightens him. But 'see' is surely what he did. A 'heavenly vision' is how he describes it. 'Have I not seen Jesus our Lord?' he asks the Corinthians (1 Cor. 9:1); and 'last of all he appeared to me' – out of sync, as it were, but on a par with the other post-resurrection appearances (1 Cor. 15:8).

However it happened, the God-light shone into Paul's heart to 'give the light of the knowledge of the glory of God in the face of Jesus Christ' – just as in some other, less dramatic way, no doubt, in some other time and place, that light shone in your heart and mine.

In this intense and profound bit of apostolic text, the visual and auditory are again intriguingly merged. What began as the 'face' became a 'gospel' – 'the light of the gospel of the glory of Christ ...' (2 Cor. 4:4). The 'face of Christ' is a symbol for the gospel. In David Ford's words, the face once seen is now 'a face that is heard'. In this light we see His light.

In the light of Easter, told as gospel, we see light so that everything looks completely different. 'So from now on we regard no-one from a worldly point of view. Though we once regarded Christ in this way, we do so no longer' (2 Cor. 5:16). In the light of Easter, and the Easter gospel, *Jesus* is no longer to be seen as a discredited Messianic pretender, but as the very 'image of God' – the one in whom God is faithfully represented, is fully present and truly revealed. C.H. Spurgeon preaching on this text on Sunday morning, 4 June 1882, said:

> There is wondrous light in the gospel, both for the future and the present. It sets forth to us the glory of Christ, the glory of love, the glory of mercy, the glory of a blood which can wash the blackest white [the sinner clean], the glory of a plea which can make the poorest prayer acceptable, the glory of a living and triumphant Saviour, who having put his hand to the work will not fail nor be discouraged till all the purposes of infinite love shall be achieved by him. This is the 'gospel of the glory of Christ', and the light of it is exceeding clear and bright.

The Easter light that shines 'exceeding clear and bright' in the gospel is the '*light of the knowledge of the glory of God*' so that we see *God* in an entirely new way. We discover what God is like as never before. That face – Paul assures the Corinthians – is the 'human face of God', a human face ravaged by suffering, now radiant with the outshining of the glory of the One Creator God.

In the light of Easter, the *story of Israel* is reconfigured. In this section of the letter Paul is shadowing the prophetic sequence – most clearly patterned in Isaiah – of *new Exodus, new covenant, new kingship, new creation.* The crucified carpenter from Nazareth, executed as an insurrectionist, is now seen to be truly 'the Christ'; He has successfully completed His forty-day journey from cross to crown, from spilling blood to pouring out Spirit, and so is scandalously and gloriously vindicated as the long-awaited Messianic King of God's people who ushers in God's peaceable kingdom.

In the light of Easter, the *landscape of the Roman Imperial world* is also redrawn, for Jesus, not Caesar, is 'Lord'. Rome's vaunted pretensions are punctured, its love of power is subverted by the power of love, and its arrogant claims on human lives are vetoed by a higher authority – bent not on enslaving but on setting free.

In effect, Paul's *entire world is redrawn*. He found that the face of Jesus, marred by suffering but transfigured by resurrection glory, changed his life and reconfigured his world. Like Jacob *before him*, in fighting with God's man he suffers a magnificent defeat, becoming among the first to know that through deadly but life-giving engagement with Christ, we are more than conquerors, we are conquered. Like John Newton *after him*, he succumbs to amazing grace and becomes the chief protagonist of the faith he had once laboured to destroy.

All in all, Easter, in its effect on the world and on us, is an event comparable only to the first morning of creation: 'For God, who said, "Let light shine out of darkness," made his light shine in our hearts.' If Christ's atoning cross is foolishness to Greeks and a scandal to Jews, and if 'the resurrection', as Lesslie Newbigin characteristically put it, 'cannot be accommodated in any understanding of the world except one of which it is the starting point …'[2] and if the Holy Spirit of new covenant can turn Pharisees into apostles, sinners into saints, then – if all this be true – we have stepped over 'in Christ' into what Paul can only describe as a *whole 'new creation'*. 9/11 did not change the world: Easter did. The Enlightenment was pre-empted by about 1,800 years. Knowing this, we need not lose heart. *Nothing upstages Easter.*

In 2006, Mary and I celebrated our fortieth wedding anniversary.[3] The guests at our wedding might well remember that what threatened to upstage our big day was that, for some unaccountable reason, we got married on 30 July 1966, the day England won the World Cup. Never in the course of human conflict have so many Spurgeon's men fled a wedding reception so quickly and left so few relatives behind as on that day. *But nothing can upstage Easter!*

2006 also marked the fortieth anniversary of the *last time* I was asked to speak in this august place. It was my second sermon class. 'Sermon classes' may be described, for the sake of the uninitiated and unscarred, as sacrificial occasions when student preachers offered up their innocent sermons on the altar of judgment to be slain by the withering comments of fellow students and faculty members alike. My second time around at this took place on the same morning as the Aberfan disaster when a mountain of coal slurry slid down and engulfed a primary school in Wales, burying over a hundred small children and their teachers. I learned then that however dark the circumstances, we may never be embarrassed to proclaim the Easter gospel.

Three years earlier, when I stood to preach in sermon class for the *first time*, I found myself speaking within hours of the assassination of John F. Kennedy. I learned then the crucial and enduring truth that we need never be embarrassed to preach this gospel or to name this name or to show this face however awful the world becomes. Easter and its gospel shines its light in the darkest days. People sometimes buttonhole me at Waverley with news of the latest sensation. 'Have you heard, isn't it amazing ... worshippers are receiving gold fillings to their teeth ... don't you think it's wonderful?' Well, I'm quite prepared to be *wonderfulled*, and yield to no one in saying that whatever the Holy Spirit can do and wants to do, He can and will do, and that's fine by me, but I have to admit to being a tad *under*whelmed: 'Well ... yes, it's wonderful ... but actually, I haven't got over the resurrection yet!'

And all this is a *treasure we have in clay pots* (4:7). Clay pots? Small earthenware containers perhaps to serve as oil lamps. Not terribly flattering and in any case quite a put down for an evangelical culture obsessed with celebrity. But clay pots? Is that to emphasise *cheapness or weakness*? Cheapness – what is inferior and ordinary, in contrast with the treasure; weakness – what is fragile and vulnerable, in contrast with the power of God? Perhaps both. I confess to both. Paul Beasley-Murray once introduced me as a conference speaker by saying, 'Philip has had a chequered career.' I suspect that should I, by grace, reach the goal, I may be greeted with a wry smile that says, 'So you made it after all?' From the worst that happens to us, the best is wrought, as I can personally testify. Forsyth was in typically prophetic mood when he wrote:

> You will come to a pass one day when the glorious world falls from you, the dearest must leave you, your nerve perhaps is broken, you have no witness of a good conscience, and your self-respect no more sustains you. Poetry and happiness, knowledge and sensibility end, perhaps in moral wreck. That is the time for real revelation. Man's extremity is God's great opportunity. Then, as never before, you need a light that does not fail. You need the revelation indeed, the one certainty for which you would exchange all the mere impressions you ever felt. And then, as when the first light arose, it rises with a new creation ...[4]

So it has proved to be for me. There is so much to be thankful for that I wonder, as Chesterton did, what atheists do with their gratitude.

Like you, then, I've had my fair share of hardships and knocks – none on an apostolic scale and many of them self-inflicted wounds. But despite the fragility and failure, the light still shines through. We have often been hard pressed and overstressed but somehow not crushed and the light has still shone through. More often than perhaps we care to admit, we are perplexed and have no idea what to do, but somehow the bafflement has stopped short of utter despair and the light still shines through. Though sometimes at our wits' end, we have surprisingly not found ourselves at faith's end, and the light has still shone through.

And, in the strange sacramental mystery that is Christian ministry, we become broken bread and poured out wine for others so that our last drop of energy seems squeezed out of us that others might live. Easter dying in us; Easter rising in them – that's how the light shines through.

On the BBC's popular programme, *The Antiques Roadshow,* members of the public bring family heirlooms and attic-stored collectables to be valued by experts in the field. On one episode, a woman brought two stained, cracked porcelain pots and presented them for valuation. They were identified as commonplace houseware from Japan, dated to the 1930s. When the atomic bomb was dropped on Hiroshima, the porcelain was fired again, this time to over 1,300 degrees centigrade so that the pots had begun to crack and the glaze had started to crystallise. The valuer said two things: these were two very ordinary domestic utensils and in themselves they were worth nothing. Then he added, but *in connection with the story they tell, they are priceless.*

And so it is with you and me, for we are entrusted with the treasure of a story to tell; only let us not undervalue this precious gospel, for if we take it at its full 'face value' and do not undersell it, then so might the world. We are called to live always before the face of Christ and to show His face to the world – always praying 'Shine, Jesus, Shine'. Since we have this ministry and the light entrusted to it, we do not lose our nerve. And when we see Him we shall be like Him. As Buechner says, the face of Jesus is *'the face of our own secret and innermost destiny …'*

18
SECOND SIGHT

My heart is not proud, O Lord; my eyes are not haughty;
I do not concern myself with great matters or things too wonderful
for me. But I have stilled and quieted my soul; like a weaned child
with its mother, like a weaned child is my soul within me.
O Israel, put your hope in the LORD both now and for evermore.
(Psalm 131:1–3)

This short psalm may be read first at the most personal and intimate level. It is the testimony of a man whose 'eyes are not raised too high' (v.1b, ESV) who has achieved a *modest* faith. He has come to a humble trust in God by renouncing grandiose ideas and plans – those 'great matters' which are 'too wonderful' for him (v.1b). Big ideas can produce big heads. Impulsive and far-fetched vision often overinflates our faith, and then only time and trouble teach us a deeper and maturer trust. To achieve this is to reverse the trend. Chesterton's judgment still applies:

> what we suffer from today is humility *in the wrong place*. Modesty has moved from an organ of ambition. Modesty has settled on the organ of conviction; where it was never meant to be. A man was meant to be doubtful about himself, but undoubting about the truth; this has been exactly reversed. Nowadays the part of a man that a man does assert is exactly the part he ought not to assert – himself. The part he doubts is exactly the part he ought not to doubt – the Divine Reason.[1]

And the psalmist has received grace to do just that. To risk being less sure of ourselves is to become more sure of God. We may then accept limitation without becoming frustrated. We may come to terms with what is and what is not our 'measure of faith'; we may arrive at a more precise understanding of our particular gifts and how this realisation both fulfils and limits us and, as a consequence, frees others with different gifts to flourish; we will not 'boast beyond our proper limits' but come to embrace a more restricted sphere of ministry without losing our expansiveness of heart.[2]

In all such ways, the agitated excitement of youthful faith gives way to a calmer, less frenetic confidence. In short, the psalmist is growing out of an infantile dependency on God (v.2).

Like a 'weaned child' the psalmist is no longer fretful and demanding, no longer clamouring to have his needs met – and met sooner rather than later. But now the psalmist is beginning to trust that God knows what he needs before He is asked. As commentator Artur Weiser puts it:

> … just as the child gradually breaks off the habit of regarding his mother as a means of satisfying his own desires and learns to love her for her own sake, so the worshipper after a struggle has reached an attitude of mind in which he desires God for himself and not as a means of fulfilment of his own desires.[3]

Famed writer Frederick Buechner was consoled by this psalm when he and his wife spent many agonising hours pacing the corridor outside their gravely ill daughter's hospital room. 'I loved God,' Buechner says,

> not so much in spite of there being nothing in it for me, but almost because there was nothing in it for me. For the first time in my life, there in the wilderness, I caught a glimpse of what it must be like to love God for his own sake, to love him no matter what.[4]

When grief is exhausted, when anxiety has grown numb, beyond the screamingly desperate praying, when there is nothing left … there arrives almost unbidden a strange empowerment to calm the soul and quiet the spirit that enables us to love, or at least, survive. Miraculously, it seems to us, and against the odds, we may achieve what the hymn writer Anna Waring called, 'a heart at leisure from itself'.[5]

So far, we have interpreted 'great matters' as having to do with personal ambition which gets above itself and ventures into realms beyond its remit. As such, the psalm offers a lesson in humility. But other interpreters suggest that 'great matters' may refer not only to personal ambition but to the great things *God* might do to save His people. In certain contexts, even this expectation must be given up if faith is to stay realistic and genuine.

The psalmist's experience mirrors that of Baruch, Jeremiah's trusted secretary and friend, who was told by the prophet: 'This is what the LORD says: I will overthrow what I have built and uproot what I have planted, throughout the land. Should you then seek great things for yourself? Seek them not. For I will bring disaster on all people, declares the LORD, but wherever you go I will let you escape with your life' (Jer. 45:4–5). Some comfort! Baruch realises that Israel's doom is settled and that God's judgment on His rebellious nation is too well set to expect God to effect a last-minute reversal of events. In such dire circumstances, faith is salted with realism.

Jeremiah chapter 45 was a favourite biblical text for Dietrich Bonhoeffer during his incarceration by the Nazis which led to his martyrdom. Bonhoeffer wrote in his prison diary:

> It will be the task of our generation not to 'seek great things', but to save and preserve our souls out of the chaos ... We shall have to keep our lives rather than shape them, to hope rather than plan, to hold out rather than march forward. But we do want to preserve for you, the rising generation, what will make it possible for you to plan, build up, and shape a new and better life.[6]

And so Bonhoeffer did. And so may we. In putting away 'childish things' for adulthood, we do not need to replace them with cynical things. By grace, we can combine adult faith with childlike wonder. Without illusion or fantasy, we may still call upon God who has the 'eternal appetite of infancy' to 'do it again' and to do 'great things' again.[7] To know this is to know something at least of what philosopher Paul Ricoeur called a 'second naiveté'. This describes an attitude of heart which lies on the other side of disillusionment and which tentatively opens itself to new surprises of God. Such a stance represents not a passive resignation but a quiet determination. We may not be breastfed all the way to eternity, but we can be sustained in a mature if modest faith, calm and unafraid.

If we lower our sights from overinflated ambitions, we may hope more truthfully in the Lord and model hope for the whole people of God (v.3). Kierkegaard said, 'Life can only be understood backwards but it must be lived forwards.' So the psalmist's reflections do not deter him from still being a pilgrim to Zion; this psalm is still a 'song of ascents'. Our 'second childhood' is but a fresh invitation to press on towards the goal for the prize of the upward call of God in Christ Jesus; a renewed incentive to give 'my utmost for his highest'. In the latter stages of the journey, less is more. Less self-promotion, more soul greatness. Loosening our grip on our need to control, we find firmer attachment to God's freedom of action which guarantees ours. Limiting our ambitions, we enter more deeply into the joy of God's plans and start to dream God's dreams. Laying down the burden of disappointment, we lift up our heads and find that our redemption draws nigh. Which is why *hope* is the strong outcome of *humility*.

The eyes that were not raised too high are now lifted up to the Lord (as in Psalm 123).
Lowering our eyes we see further, looking beyond distant things to God's future. Second childhood gives us 'second sight'. And hope is reborn.

Humility acts as spiritual buoyancy – a way of yielding to the waves which enables us to ride out the storm and even make progress against the tide. This is the secret of the resilient life: less cocksure but more confident; less gullible but more trusting; less optimistic but more hopeful. If we dare to drop back from presuming too much we will receive more; if we rest from unrealised dreams, we may find rest for our souls and a legacy for the future.

NOTES

Preface

1   This is part of a wider concern that I share with Ian Stackhouse which is expressed well in his *Gospel-Driven Church* (Milton Keynes: Paternoster, 2004).

SECTION 1

Chapter 1: Seeing Things from His Point of View

1   Oswald Chambers, *My Utmost for His Highest* (Newton Abbot: Newton Publishing, 1991) March 15th.

2   Henri Nouwen, *In The Name of Jesus* (London: Darton, Longman and Todd, 1989) pp.65–67.

3   Oswald Chambers, *Christian Discipline* Vol. I (London: Marshall, Morgan and Scott, 1934/1965) p.34.

4   Gordon D. Fee, *Gospel and Spirit: Issues in New Testament Hermeneutics* (Peabody: Hendrickson Publishers, 1991) p.130, n.19.

5   Oswald Chambers, *Christian Discipline* Vol. I, op. cit. pp.33–34.

6   George R. Hunsberger, 'Missional Vocation: Called and Sent to Represent the Reign of God' in ed. Darrell L. Gruder, *Missional Church: A Vision for the Sending of the Church in North America* (Grand Rapids: Eerdmans, 1998) p.88.

7   Gordon D. Fee, *Gospel and Spirit*, op. cit. p.143.

8   John H. Yoder, *For the Nations: Essays Evangelical and Public* (Grand Rapids: Eerdmans, 1997) p.209.

9   Ibid., p.209.

10 G.B. Caird, ed. L.D. Hurst, *New Testament Theology* (Oxford: Clarendon Press, 1994) p.288.

11 Ibid., p.316.

12 See John Yoder, *For the Nations*, op. cit. p.86.

13 In this whole section I am indebted to Donald Messer's discussion in *Contemporary Images of Christian Ministry* (Nashville: Abingdon Press,

1991) pp.97–115.

14 Ronald Sider, *Living Like Jesus* (Grand Rapids: Baker, 1999) p.173.

15 John Yoder, *The Politics of Jesus* (Grand Rapids: Eerdmans, 1972/1994) p.38.

16 Ibid., p.39.

17 Andrew Purves, *Reconstructing Pastoral Theology: A Christological Foundation* (Louisville: Westminster John Knox Press, 2004) p.xxx. This is the theme of Purves' excellent book written from a robust but sensitive Barthian standpoint.

18 P.T. Forsyth, *The Person and Place of Jesus Christ* (London: Independent Press, 1909/1961) pp.7,163.

19 Stephen J. Kraftchick, 'Death in Us, Life in You: The Apostolic Medium' in ed. David M. Hay, *Pauline Theology*, Vol. II (Minneapolis: Fortress Press, 1993) p.166.

20 Ibid., p.173.

21 Michael J. Gorman, *Cruciformity: Paul's Narrative Spirituality of the Cross* (Grand Rapids: Eerdmans, 2001) pp.4–5,213.

22 Ibid., p.213.

23 Stephen J. Kraftchick, 'Death in Us, Life in You: The Apostolic Medium' in ed. David M. Hay, *Pauline Theology*, Vol. II, p.177.

24 See Wink's influential Powers trilogy now neatly summarised in *The Powers that Be* (New York: Doubleday, 1998).

25 Michael P. Knowles, *We Preach Not Ourselves: Paul on Proclamation* (Grand Rapids: Brazos Press, 2008) p.111.

26 Alan E. Lewis, *Between Cross and Resurrection: A Theology of Holy Saturday* (Grand Rapids: Eerdmans, 2001) p.367.

Chapter 2: Ministering Grace to Establish Justice

1 Henri Nouwen, *Life of the Beloved: Spiritual Living in a Secular World* (London: Hodder & Stoughton, 1992) pp.45,47.

2 Samuel Chadwick, *Humanity and God* (London: Hodder & Stoughton, 1904) pp.100-101.

3 Eugene Peterson, *Under the Unpredictable Plant: An Exploration of Vocational Holiness* (Grand Rapids: Eerdmans, 1992) p.139.

4 Henri Nouwen, *The Living Reminder* (Dublin: Gill and Macmillan, 1982) p.45.

5 Paul D. Hanson, *Isaiah 40–66; Interpretation Series* (Louisville: John Knox Press, 1995) p.45.

6   John N. Oswalt, *The Book of Isaiah: Chapters 40–66, The New International Commentary on the Old Testament* (Grand Rapids: Eerdmans, 1998) p.111.

7   Walter Brueggemann, *Isaiah 40–66, Westminster Bible Companion* (Louisville: Westminster John Knox Press, 1998) p.42.

8   For an inspiring example see Gary Haughen's work with the International Justice Mission as told in his book, *Good News About Injustice* (Downers Grove: IVP, 1999).

9   Paul D. Hanson, *Isaiah 40–66*, op. cit. p.42.

10 John Yoder, *For the Nations*, op. cit. p.228.

Chapter 3: Making a Secret Life Count for Public Ministry

1   John Yoder, *For All Nations*, op. cit. p.229. I am indebted to Yoder for the framing of ideas in this section.

2   John N. Oswalt, *The Book of Isaiah: Chapters 40–66*, op. cit. p.291.

3   Ibid., p.304.

4   Paul D. Hanson, *Isaiah 40–66*, op. cit. p.135.

5   Robert Murray M'Cheyne, *Memoirs and Remains* (Edinburgh: Banner of Truth, 1960).

Chapter 4: Being Tough-minded and Tender-hearted

1   Walter Brueggemann, *Isaiah 40–66*, op. cit. p.122.

2   J. Randall Nichols, *The Restoring Word: Preaching as Pastoral Communication* (San Francisco: Harper & Row, 1987) p.77.

3   Paul D. Hanson, *Isaiah 40–66*, op. cit. p.141.

Chapter 5: Bearing Wounds that Bring Wholeness

1   Hanson and Brueggemann respectively.

2   William L. Lane, *The Gospel of Mark: The New International Commentary on the New Testament* (Grand Rapids: Eerdmans, 1974) p.385.

3   See most recently, Michael Gorman, *Cruciformity: Paul's Narrative Spirituality of the Cross* (Grand Rapids: Eerdmans, 2001) especially pp.164–169,186–188,316–321, and Richard Bauckham, *Jesus and the God of Israel* (Milton Keynes: Paternoster, 2008) especially pp.44–45,197–210.

4   Cited by Elizabeth Achtemeier, *Nature, God, and Pulpit* (Grand Rapids: Eerdmans, 1992) p.38.

5   John N. Oswalt, *Isaiah 40–66*, op. cit. p.391.

6   P.T. Forsyth, *God the Holy Father* (London: Independent Press,

1901/1957).

7   Eugene Peterson, *Five Smooth Stones for Pastoral Work* (Atlanta: John Knox Press, 1980) p.110–112.

8   John Yoder, *For the Nations*, op. cit. p.109.

SECTION 2

Chapter 6: Cross-eyed Visionaries

1   William Willimon, *Peculiar Speech: Preaching to the Baptized* (Grand Rapids: Eerdmans 1992) pp.32,46.

2   Martin Hengel, *The Cross of the Son of God* (London: SCM, 1986).

3   Jürgen Moltmann, *The Crucified God* (London: SCM, 1974) p.65.

4   Richard B. Hays, *First Corinthians: Interpretation Series* (Louisville: John Knox Press, 1997) p.27. For more on the epistemological effect of the cross, see Alexandra Brown, *The Cross and Human Transformation* (Minneapolis: Fortress Press, 1995).

5   Alistair McGrath, *The Enigma of the Cross* (London: Hodder & Stoughton, 1987) p.102.

6   Victor Furnish, 'Theology in 1 Corinthians' in ed. David Hay, *Pauline Theology, Vol. II: 1 and 2 Corinthians* (Minneapolis: Fortress Press, 1993) p.68. See also Gordon Fee in the same symposium.

7   Dietrich Bonhoeffer, *Letters and Papers from Prison* (London: Collins, 1963) p.122.

8   John V. Taylor, *The Go-Between God: The Holy Spirit and the Christian Mission* (London: SCM, 1972) p.222. For my comment, see Acts 2:43.

9   Ben Witherington III, *Jesus the Sage: The Pilgrimage of Wisdom* (Edinburgh: T&T Clark, 1994) p.7.

10 Ibid., p.313.

11 Ibid., p.310.

12 John V. Taylor, *The Go-Between God*, p.19. See my further reflections on this point in a Johannine context of the 'Farewell Discourse' of John 16–17 in my *Legacy of Jesus* (Farnham: CWR, 2005) pp.114–117. See also the insightful work of Edith Humphrey, *Ecstasy and Intimacy: When the Holy Spirit Meets the Human Spirit* (Grand Rapids: Eerdmans, 2006).

13 See Gordon Fee, *The First Epistle to the Corinthians* (Grand Rapids: Eerdmans, 1987) p.110.

14 Alexandra Brown, *The Cross and Human Transformation*, op. cit. pp.145–146.

15 Douglas D. Webster, *A Passion for Christ: An Evangelical Christology* (Grand Rapids: Zondervan Books, 1987) pp.176–177. See Philippians 3:10 for the spiritual sequence this reflects.

16 Alistair McGrath, *The Enigma of the Cross* (London: Hodder & Stoughton, 1987) pp.32–33. See also Alan E. Lewis' profound reflections on this theme: *Between Cross and Resurrection: A Theology of Holy Saturday* op. cit.

17 Alan E. Lewis, op. cit. p.465.

Chapter 7: Servant-leaders

1 The judgment is that of Ben Witherington, *The Paul Quest* (Downers Grove: IVP, 1998) p.170.

2 Ibid., p.168.

3 William J. Webb, *Returning Home: New Covenant and Second Exodus as the Context for 2 Corinthians 6:14–7:1* (Sheffield, JSNT: Sheffield Academic Press, 1993) p.100.

4 Tim Savage, *Power Through Weakness: Paul's Understanding of the Christian Ministry in 2 Corinthians* (Cambridge: Cambridge University Press, 1996) p.112. (For the technically minded, Savage notes that the term φυς λαμψει is an indicative future of prophecy and not like γενηθητωφως a subjunctive of command.) No other resource has proved as stimulating and helpful as Savage's fine study, especially for contextualising Paul's letter.

5 Ronald Sider, *Living Like Jesus* (Grand Rapids: Baker Books, 1996) pp.174–175. During my visit, I met staff from a church in Kuala Lumpur which, at the time, was operating the only kidney dialysis machine available in the country and was doing so in Christ's name.

6 Timothy Savage, *Power Through Weakness: Paul's Understanding of the Christian Ministry in 2 Corinthians*, op. cit. p.126.

7 2 Corinthians 6:4,9–10 'Amalgamised' version (J.B. Phillips and Eugene Peterson).

8 David Wenham, *Paul, Follower of Jesus or Founder of Christianity?* (Grand Rapids: Eerdmans, 1995) pp.266–271. Wenham's is a much neglected study.

9 James Denney, *The Second Epistle to the Corinthians, The Expositor's Bible* (London: Hodder & Stoughton, 1894) pp.186–187.

10 Ibid., pp.196–197.

Chapter 8: Competent Inadequates

1 Larry Crabb, *Shattered Dreams: God's Unexpected Pathway to Joy* (Colorado Springs: Waterbrook Press, 2001) p.80.

2 Michael P. Knowles, *We Preach Not Ourselves*, op. cit. p.93.

3 Larry Crabb, *Shattered Dreams*, op. cit. p.81.

4 Donald Messer, *Contemporary Images of Christian Ministry*, op. cit. pp.142–143.

5 Stanley Hauerwas, *The Peaceable Kingdom: A Primer in Christian Ethics* (London: SCM Press, 1983) p.31.

6 Frances Young and David Ford, *Meaning and Truth in Second Corinthians* (London: SPCK, 1987) p.245.

7 Larry Crabb, *Shattered Dreams*, op. cit. p.80.

8 Ibid., p.80.

9 Ibid., p.81.

10 Michael P. Knowles, *We Preach Not Ourselves*, op. cit. p.100.

Chapter 9: Wounded Healers

1 Henri Nouwen, *The Wounded Healer* (London: Darton, Longman and Todd, 1979, 1994) p.xvi.

2 Ibid., p.xvi.

3 Ibid., p.44.

4 Ibid., p.88.

5 Ibid., p.88.

6 Donald E. Messer, *Contemporary Images of Christian Ministry* (Nashville: Abingdon Press, 1991) p.88.

7 L. Gregory Jones and Kevin R. Armstrong, *Resurrecting Excellence: Shaping Faithful Christian Ministry* (Grand Rapids: Eerdmans, 2006) pp.89–93.

8 Ibid., p.91.

9 Ibid., p.92.

10 A.E. Harvey, *Renewal through Suffering* (Edinburgh: T&T Clark, 1996) p.79.

11 Ben Witherington, *The Paul Quest* (Downers Grove: IVP, 1998) p.171.

12 See, for example, Scott Hafemann, *2 Corinthians, the NIV Application Commentary* (Grand Rapids: Zondervan, 2000).

13 Ben Witherington, *Conflict and Community in Corinth: A Socio-Rhetorical Commentary on 1 and 2 Corinthians* (Grand Rapids: Eerdmans, 1995) p.366.

14 James M. Scott, *2 Corinthians: New International Biblical Commentary* (Peabody: Hendrickson, 1988) pp.60–64.

15 Paul Barnett, *The Second Epistle to the Corinthians: the New International Commentary on the New Testament* (Grand Rapids: Eerdmans, 1997) p.149.

16 André Resner, *Preacher and Cross: Person and Meaning in Theology and Rhetoric* (Grand Rapids: Eerdmans, 1999) p.6.

17 Michael P. Knowles, *We Preach Not Ourselves: Paul on Proclamation* (Grand Rapids: Brazos Press, 2008) p.61.

Chapter 10: Treasure in Clay Pots

1 Stephen J. Kraftchick, 'Death in Us, Life in You: The Apostolic Medium' in ed. David Hay, *Pauline Theology*, Vol. II (Minneapolis: Fortress Press, 1993), p.172.

2 Henri Nouwen, *The Living Reminder*, op. cit. pp.24–25.

3 Frances Young and David Ford, *Meaning and Truth in Second Corinthians* (London: SPCK, 1987) p.240.

4 Ibid., p.240.

5 Ibid., p.240. I am indebted to Young and Ford's whole discussion here.

6 Scott Hafemann, *2 Corinthians: the NIV Application Commentary* (Grand Rapids: Zondervan, 2000) p.465.

7 Andrew Purves, *Reconstructing Pastoral Theology* (Louisville: Westminster John Knox Press, 2004) pp.210,xi.

8 Douglas John Hall, *The Cross in Our Context: Jesus and the Suffering World* (Minneapolis: Fortress Press, 2003) p.82; n.8 p.239.

9 Ben Witherington, *Conflict and Community in Corinth*, op. cit. p.464.

10 André Resner, *Preacher and Cross*, op. cit. p.154. The citation is from Alan Lewis.

11 Timothy B. Savage, *Power through Weakness: Paul's Understanding of the Christian Ministry in 2 Corinthians*, op. cit. p.190.

Chapter 11: Undiminished Flames

1 John Sanford, *Ministry Burnout* (Evesham: Arthur James, 1982).

2 Henri Nouwen, *The Living Reminder*, op. cit. p.45.

3 William Willimon, *Clergy and Laity Burnout* (Nashville: Abingdon Press, 1989) p.41.

4 William Willimon, *Pastor: The Theology and Practice of Ordained Ministry* (Nashville: Abingdon Press, 2002) p.326. See also Willimon's *Clergy and*

Laity Burnout where Willimon acknowledges Sanford's earlier study.

5 Tom Wright, *Reflecting the Glory* (Oxford: Bible Reading Fellowship, 1997) p.27.

6 Philip Hughes, *Paul's Second Epistle to the Corinthians* (Edinburgh: Marshall, Morgan, and Scott, 1961) p.121.

7 Michael Esses, *Jesus in Exodus* (Plainfield: Logos Publishers, 1997) pp.245–246.

8 William Willimon, *Clergy and Laity Burnout*, op. cit. p.25.

9 Ray Anderson, *The Shape of Practical Ministry: Empowering Ministry with Theological Praxis* (Downers Grove: IVP, 2001) p.286.

10 David Ford, *The Shape of Living* (Grand Rapids: Baker, 1997) pp.45–47.

11 Marva J. Dawn, *A Royal 'Waste' of Time: The Splendour of Worshipping God and Being Church for the World* (Grand Rapids: Eerdmans, 1999) p.237.

12 Stephen J. Kraftchick, 'Death in Us, Life in You: The Apostolic Medium' in ed. David Hay, *Pauline Theology*, Vol. II, pp.172–173.

13 Martyn Lloyd-Jones, as ever, was astute about this habit. See *Spiritual Depression: Its Causes and Cure* (London: Pickering and Inglis, 1965) pp.195–196.

14 Tim Savage, *Power Through Weakness*, op. cit. p.180.

15 Thomas F. Torrance, *The Apocalypse Today* (Grand Rapids: Eerdmans, 1969) p.11.

16 Martyn Lloyd-Jones, *Expository Sermons on 2 Peter* (Edinburgh: The Banner of Truth Trust, 1983) p.194.

17 See John Piper, *The Purifying Power of Living by Faith in Future Grace* (Leicester; IVP, 1995) pp.171–172 and his reflections on the story.

17 J.R.R. Tolkien, *Lord of the Rings* (London: HarperCollins Publishers Ltd) © 1954 J.R.R. Tolkien.

SECTION 3

Chapter 12: Idolatrous Relevance

1 See Luke 6:26. I have offered further thoughts on this in my reflections on the Sermon on the Mount, *Voice from the Hills* (Farnham: CWR, 2008) pp.41,61.

2 John Oman, *Grace and Personality* (London: Collins, 1917/1962) p.21.

3 Os Guinness, *Prophetic Untimeliness: A Challenge to the Idol of Relevance* (Grand Rapids: Baker Books, 2003) p.15. It will be obvious that I am heavily indebted to Guinness' insights which are those of a true 'watchman on the walls'.

4 Dietrich Bonhoeffer, *No Rusty Swords* (London: Collins, 1965) p.308.

5 Ibid., pp.309–310.

6 Ibid., p.310.

7 Ibid., p.310–311.

8 Peter L. Berger, *A Far Glory: The Quest for Faith in an Age of Credulity* (New York: Doubleday, 1992) p.10.

9 Ibid., pp.10–12.

10 Mark Buchanan, *Your God is Too Safe* (Oregon: Multnomah, 2001) p.56.

11 Jaroslav Pelikan, *The Christian Tradition: A History of the Development of Doctrine*, Vol. I. *The Emergence of the Catholic Tradition (100–600)* (Chicago: University of Chigago Press, 1971) p.9.

12 Pelikan in an interview in US News and World Report, June 1989.

13 Eugene Peterson, *Run With The Horses* (Downers Grove: IVP, 1983) pp.175–176.

14 Henri Nouwen, *In the Name of Jesus* (London: Darton, Longman and Todd, 1989) p.17.

15 Richard Lischer, 'Resurrection and Rhetoric' in eds. Carl Braaten and Robert Jenson, *Marks of the Body of Christ* (Grand Rapids: Eerdmans, 1999) p.23.

16 Cited in Os Guinness, *Time for Truth* (Grand Rapids: Baker Books, 2000) p.75.

Chapter 13: Prophetic Untimeliness

1 Os Guinness, *Prophetic Untimeliness*, op. cit. p.19.

2 Ibid., p.106.

3 Walter Brueggemann, *A Commentary on Jeremiah: Exile and Homecoming* (Grand Rapids: Eerdmans, 1998) p.92.

4 Ibid., p.181.

5 Dietrich Bonhoeffer, *The Cost of Discipleship* (London: SCM Press, 1959) pp.98–99.

6 Pope Benedict XVI, *A New Song for the Lord* (New York: Crossroad, 1996) p.189.

7 John Goldingay, *Models for Scripture* (Grand Rapids: Eerdmans, 1994) p.204.

8 Walter Brueggemann, *A Commentary on Jeremiah*, op. cit. p.353.

9 William Willimon, *Peculiar Speech: Preaching to the Baptised* (Grand Rapids: Eerdmans, 1992) p.19.

Chapter 14: Premature Ambassadors

1   Richard John Neuhaus, *Freedom in Ministry* (Grand Rapids: Eerdmans, 1979) p.71.

2   George Weigel, 'The Church's Political Hope for the World' in eds. Carl Braaten and Robert Jenson, *Two Cities of God: The Church's Responsibility for the Earthly City* (Grand Rapids: Eerdmans, 1997) p.61.

3   H. Richard Niebuhr, *Christ and Culture* (New York: Harper and Row, 1951).

4   See in particular, John Howard Yoder, 'How H. Richard Niebuhr reasoned: A Critique of Christ and Culture' in eds. Glen H. Stassen, D.M. Yeager and John Howard Yoder, *Authentic Transformation: A New Vision of Christ and Culture* (Nashville: Abingdon Press, 1996).

5   Craig A. Carter, *The Politics of the Cross: The Theology and Social Ethics of John Howard Yoder* (Grand Rapids: Brazos Press, 2001) pp.221–222.

6   G.K. Chesterton, *The Everlasting Man* (London: Hodder & Stoughton, 1925) p.247.

7   See for example N.T. Wright, 'On Becoming the Righteousness of God: 2 Corinthians 5:21' in ed. David Hay, *Pauline Theology, Vol. II: 1 and 2 Corinthians* (Minneapolis: Fortress Press, 1993) pp.200–208. For further arguments to press this case, see Tom Wright, *Justification* (London: SPCK, 2009) pp.135–144.

8   Karen Onesti and Manfred Brauch, 'Righteousness of God' in eds. Gerald Hawthorne, Ralph P. Martin and Daniel G. Reid, *Dictionary of Paul and His Letters* (Downers Grove: IVP, 1993) p.836.

9   Richard B. Hays, *The Moral Vision of the New Testament: A Contemporary Introduction to Christian Ethics* (Edinburgh: T&T Clark, 1996) p.24. Further voices in support of what is still a minority position include James W. Thompson, *Pastoral Ministry in Paul: A Biblical Vision* (Grand Rapids: Brazos Press, 2006) p.144.

10 Cited by Ray Anderson, *Self Care: A Theology of Personal Empowerment and Spiritual Healing* (Wheaton: Bridgepoint/Victor Books, 1995) p.153.

11 Richard B. Hays, *The Moral Vision of the New Testament*, op. cit. p.24.

12 Richard John Neuhaus, op. cit. *Freedom in Ministry*, p.74.

13 Ibid., p.77.

14 Throughout this piece, the cultural colour and some of the language depends heavily on Tim Savage's fascinating research.

15 Ben Witherington, *Conflict and Community in Corinth*, op. cit. pp.393–394.

16 Eugene Peterson, *Subversive Spirituality* (Grand Rapids: Eerdmans, 1997) pp.188–189.

17 William Willimon, *Shaped by the Bible* (Nashville: Abingdon Press, 1990) pp. 62–63.

18 Richard Lischer, 'Resurrection and Rhetoric' in eds. Carl Braaten and Robert Jenson, *Marks of the Body of Christ* (Grand Rapids: Eerdmans, 1999) p.15.

19 James Thompson, *Preaching Like Paul* (Louisville: Westminster John Knox Press, 2001) p.161.

20 Richard Lischer, 'Resurrection and Rhetoric', op. cit. pp. 23,21.

21 Craig A. Carter, *The Politics of the Cross: A Theology and Social Ethics of John Howard Yoder* (Grand Rapids: Brazos Press, 2001) p.147.

22 G.K. Chesterton, 'The Ballad of the White Horse' in *The Collected Poems of G.K. Chesterton* (London: Methuen and Co. Ltd., 1958).

23 Alan Lewis, *Between Cross and Resurrection: A Theology of Easter Saturday* (Grand Rapids: Eerdmans, 2001) p.65.

Chapter 15: Only Fools and Martyrs

1 For what follows I am again heavily indebted to Tim Savage, *Power through Weakness,* op. cit.

2 Ibid., pp.29–31.

3 Ibid., p.51.

4 Ibid., p.31.

5 Ibid., p.47.

6 Ibid., p.66.

7 Ibid., p.73.

8 Ibid., p.99.

9 Ben Witherington, *Conflict and Community in Corinth*, op. cit. p.348.

10 Ibid., p.431.

11 Don Carson, *From Triumphalism to Maturity: A New Exposition of 2 Corinthians 10–13* (Leicester: Inter-Varsity Press, 1984) p.46.

12 Ibid., p.77.

13 Ibid., p.18.

14 Ben Witherington, *Conflict and Community in Corinth*, op. cit. p.442.

15 Os Guinness, *The Call: Finding and Fulfilling The Central Purpose of Your Life* (Nashville: Word Publishing, 1998) pp.214–215.

16 James Houston, *I Believe in the Creator* (London: Hodder & Stoughton, 1979) pp.222–225.

17 Harry Blamires, *Meat Not Milk* (Eastbourne: Marc, 1988) pp.105–107.

18 Os Guinness, *The Call*, op. cit. p.217.

19 Dietrich Bonhoeffer, *The Way to Freedom* (London: Collins, 1966) p.246.

20 Os Guinness, *The Call*, op. cit. p.221.

21 E.G. Rupp and Benjamin Drewery, *Martin Luther: Documents of Modern History* (London: Edward Arnold, 1970) p.75.

22 Austen Farrer, *A Celebration of Faith* (London: Hodder & Stoughton, 1970) p.111.

REVIEW
Chapter 16: Through a Glass, Darkly

1 Gordon Fee, 'Some Reflections on Pauline Spirituality' in eds. J.I. Packer and Loren Wilkinson, *Alive to God: Studies in Spirituality* (Downers Grove: IVP, 1992) p.105. More recently Fee has established the point through detailed exegesis and exposition in his magisterial study, *God's Empowering Presence: The Holy Spirit in the Letters of Paul* (Peabody: Hendrickson Publishers, 1994). Also, Alexander Schmemann, *Of Water and Spirit: A Liturgical Study of Baptism* (London: SPCK, 1974) p.107.

2 Dallas Willard, *In Search of Guidance* (New York: HarperCollins, 1993) pp.51–52.

3 Mark Buchanan, *Your God is Too Safe*, op. cit. pp.56–57.

4 Eugene Peterson, *Five Smooth Stones for Pastoral Work* (Atlanta: John Knox Press, 1980) p.140.

5 Lewis Smedes, *A Pretty Good Person* (San Francisco: Harper and Row, 1990) chapter 3. Smedes is a long-time favourite author for his honesty and his ability to make goodness attractive.

6 Cited by Craig Barnes, *When God Interrupts* (Downers Grove: IVP, 1995) p.112.

7 William Clow, *The Cross in Christian Experience* (London: Hodder & Stoughton, 1910) pp.226–229.

8 On this subject, Tom Schreiner and Ardel Caneday's *The Race Set Before Us: A Biblical Theology of Perseverance and Assurance* (Downers Grove: IVP, 2001) has been lent me by a friend and comes well recommended. But I have not yet studied it in any detail except to notice that the 'existential' view I am offering here merits only a footnote on page 38!

9   Jacques Ellul, *What I Believe* (Grand Rapids: Eerdmans, 1989) pp.73–86.

10 Richard B. Hays, *First Corinthians* (Louisville: Westminster John Knox Press, 1997) p.233.

11 R.S. Thomas, 'The Absence' in *Collected Poems, 1945–1990* (London: Phoenix, 1995).

12 E. Stanley Jones, *The Unshakeable Kingdom and the Unchanging Christ* (Nashville: Abingdon Press, 1972) p.275.

13 Samuel Wells, *Improvisation: The Drama of Christian Ethics* (London: SPCK, 2004) p.78.

14 L. Gregory Jones and Kevin R. Armstrong, *Resurrecting Excellence* (Grand Rapids: Eerdmans, 2006) pp.136–137.

15 For more on this, see my *Worship in the Best of Both Worlds* (Milton Keynes: Paternoster, 2009).

Chapter 17: Face Value

1   Frederick Buechner, *The Faces of Jesus* (New York: Harper and Row, 1989).

2   Lesslie Newbigin, *Truth to Tell* (London: SPCK, 1991) p.11.

3   Spurgeon's College held its 150th Anniversary Conference in June 2006, hosted by my long-time friend, David Coffey, who presided over the event, and who had been best man at our wedding.

4   P.T. Forsyth, *Revelation, Old and New* (London: Independent Press, 1962) p.15.

Chapter 18: Second Sight

1   G.K. Chesterton, *Orthodoxy* (London: The Bodley Head, 1908) p.53.

2   See Romans 12:3–8; 2 Corinthians 10:13–18.

3   Artur Weiser, *The Psalms* (London: SCM, 1962) p.777.

4   Frederick Buechner, *Secrets in the Dark: A Life in Sermons* (San Francisco: Harper, 2006) pp.101–103.

5   Anna Laetitia Waring, 'Father I know that all my life', *Baptist Hymn Book*, no.468.

6   This is from the new translation of *Letters and Papers From Prison*. The citation appears on p.157 of the earlier Fontana Edition in my possession. Elsewhere, he recommends repeating Jeremiah 45 to ourselves every day (see p.90).

7   See G.K. Chesterton, *Orthodoxy*, op. cit. p.107.

Day and Residential Courses
Counselling Training
Leadership Development
Biblical Study Courses
Regional Seminars
Ministry to Women
Daily Devotionals
Books and Videos
Conference Centre

Trusted all Over the World

CWR HAS GAINED A WORLDWIDE reputation as a centre of excellence for Bible-based training and resources. From our headquarters at Waverley Abbey House, Farnham, England, we have been serving God's people for over 40 years with a vision to help apply God's Word to everyday life and relationships. The daily devotional *Every Day with Jesus* is read by nearly a million readers an issue in more than 150 countries, and our unique courses in biblical studies and pastoral care are respected all over the world. Waverley Abbey House provides a conference centre in a tranquil setting.

For free brochures on our seminars and courses, conference facilities, or a catalogue of CWR resources, please contact us at the following address. **CWR, Waverley Abbey House, Waverley Lane, Farnham, Surrey GU9 8EP, UK**

Telephone: **+44 (0)1252 784700**
Email: **mail@cwr.org.uk**
Website: **www.cwr.org.uk**

CWR Applying God's Word
to everyday life and relationships

GET A DEEPER UNDERSTANDING OF SCRIPTURE

Cover to Cover Every Day daily Bible-reading notes provide thought-provoking study of Bible books, stories and characters.

Over a five-year period, you will be taken through each book of the Bible. Every issue includes contributions from two different authors.

- Short, in-depth Bible study every day
- Rolling, five-year curriculum will cover every book of the Bible
- A psalm for each weekend
- Contributions from well-known authors including R.T. Kendall, Joel Edwards and Philip Greenslade.

Cover to Cover Every Day
Daily Bible-reading notes by various authors

170x120mm booklet – six issues per year published bimonthly

£13.80 for a one-year subscription (UK)

£2.49 each (exc P&P) for individual issues

NOV/DEC 2009
Ecclesiastes &
Song of Songs
1, 2 & 3 John

cover to **cover**
Every Day

Ecclesiastes & Song of Songs
John Houghton

1, 2 & 3 John
Peter Hicks

WITH REFLECTIONS ON A PSALM EACH WEEKEND

BRINGING YOU DEEPER BIBLICAL UNDERSTANDING CWR

DEFINE CHRISTIAN LEADERSHIP GOD'S WAY

Survey some of the ways in which leadership operates today and discover more biblical – and effective – structures to the Church's life and ministry.

Philip Greenslade draws on his experience and enthusiasm to outline the characteristics of a true leader, reminding us of those biblical ideals found in Christ, as well as Paul and other great leaders in Scripture and history.

Leadership
by Philip Greenslade

208-page paperback, 130x195mm
ISBN: 978-1-85345-202-4

£12.99

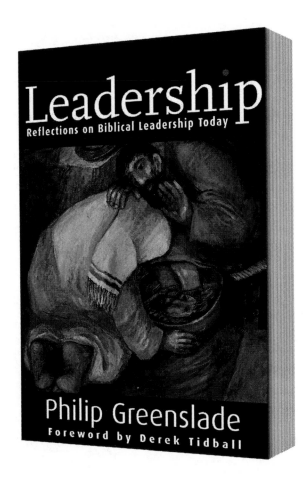

FRESH INSIGHTS AND NEW POWER

With his characteristic original thinking, Philip Greenslade
expounds on Christ's messages from the mounts, the 'voice
from the hills', and reveals the profound connection between
the Sermon on the Mount and Jesus' seven 'words' from the
cross; between Jesus' call to holiness and His crucifixion.

You will be empowered by the Holy Spirit afresh as you
understand why 'it takes nothing less than the cross of God's
Son to implement in us the Sermon on the Mount'.

Voice from the Hills - Costly grace, crucial words
by Philip Greenslade

234-page paperback, 230x172mm
ISBN: 978-1-85345-469-1

£9.99

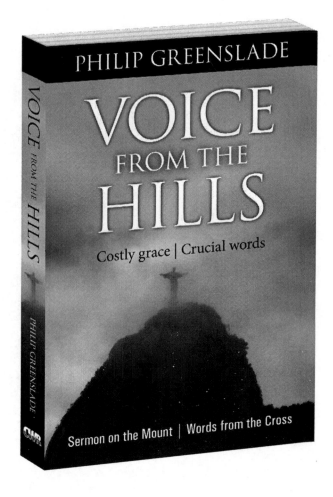